Twenty Years
in a Siberian Gulag

Twenty Years in a Siberian Gulag

Memoir of a Political Prisoner at Kolyma

LEONID PETROVICH BOLOTOV

Translated and edited by
IRINA YEVGENIEVNA BARCLAY

McFarland & Company, Inc., Publishers
Jefferson, North Carolina

LIBRARY OF CONGRESS CATALOGUING-IN-PUBLICATION DATA

Names: Bolotov, Leonid Petrovich, 1906–1987, author. |
  Barclay, Irina Yevgenievna, editor, translator.
Title: Twenty Years in a Siberian Gulag : Memoir
  of a Political Prisoner at Kolyma / Leonid Petrovich Bolotov ;
  translated and edited by Irina Yevgenievna Barclay.
Other titles: Memoir of a political prisoner at Kolyma
Description: Jefferson, North Carolina : McFarland & Company, Inc.,
  Publishers, 2020 | Includes bibliographical references and index.
Identifiers: LCCN 2020023872 | ISBN 9781476682211
  (paperback : acid free paper) ∞
  ISBN 9781476640396 (ebook)
Subjects: LCSH: Bolotov, Leonid Petrovich, 1906-1987. |
  Political prisoners—Soviet Union—Biography. | Soviet Union—
  History—1925-1953. | Political persecution—Soviet Union. |
  Forced labor—Soviet Union. | Kolyma (Concentration camp)—
  Biography. | Political prisoners—Family relationships—Soviet Union—
  History. | Penal colonies—Russia (Federation)—Kolyma Mountains
  Region—History—20th century.
Classification: LCC HV9712.5.B65 A3 2020 | DDC 365/.45092 [B]—dc23
LC record available at https://lccn.loc.gov/2020023872

BRITISH LIBRARY CATALOGUING DATA ARE AVAILABLE

ISBN (print) 978-1-4766-8221-1
ISBN (ebook) 978-1-4766-4039-6

© 2020 Leonid Petrovich Bolotov. All rights reserved

No part of this book may be reproduced or transmitted in any form or by any means, electronic or mechanical, including photocopying or recording, or by any information storage and retrieval system, without permission in writing from the publisher.

Front cover: Leonid Bolotov; a mine trolley (Dal'stroi Territories Photo Album of 1942–1943, Ministry of Inner Affairs, State Archive, Russian Federation, Moscow)

Printed in the United States of America

McFarland & Company, Inc., Publishers
  Box 611, Jefferson, North Carolina 28640
    www.mcfarlandpub.com

To my wife,
Nina Alekseevna Bolotova

The sun rose; the day begins.
—Nekrasov

Table of Contents

Translator-Editor's Acknowledgments — x
Translator-Editor's Preface — 1
Translator-Editor's Introduction — 3

Part I: Defeat of the Working Family

One—My Arrest — 10
Two—Shpalernaia Prison — 12
Three—My Interrogation — 16
Four—Pruss and Aleksandrov — 21
Five—The Sailor — 25
Six—The Pilot — 31
Seven—I'm Held in Captivity — 36
Eight—The Hundredth Prisoner — 43
Nine—My 60th Day in Prison — 48
Ten—My Stay in Two Prisons — 53
Eleven—The Night Before the Trial — 57
Twelve—The Trial — 63
Thirteen—I Meet My Convicted Friends — 67
Fourteen—Second Transit Prison for Men — 70
Fifteen—The Train: Leningrad to Vladivostok — 73
Sixteen—Vladivostok Transit Camp — 85
Seventeen—Behind Barbed Wire — 88
Eighteen—Kulu — 92

Part II: My Stay and Work in Kolyma

Nineteen—From Magadan to the Taiga	96
Twenty—The New Power	101
Twenty-One—Baptism of Fire	104
Twenty-Two—Panning Season	109
Twenty-Three—Music While We Worked	115
Twenty-Four—My Father's Letter	120
Twenty-Five—My Search for Firewood	124
Twenty-Six—My Broken Leg	127
Twenty-Seven—My New Friends	130
Twenty-Eight—The Competition	133
Twenty-Nine—World War II in the Gold Mine	136
Thirty—The Cave-In	139
Thirty-One—The Unexpected Meetings	142
Thirty-Two—Investigator Kulakov	146
Thirty-Three—The New Accusation	149
Thirty-Four—Jail	154
Thirty-Five—Brevda's Story	157
Thirty-Six—My Last Judgment	160
Thirty-Seven—The Finnish Shingles	163
Thirty-Eight—Glass Factory	167
Thirty-Nine—Young Thieves	173
Forty—Katia Maksakov's Story	176
Forty-One—Ivan Zelenin's Story	182
Forty-Two—Our Raskolnikov	184
Forty-Three—The Blue-Eyed Blonde	186
Forty-Four—Bears and Berries	191
Forty-Five—Special Camp 5	193
Forty-Six—A New Order	198
Forty-Seven—Freedom—with Restrictions	203
Forty-Eight—Dishwashing	210

FORTY-NINE—The Family Cares	213
FIFTY—Nina's Arrival	216
FIFTY-ONE—Nina's Arrest	221
FIFTY-TWO—Tomsk's Jail	226
FIFTY-THREE—Nina's Release and Meeting with Children	231
FIFTY-FOUR—The First Thawed Patch	237
FIFTY-FIVE—In Leningrad	239
FIFTY-SIX—Our New Lives Begin	244
Translator-Editor's Afterword	247
Glossary	251
Abbreviations	254
Bibliography	257
Index	263

Translator-Editor's Acknowledgments

I wish to thank Lana Bourret and the Bolotov family for sharing their grandfather's manuscript and family pictures, which added color and depth to the translation and threw light on my own grandfathers' arrests.

To Vasilii Niemets, my cousin from Mukachevo, Zakarpattia Region, who added details of the arrest of our paternal grandfather, and my mother, Valentina Papp (Pavlova), for similar stories of my maternal grandfather's arrest.

As for research, I want to thank Russian, German, and American museums, libraries, archives, and their staffs for assisting me in this endeavor. Arzamas Museum of History and Art and the Arzamas Gaidar Museum in Nizhnii Novgorod Province for providing me official documentations, genealogy, and photographs of the Doroshevskiie and Poliakov families. Their input brought 1930s Leningrad and beyond to life and embellished impressions of Russian life during those years. The Saratov Radishchev Art Museum for allowing me to use Nina Lekarenko's extraordinary drawings of the women's jail in Tomsk. Nina Liberman, daughter of Nina Lekarenko, who confirmed in an email her mother's arrest and exile in 1937. Nina Molchanova, head of the Lyceum No. 40 Museum, Saint Petersburg, for her email documenting that Georgii Zhurba, Red Triangle Manager, defended Leningrad during its blockade. Aleksandr Vinnikov, a Tomsk Province historian and medical doctor, for sending me his descriptions and father's stories of railroad transportation during World War II. Marina Provotorova, Saratov State Museum of Regional Studies, for assisting me with sources dedicated to Saratov revolutionary life during 1919. Ivan Panikarov, founder of the Gulag Museum in Yagodnoye, Magadan Province, for background of the lives of Kolyma prisoners. Special thanks go to Ivan Utenkov, Russian State Archive, for providing Kolyma pictures; Aleksandr Makeev, Tatyana Polianskaia, and Pavel Shirokov, Gulag Museum

Translator-Editor's Acknowledgments

in Moscow scholars, for responding to my many queries concerning arrests in 1937; Angelina Azieva for her Tomsk photos; Bertram Seidel, Chemnitz, and Valerian Welm of the Dresden Documentation Center, Saxony, Germany, for sharing information about Fridolin Seydewitz; and the archives in Srednekanskii and Khasyn Districts, Magadan Province, for proofs concerning glass factory employees.

Dianne Johnson, Appalachian State University interlibrary loan specialist, and the College of Arts and Sciences at Appalachian State for their unwavering financial support. Finally, my husband, Ceylon Lorenzo Barclay, for his untiring assistance.

Translator-Editor's Preface

As a child growing up in Tver, Russia, I often overheard my parents speak of the arrests of their fathers along with other innocents who were sentenced to Stalin's Gulags.[1]

My mother's father, Vasilii Egorovich Pavlov (1899–September 16, 1966), managed a collective farm in Tver Province; he was arrested in 1938 and spent a year in Bezhetsk NKVD Prison.[2] His wife, Evdokiia Dmitrievna Pavlova (February 5, 1897–December 12, 1956), illiterate, asked my mother's teacher to write petitions that helped release the weakened man in 1939, but he was then conscripted into World War II.

My dad's father, Illesh Ianoshevich Papp (July 20, 1902–1968), was arrested June 23, 1948, in Novaia Botrad' for refusing to hand over, for collectivization, his 32-acre farm, four horses, three cows, four pigs, two tillers, and a new suit. On August 12, 1948, the Zakarpattia Region Court sen-

This drawing of Illesh Ianoshevich Papp was made in 1949 in Irkutsk Gulag (Collection of Irina Y. Barclay).

---

1. Stalin, Iosif Vissarionovich (1878–1953), General Secretary of the Party, expanded Gulags, *Glavnoe Upravlenie Lagerei*, or Main Administration of Camps. Wieczynski, Joseph L., ed. *The Modern Encyclopedia of Russian and Soviet History*, vol. 37 (Gulf Breeze, FL: Academic International Press, 1984), 63–72.

2. NKVD, or *Narodnyi komissariat vnutrennikh del*, Commissariat of Internal Affairs, was the main organ of Soviet government control, established in 1917. Wieczynski, *The Modern Encyclopedia of Russian and Soviet History*, vol. 7 (1978), 192–195.

tenced him to 10 years at an Irkutsk Camp, with an additional five years in Siberian exile.³ His daughter, Maria Papp (September 20, 1927–May 19, 2004), sent appeals until, after Khrushchev's 1956 Secret Speech,⁴ he was freed and returned to his wife, Maria Zherebak (August 8, 1903–January 19, 1995). He suffered the rest of his life with traumatic brain injuries from severe prison beatings. Illesh's son, Ivan Papp (June 9, 1922–January 12, 2010), witnessing collectivization of his father's farm, fled to Czechoslovakia in 1947 with only a backpack and loaf of bread.⁵

On January 1, 2003, I moved from Tver to Florida, with my husband Ceylon and daughter Anastasia. It was there I met Lana Bourret whose grandfather, Leonid Bolotov, survived 20 years in Kolyma Gulags. He wrote a 400-page memoir of his ordeal, which threw vivid light on Soviet rule, embellished with slogans, sounds, and the names of leaders that added color and authenticity to my parents' stories of my grandfathers' lives.

For my curiosity, armed with this manuscript, I expanded my knowledge of the Gulag as my generation had only heard of Aleksandr Solzhenitsyn's story *One Day in the Life of Ivan Denisovich*, the barbed-wire-life of convicts, grueling labor, and deaths.

---

3. Rizak, I.M., et al. *Reabilitovani istorieiu. Zakarpatska oblast.'* [Rehabilitation Through History. Zakarpatskaia Province]. Kniga 1 (Uzhgorod: Vidavnictvo "Zakarpattia," 2003), 576.

4. On February 14–25, 1956, Nikita Khrushchev denounced Stalin's politics and released prisoners from the Gulags. Wieczynski, *The Modern Encyclopedia of Russian and Soviet History*, vol. 16 (1980), 197.

5. Petra Přerostová. Podporučik Ivan Pap (1922–2010). "Kdybych byl stál přímo, tak jsem to dostal do hlavy." Teplice, October 26, 2007. *Projekt: Příběhy 20. Století*. Post Bellum, Prague, Czech Republic, October 21, 2018, http://pametnaroda.cz/story/pap-ivan-1922-69.

Translator-Editor's Introduction

Bolotov and His Memoirs

Leonid Petrovich Bolotov was born in Saratov, Russia, in 1906, the third son of Varvara Ivanovna Cherntsova and Petr Antonovich Bolotov, a stove-maker and soldier in the Tsarist Army 1914–1918. Varvara Ivanovna, a merchant's daughter, had five children; the other four were Anna, Aleksandr, Zenaida, and Boris. In Saratov, Petr Antonovich owned a tiny house at 16 Kamyshinskaia Street.

Petr and Varvara Bolotov, the couple at center, with their children and grandchildren, circa 1928. Petr holds their granddaughter Klara. Standing among unidentified siblings are Leonid (right) and his youngest brother Boris (third from left) (Collection of Lana Bourret).

Cherntsov, a merchant, and his family in Saratov. Seated: Ivan Cherntsov and Anna Cherntsova, Leonid's maternal grandparents. Back, left to right: Varvara Cherntsova, Petr Bolotov, Mikhail Ivanovich Chertntsov, and an unknown woman (Collection of Lana Bourret).

Bolotov's memoir shows his father's persuasive influence. Petr Antonovich joined the Bolshevik Party before the October Revolution, participated in grain collection for Lenin in Saratov Province, and served on political and military committees. Bolotov's political inclinations began early, and they stayed related to Bolsheviks' policies. At 13, he was captured by White Cossacks in Saratov steppes and witnessed the anti–Bolshevik rebellion in his hometown. He propagandized Lenin's principles in Middle School 8 and attended Saratov State University (1924–1928), majoring in engineering. At graduate school, Bolotov studied in Moscow and then was ordered, by the State Department of Chemistry, to take a position as an engineer at the Red Triangle Factory.

In 1928, Leonid married Nina Alekseevna Temiakova (1910–1979), also from Saratov. She came from a tailor's family, and they had two children, Gennadii and Valeria.

In 1931, Leonid became a member of All-Russian Communist Party (Bolsheviks), reflecting his conviction in the new ideology that controlled all aspects of life.[1] Both Leonid and Nina warmly greeted all

---

1. The official name for the Communist Party, 1903–1952. Wieczynski, *The Modern Encyclopedia of Russian and Soviet History*, vol. 7 (1978), 217.

Leonid Bolotov's 1936 Leningrad apartment in 2015 (Collection of Irina Barclay).

Soviet innovations as they brought truth, fairness, equality, and justice to the people who had long suffered the Tsarist government and similar politics in the West.

Leningrad, Lenin's name for Saint Petersburg, meant for them not only the industrial and artistic progress in the former capital, but also the human achievements of state power over its citizens.[2] Thus, they admired the present *and* acknowledged the past, the present Communist ideas *and* past tsars' triumphs. These divergent forces were interwoven in people's minds, but, in 1937, the young couple's views were altered as new authorities launched the Great Purge. This year bifurcated Leonid's life: everything was either *before* or *after* 1937.

Arrested on June 17, 1937, Leonid was taken to Leningrad's Shpalernaia Prison. In September, without a trial, he was sentenced to death for having refused to sign a false confession. Weeks later, the Soviet Supreme Court set aside his death sentence, replacing it with a 10-year sentence of hard labor in the Arctic Kolyma penal camps.

In Kolyma Leonid's term was expanded another decade; he worked in

---

2. Leningrad was the name for Saint Petersburg, 1924–1991. Wieczynski, *The Modern Encyclopedia of Russian and Soviet History*, Supplement, vol. 49 (1988), 233.

Left to right: Valeria, Nina, and Gennadii in 1953 (Collection of Lana Bourret).

gold and uranium mines, the taiga, cutting trees, and a glass factory. This vast Gulag panorama gave him the background to describe and analyze convict lives, verdicts, and Soviet justice. Also, Leonid speaks about Nina's arrest and exile in Tomsk and Anzhero-Sudzhensk. These unforgettable horrors created the backdrop for Bolotov's memoir and his version of 1937 with its slavery, humiliation, deaths, and separation.

Throughout his long confinement, Leonid came to see, first-hand, that the term Communism was synonymous with NKVD officers seizing the property and belongings of others. Millions of Soviets lost their respect for and confidence in their leaders. After Stalin's death on March 5, 1953, and the findings of the Twentieth Party Congress in 1956, Bolotov was declared innocent of his 1937 conviction.

In Bolotov's memoir, each chapter points to an exact time and place of events; this attention to detail allows readers to reconstruct the Kolyma chronicles and comprehend the vast actions of Soviet penitentiary system. The memoir is written in Bolotov's unique style and reflects his rage and anger, love and tenderness, and restraint and thoughtfulness in his past.

A Note on the Translation

Bolotov's memoir should be included in Gulag literature as a valuable document of Stalin's failed leadership. In it, the names of people are real, and I found most of them in publications dedicated to victims of Stalin's repressions and through my personal contacts with museums, archives, and local historians.

The dates of Bolotov's arrest and release and his occupation and home address in Leningrad were confirmed by official emails received from the Federal Service of State Security in Saint Petersburg and Leningrad Province on May 31, 2018.

All notes to the text are mine. Because this book is intended for English speakers, I concentrated on an English language tradition in translation of Soviet Gulag literature and converted kilometers to miles, yards, and feet and Celsius to Fahrenheit.

Since Russian names are often difficult for English speakers, it is worth noting that in the text, Bolotov called himself Leonid Petrovich Bolotov, Leonid Bolotov, and sometimes by his father's name, Petrovich.

Part I

Defeat of the Working Family

ONE

My Arrest

156 Obvodnii Canal, Apartment 223
Thursday, June 17, 1937, 2:00 a.m.

On the pivotal white night I was arrested, we were all soundly asleep. Someone pounded on our apartment's outer door. I pulled on my Boston suit pants[1] and rushed to open both doors before my family awoke, swinging the inner door in and pushing the outer door into the hall. There stood two glaring secret agents in dreaded blue caps with crimson bands and khaki uniforms: NKVD! With them stood our street sweeper, a stocky man of fifty twisting his cheek-to-cheek mustache and winking at the agents. He nodded at me with hardened eyes.

"That's Bolotov!" he snarled, jabbing his finger at me. "Arrest him!"

I was dumbfounded. Despite rumors of the seizures of Leningrad top party leaders since January 1937, I never expected to see secret agents at our door. How wrong I was.

The agents shoved through the door and stomped into our small entryway.

I heard Nina rise from our bed, and her bare feet padded across the living room's wooden floor behind me and stopped.

The taller of the officers strutted into the living room and switched off the radio. The shorter agent followed. With no provocation from me nor comment from them, the agents searched our room and its three little storage drawers. They flipped over two chairs and tore out the bottoms.

"Bolotov, you'll receive the order for your arrest tomorrow!" the tall investigator sneered.

The agents glared unflinchingly at Valeria's carriage. Nina rushed to

---

1. The Boston suit was, and still is, a classic men's suit made of high-quality wool, usually in dark colors. Kirsanova, R.M., et al. *Kostium v russkoi khudozhestvennoi kul'ture 18—pervoi poloviny 20 vv: opyt enciclopedii* (Moskva: Nauchnoe izdatel'stvo "Bol'shaia Rossiiskaia entsyclopedia," 1995), 47.

One. My Arrest

get the baby. The agents flipped the carriage over, pulled out knives, and slashed its bottom, looking for but not finding a thing. Their harsh sneering quips woke my parents in the adjoining room.

Nina gazed at me. Her blue eyes, always cheerful, glittered with horror. In seven years of marriage, I had never seen that look but once, the day in 1930 she received the telegram of her mother's death. Calling up inner strength, she neither fell into hysterics nor screamed outrageously. With head high, back straight, and a determined look in her eyes, she went to the kitchen to make me a sandwich. My mother turned from the bedroom door and stepped into her room to get me a change of underwear. As I stuffed the sandwich in my Boston suit pocket, Nina tied her red silk scarf around my neck and kissed me.

My son Gena awoke, crying, "Daddy, are you going on a trip?"

"Yes, son," I replied with all the zest I could muster.

Unlike the women, my father stood motionless as a mannequin.

"My father and I are members of the Party," I told the NKVD duo.

They ignored me and said, "Bolotov, you won't need a sandwich; we serve meals three times a day in NKVD."

Without another word, the agents shoved me out the door, poked me, walking down the stairs and toward their Black Raven.[2] The sight of it made me shudder.

The tall agent ordered, "Bolotov, in the back!"

They drove along the Obvodnii Canal, through the industrial part of Leningrad to the Big House on Volodarskii Prospect.[3] I remembered well, during our first tour of Leningrad, how Nina and I showed this massive, six-story building to my parents. The Big House was a momentous achievement of Soviet architects, then and now; it remains a tourist attraction.[4]

How could I dream this long, white, June night would change my destiny forever?

---

2. The Black Raven was the NKVD black car used to take enemies of the people to prison. Kravchenko, Victor. *I Choose Freedom: The Personal and Political Life of a Soviet Official* (New York: Charles Scribner & Sons, 1946), 485.
3. The name Volodarskii Prospect was used for Liteinii Prospect from 1918 to 1944. Levtov, V.E. *Bol'shaia toponimicheskaia entsiklopediia Sankt-Peterburga:15 000 gorodskikh imen* (Sankt-Peterburg: Informatsionno-izdatel'skoe agentstvo "LIK," 2013), 245.
4. The detention house, constructed in 1933 under a project by Gegello, Trotskii, and Ol', represents the successful achievement of constructivism and is a replica of the competitive project, the Palace of Soviets, designed by American architect Hector Hamilton. *Ves' Leningrad: adresnaia i spravochnaia kniga* [1935 Leningrad Yellow Pages] (L: Lenoblispolkom i Lensovet, 1935), 506–507.

Two

Shpalernaia Prison

25 Voinov Street
Thursday, June 17, 1937, 3:00 a.m.

Shortly after sunrise that morning, the agents drove through the massive gate of the sprawling Shpalernaia Prison. I was searched, issued an identity card, and taken to the *sobachnik*, or dog kennel. Later, a burly guard appeared to process me. He opened the door and walked me across the yard to a duty officer who took my picture, profile and full-face, then rolled my fingers, side to side, on what prisoners called the "grand piano," a fingerprint inkpad.

He shouted, "Strip naked." I did. "Bend over!" I did.

Another guard stepped behind me, pulled on gloves, and probed *all* my orifices. Degradation is an integral part of prisoners' *sobachnik* treatment, aka prison etiquette. My *sobachnik*, a windowless cell a little larger than a coffin, had a narrow bench to sit on, leaving my knees almost touching the door. Just in front of me was a Judas-hole. Every few minutes it was opened and revealed an unwinking eyeball.[1]

Then guards cut off the buttons of my Boston suit, yanked off my belt, and ordered me to redress. Once dressed, they pushed me down a long, dim hall lined with thick steel doors, stopping at cell 20. The guard opened the door and shoved me inside. The cell was sprawling, but there was barely any room to stand. A crowd of men gaped at me; most couldn't be bothered. The door clanged shut. The lock clicked.

I wormed to the back of the cell where a grimy, barred window overlooked the prison yard. It was about five a.m. The sun glowed red a finger-width above the eastern horizon. There was no room to lay and

---

1. "Kennel" is a special prison section or separate cell therein for newly-arrested individuals prior to their assignment to their cells in a given prison or to other prisons. Rossi, Jacques. *The Gulag Handbook: An Encyclopedia Dictionary of Soviet Penitentiary Institutions and Terms Related to the Forced Labor Camp* (New York: Paragon House, 1989), 401.

Two. Shpalernaia Prison

The front page of *The Red Triangle* on Thursday, June 17, 1937, made no mention of the vast number of arrests made that day, including Bolotov's (Russian National Library, St. Petersburg).

sleep, but I could not sleep with the clanging of keys, slamming of cell doors, and shoving and stink of prisoners curled on the cement floor like animals. Soon, an electric bell buzzed as loudly as a beehive. Prisoners rose and pushed into a reeking line, time for the *parasha*, or shit barrel. *How many gallons did it contain? How many times had it spilled on the floor?* The *parasha* made me realize Soviet leaders ignored our bodily needs and debased our lives. *Was this my future?*

I stood, holding up my beltless pants, and thought how yesterday we strolled through the Ekaterininskii Public Garden on Nevskii Prospect and talked about industrial development in Leningrad. I knew my Red

Part I—Defeat of the Working Family

Triangle Factory had fulfilled Ordzhonikidze's work order,[2] making new, synthetic rubber products developed by the academic Lebedev.[3] But now I was a prisoner among strangers; few men talked to me. *I'll be home for supper. Prisons are for criminals!*

In the *parasha* line, a clutch of prisoners squashed me. Some fired questions. "Where are you from, comrade?" a gnarled face growled like a tiger. "Are you a Bolshevik?" another asked. "What's going on outside?" "Who's been arrested or shot lately?" "Is it true comrade Kodatskii admitted he was an enemy of the people?"[4] I was shocked and confused, stunned, really, at the rapid-fire questions. I stood speechless, holding up my pants, my head a jumble of thoughts.

An old man with grizzly gray hair touched my arm. "When did they arrest you, son?"

He seemed sincere, and I replied, "This morning, at two o'clock."

"This place is going to jangle your nerves with its all-night questioning. But tell me, what do you do and where are you from?"

I relaxed. "I'm an engineer at the local Red Triangle factory; I was born in Saratov."

"Ahh." The old man looked up, grunting understandingly, "An engineer…"[5]

Another man snarled over his shoulder, "They know how to pick who they arrest."

"Yeah," another scoffed. "Authorities know their business. You're an engineer; they'll call you a saboteur."[6]

Within moments, I heard keys rattle, locks turn, and the screech of

---

2. Ordzhonikidze, Grigorii Konstantinovich (1886–1937), leader of the Industrial Revolution in the 1930s. Wieczynski, *The Modern Encyclopedia of Russian and Soviet History*, vol. 26 (1982), 74–81.

3. Lebedev, Sergei Vasil'evich (1874–1934), discovered the method of making synthetic rubber. Streltsova, A.L. *Krasnyi Treugol'nik* (Leningrad: Lenizdat, 1978), 96–102.

4. Kodatskii, Ivan Fedorovich (1893–1937), Chairman of the Leningrad Executive Committee from 1930, was executed October 10, 1937. Kodatskaia, N.I. "Ivan Fedorovich Kodatskii." Vol'skii, E.V., et al. *Leningradskii martyrolog: 1937–1938: kniga pamiati zhertv politicheskikh repressii*, t.5, *1937 god* (Sankt-Peterburg: Rossiiskaia natsional'naia biblioteka, 2002), 531–535.

5. Repressions at the Red Triangle Factory started in 1930, when Bitker, German Samoilovich (1895–1937), became the head of the rubber industry and befriended its director, Vasil'ev Naum. Earlier, both supported Trotskii, and they were convicted for ignoring methods of producing synthetic rubber as an excuse. Zakovskii, L.M. *O nekotorykh metodakh i priemakh inostrannykh razvedyvatel'nykh organov i ikh trotskistsko-bukharinskoi agentury* (Leningrad: Partizdat TSK VKP (b), 1937), 1–52.

6. Sabotage was one of the most expressive and capacious terms in official Soviet verdicts. In July 1931, Stalin said, "Two years ago we all learned that the majority of qualified old intelligentsia poisoned themselves with the sabotage virus." Iablokov, A. *Istoriia glazami Krokodila. XX vek. Slova 1922–1937* (Moskva: OOO "XX Cenchury Krokodila," 2014), 66.

Two. Shpalernaia Prison

iron-on-iron as the cell's hinges opened. Two scowling guards pushed in, knocking over several *zeks*.[7]

"Bolotov!" one yelled. "Where are you?"

"Right here," I replied, standing and gathering my wit.

"Outside, NOW!" he commanded.

Clinging to my pants, I stepped over legs and arms and jostled to the door.

"Hey, Leonid, just a second," some guy said politely. He tore a strip of fabric from his shirt and held it out. "Take this for a belt. It'll hold up your pants. You'll need your arms to protect yourself when the investigators start beating."

"Thanks," I said, threading the strip through my pant loops. I stepped out of the cell.

A guard with a thick, red neck relocked the door. His partner glanced at me. "Arms behind your back! Head down! Don't turn! Don't talk! Don't drop your arms!" His speech sounded like that of a peasant who left for the city to work for the NKVD.

We walked down a hall as quiet as a midnight graveyard, passing barred cells crammed with silent, child-innocent faces. I barely made out the guards' commands due to the clunking of their heavy boots striking behind me. They shoved me repeatedly. "Arms behind you!"

With fingers laced behind my back, my grip kept slipping and my arms kept dropping. I hurried along, knowing: *Today, they'll read my file. Tonight, I'll be home.*

Finally, at the end of a long hallway, I saw a vestibule, elevator, and staircase. We took the elevator and stopped on the fourth floor. *"Ah-ha, now! After a few questions, they'll see their mistake and let me go!"*

---

7. The abbreviation *zek* is derived from *zakluchennii*, or prisoner. Margolin, Ju. B. *Puteshestvie v stranu Ze-ka* (New York: Izdatel'stvo imeni Čechova, 1952), 20.

Three

My Interrogation

4 Volodarskii Prospect
Office of the NKVD Interrogator
Friday, June 18, 1937, 5:00 a.m.

"STOP!" the young guard shouted.

Filled with fear, I stopped before the fourth-floor office door. The guard rapped.

Within, a shockingly cruel voice bellowed, "Bring in the *accused*," stressing *accused*.

I stumbled over a tread-worn threshold. On my left stood a Paul Buhré grandfather clock[1]; its face exposed a sinking moon and rising sun. It chimed five times. A picture of Stalin hung behind the investigator's desk cluttered with papers, cigarettes, ashtray, matches, and an ink bottle and pen. A safe stood in the far corner beneath a shelf heavy with files. A cool, soft breeze, from the Neva River, whispered through an opened window, rustling *Pravda* newspaper headlined "Soviets Blame Trotskii and Bukharin."[2]

The investigator was writing in a dossier. He did not look up. When he did, I noted the brash face of a stocky man of 40 with black hair gleaming in the long morning rays. He had wide shoulders, a broad chest, and wore a khaki uniform. I stood rigid, arms behind my back, praying I'd transfix him with my innocence. I turned my eyes to stare out the window

---

1. Buhré, Paul-Eduard (1810–1882), was a famous Swiss watchmaker in Saint Petersburg. *Ves' Peterburg: na 1913 god: adresnaja i spravočnaja kniga g. S.-Peterburga* ([SPb.]: izdaniie A.S. Suvorina, [1913], 1389).

2. Bukharin, Nikolai Ivanovich (1888–1938), an economist and theoretician in Party leadership, in 1919 published the widely-read handbook *ABC of Communism* in collaboration with Preobrazhenskii. Wieczynski, *The Modern Encyclopedia of Russian and Soviet History*, vol. 5 (1977), 237–240.

Trotskii, Lev Davidovich (1879–1940), anti-Stalin oppositionist, in 1929 became a political refuge in Turkey, France, and Mexico until Ramon Mercader murdered him. Wieczynski, *The Modern Encyclopedia of Russian and Soviet History*, vol. 39 (1985), 223–233.

Three. My Interrogation

and listen to people walking along the Neva River. *Why is the investigator remaining silent so long. Should I speak first?*

Suddenly, he straightened the dossier, dropped it in a drawer, and stared at me with eyes so angry I cringed. After a long minute, he pointed at a chair.

"Welcome to Shpalernaia Prison, Sir Bolotov."[3] His snide remark twisted open his lips to reveal fake, gold teeth. He picked up a fountain pen and turned a paper around for me to sign.

My ears had perked up at his use of "Sir" twice. I sat down, suspicious and alert.

"Well, Sir Bolotov, tell me the truth about your relatives!" He smirked. "And where you've been, who you've seen, and who you've talked to, so I can add it all to your confession."

Naïvely and cautiously, I glanced at my "confession." It relayed accurate facts about my family, friends, and colleagues, who I never blamed for my arrest.

And then the same questions began, over and over and over. My refusal to sign my confession made the investigator's face turn red. Finally, he shoved the paper aside, wiped his sweaty face on a towel, opened the drawer, and pulled out my dossier.

"You, Sir Bolotov, didn't support the October Revolution; you're a counter-revolutionary. Now, goddamn it, tell me the truth and sign this!"

I was appalled at his absurd accusations. Not only were they outrageous, but they were degrading and offensive. "I hide nothing. Your charge is a mistake. My family is anxiously awaiting my return home," I contested.

The investigator's face deepened to scarlet. His eyebrows bristled. "We, Sir Bolotov, know you're a member of the counter-revolutionary, saboteur organization at your factory. Is that clear?"

"I've told you the truth," I objected. "I've never done any of the things you write."

"Are you going to plead guilty? I'm asking for the last time?" He pounded the desk.

I remained silent. What more could I say?

After a few minutes, the investigator barked, "Well, Bolotov? The truth!"

Hour after hour this haranguing dragged on. Daylight dimmed. I was thunderstruck by the lies, overwhelmed and grief-stricken at the endless babble, which only paralyzed me with fear but strengthened my resolve.

---

3. Spoken sarcastically, the word *Sir,* in Russian, sounds like a synonym for the two words, "intellectual" and "petty bourgeoisie," which the Soviet government inferred was Western life. Iablokov, *Istoriia glazami Krokodila,* 64.

After long hours, he still insisted, "Will you plead guilty? No? Why not, Sir Bolotov?"

"I became a member of the *Komsomol* at 14[4]; I joined the Party in 1931 while a student at Saratov State University and simultaneously working as a P.E. instructor at middle-school number 8. In 1929, I worked as an economist at the Low-Volzhskii Territory.[5] In 1930, my supervisor sent me to Moscow to gain professional development in engineering while my wife graduated from Saratov Pedagogical College. After my graduation, the executive director of the college offered me a choice of three jobs at Berezniki Chemical Factory in Perm Province, Ural Mountains, the Shostkinski Factory in Ukraine, or the Red Triangle Factory. I chose Leningrad's Red Triangle where I still work. Evenings, I teach political economics at Automobile Institute."

Eyes gleaming, the investigator gave me an alligator smile. "We don't arrest the innocent!" he screamed. "Are you saying the Soviet justice system made a mistake?"

I felt hackles rise on my neck. "You made a mistake. Check my file again."

"A mistake?" he drew out the word. "You said mistake! Never!"

He shut his eyes and opened them again. "You're a fascist!"[6] The investigator waved his fists in my face and hissed, "Now sign the damn record! I don't have any more time. I'll dictate, and you write: I, Bolotov Leonid Petrovich, affirm to investigator Baryshnikov[7] that the director of the Red Triangle Factory, Vasil'ev,[8] recruited me as a saboteur for his counter-revolutionary organization and have followed his orders."

He held out his pen. I refused to take it. "Take this pen and write!" he screamed.

I would not touch the pen. "I won't sign lies," I protested.

"You'll sign, or we'll squash you like a bug and send you to Kolyma!"

I remained silent, but I started trembling.

---

4. *Komsomol*, or Communist Youth Organization, was founded for ages 15–28 on October 29, 1918. Wieczynski, *The Modern Encyclopedia of Russian and Soviet History*, vol. 7 (1978), 228–235.

5. The Low-Volzhskii Territory was established on June 11, 1928, with its capital Saratov. Buianov, D.V., et al. *Istoriia administrativno-territorial'nogo delenia Stalingradskogo (Nizhnevolzhskogo) kraia, 1928–1936gg.: spravochnik* (Volgograd: Volgogradskoye nauchnoie izdatel'stvo, 2012).

6. During the 1930s, the term *fascism* related to Mussolini and Hitler. Iablokov, *Istoriia glazami Krokodila*, 63.

7. Baryshnikov, Vladimir Iakovlevich (1900–1971), was a secret agent fighting economic sabotage and crime, 1934–1936. Petrov, N.V. *Kto rukovodil organami gosbezopasnosti 1941–1954* (Moskva: Zveniia, 2010), 182–183.

8. Vasil'ev, Naum Ivanovich (1895–1937), Plant Manager of the Red Triangle Factory 1934 to 1937, was executed August 24, 1937. Vol'skii, E.V., et al. *Leningradskii martyrolog: 1937–1938*, t.4 (2002), 77.

Three. My Interrogation 19

"Shout out the names of all the others!" he screamed. "Who did you tell? Stand up like a man and sign, and I'll save your life!"

I remained seated and quiet.

"Are you going to sit there, silent as a clam?!" The investigator screamed. Jumping from his chair, he began to pace. He waved his fist as he stomped from window to door and back. Then he kicked the chair out from under me. I hit the floor just as a door opened. I looked up at a young man with jet-black hair and soft eyes. He wore a black satin shirt with rolled up sleeves.

My investigator, Baryshnikov, addressed him, "Sapozhnikov, perhaps you can show *Sir* Bolotov a 'beautiful' life."

I stiffened. The pair began interrogating me relentlessly while smoking nervously. Sapozhnikov opened the window wider.

I looked out and thoughts flashed: *How I love Leningrad and its grand buildings on the Neva, Moika, and Fontanka Rivers; its factories: The Red Putilovets, Elektroseela, Mettallic; it's shipbuilding and dockyards. I love the straightforward, honest toil of Leningradians. I love its museums, libraries, and parks. I even love its cold, wet weather, its fog, and rain. Why must I sign lies and leave the life I love?*

After a while, Sapozhnikov left the office. I was alone with Baryshnikov again. He remained silent for an entire hour. While I waited, I watched light beams dazzle on his crystal water-bottle and play on the wall. Those reflections eased my soul.

Baryshnikov, with a quiet but careless voice, tried again, "We, Bolotov, *will save your life* if you sign the confession. If you do not, you *will rot* in a Siberian camp."

I'm exhausted. Let me go.

But then Baryshnikov changed his method of attack. He mentioned that Vasil'ev had recognized all his ideological mistakes, and I was the only one of his employees who had not. I worried: *What did this mean for me? Should I confess?* Vasil'ev endured a party purge April 2, 1937. Comrades Denisov, Kasimov, Tyrkov, and Pavlov blamed him for lack of his ideological work with the engineers. He admitted a few conflicts at the factory but added that the director could not be responsible for everything. After his 30-minute speech, factory workers clapped, and the party committee noted that comrade Vasil'ev had passed its purge without criticism. Despite this fact, Kasimov said that Vasil'ev did not take the solutions of the Central Party Committee seriously.[9] I had read this story in the *Krasnyi*

---

9. The Central Committee was the supreme body of the Party operated during the five-year plans between the Communist Congresses, 1917–1991. Wieczynski, *The Modern Encyclopedia of Russian and Soviet History*, vol. 6 (1978), 165–168.

Treugol'nik newspaper on April 4 and remembered: *Vasil'ev was born into a peasant family. Before 1917, he worked at a factory in Saint Petersburg. Why was he now labeled a saboteur if he confessed?*

Baryshnikov grew nervous, smoking non-stop, and he hurled the newspaper to the floor before starting to swear again. "*Sir* Bolotov, we know you're an instructor of political economy at the Auto Institution. You must help us. It's in your interest. Sign!"

"No," I insisted. "I'll *never* defame my family and friends. Your *'facts'* are wrong."

"Get the hell out of my office!" Baryshnikov shrieked. "Guards!"

Two men took me away. In the dark, ominous corridor I saw an old man. Guards were twisting his arms. *Is this what will be happening to me?* I realized those arrested were not our enemies, and I shared their grief over being branded as such.

We returned to the cell at 7:00 a.m. Saturday, and they shoved me into 20.

Four

Pruss and Aleksandrov

Cell 20
Saturday, June 19–Monday, July 12, 1937

Cell number 20 was dark, filthy, and reeked from the throng of unwashed prisoners with no place to move. Once inside, some men spoke to me, their grimy faces masked with shaggy beards, their breath rancid. They told me they'd been incarcerated for months and wanted to be my friends. As their questions registered, I realized these men were exactly like me. They spoke in careful words that showed respect for me and disdain for the system.

Someone asked, "Why are you here?"

I was stunned and remained silent, taken back, or, perhaps, frightened by their dirty, sad faces crowding closer to hear my reply. Time passed—I don't know how long—as I absorbed their kindness. Some men sat on the cement floor. Others rested on a few plank-beds. Most lay on the floor or squeezed beneath plank-beds or stood shoulder-to-shoulder. I was to learn there was an unspoken law here. Those with the longest terms had a sleeping plank; the newly arrested slept on the floor. Men moved to the middle of the cell for warmth and a plank when their turn arrived. Shuffling was constant, smoking, too; cigarettes rolled from scraps of newspaper around shreds of paper, butts, and trash—anything that would burn. Someone was always leaving the cell; someone is always arriving. Whenever someone left, no one could move as the crowd quickly absorbed the few square inches of space.

Along the back wall were three high, grimy barred windows. Small cracks in glass let in darts of light. Overhead, a tiny, dust-encrusted bulb laced with cobwebs barely glowed, leaving the cell in perpetual gloom. Prisoners coughed, hacked, and spit on the floor. As my eyes adjusted to its duskiness, I saw a large, old, pine table in the middle of the cell where prisoners divided black-bread, broke cubes of sugar, and ate a thin, watery gruel made of flour, bones, turnips, and rotten potatoes, known as *balanda*.[1] Sick, sad, scrawny men sat on the table's bench. I thought of the many prisoners who had sat there over the centuries. We took turns at the table, which provided a semblance of civility. Someone claimed—I couldn't make out his face—the table and bench were built fifty years ago in Aleksander II's time.[2] I didn't doubt him.

The cell door opened. Two old prisoners brought in a pot of *balanda* and set it on the table. The sick men rose from the floor and shuffled to the table; others cleared the way for them to eat. From a judas hole in the cell door, guards watched. They could see the entire cell, even the throne in the far corner. I stood silently, staring at the men from the shadows, the air was so rancid it made me choke and left a crushing foulness in my chest. While we waited to eat, men continued to speak to me. Finally, one persistent old man pushed through close enough to ask, "How are you doing, my dear son?" His voice was friendly, allaying my concerns.

I cleared my throat and said, "I'm okay."

The old man, about 70, had a long, white beard, yellow-stained around his mouth. "I worked with Dzerzhinskii,"[3] he said. "My name's Pruss; I joined the Party in 1899."[4]

I was exhausted, but he wanted to hear my story, so I said, "I didn't sign their accusations. The investigator demanded I sign it for hours, but the confession was slanderous, claiming I was a saboteur."

"You did well; you'll endure. That's important," Pruss said.

As we spoke, the cell quieted. Men whispered about my interrogation and listened. "The investigators try to humiliate and intimidate us," Pruss said. "Remember, engineers are always saboteurs; teachers are anti-government agitators; medical doctors, terrorists, and locomotive drivers are wreckers. If you were an officer in the Red Army, you get the whole bucket of Article 58 thrown at you. If you'd lived abroad, you're a spy. Everybody is an enemy of the people and counter-revolutionary. Remember this," Pruss said and he quoted the penal code:

---

1. From conversations I overheard in my family.
2. Aleksander II (1818–1881), was the all-Russian Emperor, Tsar of Poland, and Grand Duke of Finland, a continuation of the Romanov Dynasty (1613–1917). Wieczynski, *The Modern Encyclopedia of Russian and Soviet History*, vol. 1 (1976), 132–140.
3. Dzerzhinskii, Feliks Edmundovich (1877–1926), Chairman of the Cheka in the Russian Federation, was the father of the Civil War's Red Terror. Wieczynski, *The Modern Encyclopedia of Russian and Soviet History*, vol. 10 (1979), 85–90.
4. Pruss, Vladislav Aleksandrovich (1874–1937), an officer in the NKVD, Leningrad Province, was executed August 27, 1937. Vol'skii, E.V., et al. *Leningradskii martyrolog: 1937–1938*, t.1 (1995), 480.

Four. Pruss and Aleksandrov

"'A counterrevolutionary is any action directed toward the overthrow, subversion, or weakening of the power of the worker-peasant councils.'"[5]

"I know," I said. "I've done none of those things."

When Pruss finished, a handsome, blue-eyed man of 45 pushed closer. He wore a khaki top and pants. "My name is Aleksandrov," he said, studying me carefully and shook my hand. "Please come and join us at the table!"

Aleksandrov was a tall, slender man. As he spoke, he stressed the vowel *o*, and I figured he was from the Lower Volga Region where that accent prevailed. The scar on his face, likely a stab wound, moved as he spoke.

"Come over!" he insisted. "Don't be shy! It's crowded, but here you're a Bolshevik."

I stepped over arms and legs splayed on the floor. Men occupied every inch of space, but I finally reached the table. Someone passed me a tin bowl. Someone else ladled *balanda*, but I was so nervous I couldn't eat. Someone poured me tea.

I said to Aleksandrov, "Please give my meal to somebody else."

Pruss, sitting beside me, said, "I know how hard it is, son. Be steady! I was in the tsar's maximum penitentiary. It was easier at that time: we knew the reason for our arrests, we'd fought the tsar and his reign. Now we haven't a clue why we're here." The old man stayed silent awhile and then asked, "Why were you arrested?"

I admitted my bafflement. "I think someone slanders me."

"Ah, who knows. Do you think the student sitting across from us knows why he's here? Of course not. No one does."

Suddenly, a light dawned in his widening eyes. "Say, you said your name's Bolotov?"

"Yes," I replied, "Leonid Petrovich Bolotov."

"I knew it!" He exclaimed, visibly moved. "Is Petr Antonovich Bolotov, from Saratov, your father?"

"He is."

"Your father and I fought the tsarists together. Now I am sitting with Petr's son! Was he arrested too?"

I touched his arm, comforting him. "No, Dad's at home, or he was. He works in a foundry." I wanted to tell him more, but the thought of Dad choked me up, and I couldn't speak.

Pruss fell to thinking. With a knitted brow, he took a scrap of paper

---

5. Kaple, Deborah. *Gulag Boss: A Soviet Memoir* (New York: Oxford University Press, 2011), 189.

and debris from his pocket to roll a cigarette. He lit it, inhaled, and exhaled foulness.

"Listen, my dear son," he said. "How old are you? Do you have children?"

"I'm 32. We have a boy and girl."

"Whatever you do, Leonid," Pruss warned, *"don't sign their lies."*

"I won't," I vowed.

"You're in the right," he said with conviction. "You *will* win. Only sign the paper if it's honest. Resist interrogators' lies; don't argue; only speak of your life quietly."

His wisdom was helpful in the following months.

Someone in the crowd behind me, said in a strong voice, "You endured their first torture. Be a Bolshevik for as long as it lasts! That's all there is to it!"

Pruss rose and aimed for the planks. "I'm tired," he said, "I must rest." He gently eased through men, got to an empty plank, and flopped down. On the wall above his plank was an old, single-breasted military uniform with gaping crimson buttonholes, buttons removed, and a hole over the heart where investigators had cut off his ribbons. His leather soldiers' boots were beneath the plank, clean and unworn for a long time.

At the table, I spoke to several men and learned some had received different sentences though most were still interrogated nightly, tortured, and ordered to sign lies. Although each of us lived with his interests in mind, all the men were interested in the outcome of every other prisoner. The utter defeat of the investigators was, to a man, our goal, our glory.

For the next two months, I lived in cell 20 with over 100 men. I met all of them, and, to this day, remember their stories, lives, hometowns, families, and work. Sadly, when becoming exhausted by investigations, sleeplessness, beatings, and hunger, some men signed, confessing their participation in fascism, terrorism, and even to belonging to Chinese Emperor Puyi's family, though none could recall his name or ever being in China.[6]

---

6. Puyi's reign's name, Xuantong (1906–1967), was the last emperor of the Qing Dynasty, 1908–1911. Pu Yi, Henry. *The Last Manchu: The Autobiography of Henry Pu Yi, Last Emperor of China* (New York: Skyhorse, 2010).

Five

The Sailor

Shpalernaia Prison, Cell 20
Tuesday, July 13–Tuesday, July 27, 1937

 Mid-July arrived. I was still in Shpalernaia Prison. Interrogations continued. Summer's white nights often brought all-night rains. Through the cell's broken glass in three barred windows, rainwater seeped across the floor where we lay, making sleeping shivering wet and miserable. Sodden, I stayed bone-cold 24 hours a day, 850 miles north of Saratov.

 Guards tried to crush my mind and obstinacy. Unlike other exhausted prisoners who succumbed to beatings and torture and confessed to being spies of the Chinese or enemies of the people, I did not. With growing tension from snowballing confessions, the cell grew soundless, the men untrusting and despondent. A few gathered in small groups to whisper and smoke, debating if they, too, should confess to escape crushing torture. Some prisoners concluded that if a majority signed the confessions, it would force the authorities to deal with their lies. Others thought that we must uphold our rights and confess to nothing. Sadly, life continued its cruel course.

 Pruss turned to me one day and said, "Leonid, things will be changing soon."

 I was going to respond, but suddenly, as if to break our miserable monotony, we heard the bell ring once again: guards bringing a new prisoner. The cell door opened. They shoved in a fearless-looking man wearing a sailor's uniform with the rank of captain. His arrival was as welcome as a summer thunderstorm breaking a heat wave. With its high, tailored collar, his outfit appeared to be a *Komsomol* uniform, despite the blouse being in tatters where medals had been ripped off. The captain was movie-star handsome with a chiseled jaw and closely cropped beard, wide forehead, and intense blue eyes that studied us.

 I was flabbergasted: *What was a sailor doing here?*

"Hello, dear comrades!" he said in a joyous voice. "I'm a Navy captain. Seventeen years ago, I worked with Lenin. The investigators tore off my military medals, even the one from the All-Russian Central Executive Committee."[1] He pressed his chin to his chest to look down at the hole in his uniform. Vexed, he clenched his fists and vowed, "I'll never forgive them. They tore off my medals and slammed them on their table like trash! They threw away my Order of Lenin!"[2]

We were astonished. "Why did they do that?" someone asked.

The captain slapped the hole. "I told them they hadn't given me these medals, and they had no right to take them!" His hands clenched into fists, ready to assail his unreachable aggressors. "There's no doubt about it! They're on high horses, and we are..." he stammered, "must kill them! They're nothing but reptiles, scum, and rogues! I showed them just what the hell kind of an enemy of people I am!" he shouted indignantly.

"You're fearless!" a prisoner avowed.

"Well, my dear Eagles," the captain said, "The Party will listen and protect us!"

His voice renewed our hope and reanimated us. The cell grew silent as if it were holding its collective breath. Men started to comprehend that they did not have to listen to the investigators. Prisoners *could* do something: fight their lies.

Raising his fists, the sailor declared, "I brawled with the investigator for more than 24 hours and still he demanded I confess and sign that Marshal Tukhachevskii was a spy.[3] I told him, I'm not signing that abomination! Tukhachevskii was Marshal of the entire Red Army. But the investigator argued and said I was an old fogey who didn't know a thing about Tukhachevskii who became a spy at 12 and needed to have his record straightened! That's all they were asking! I argued, Are you nuts? And my investigator screwed up his face; his eyes turned menacing. He snarled and said it would not work, that Tukhachevskii was a mole having admitted his close collaboration with German intelligence! He'd lost Soviet citizenship because he did not protect the governmental military goals, and I replied, You don't know me and you don't know Marshal Tukhachevskii!"

The captain continued, "The investigator tried to intimidate me by

---

1. The All-Russian Central Executive Committee was the supreme legislative and administrative organ of the Russian Federation, 1917–1937. Wieczynski, *The Modern Encyclopedia of Russian and Soviet History*, vol. 1 (1976), 165.

2. The Order of Lenin, the highest order of the USSR, was established April 6, 1930, for outstanding activities done in the name of the government. Wieczynski, *The Modern Encyclopedia of Russian and Soviet History*, vol. 21 (1981), 160.

3. Tukhachevskii, Mikhail Nikolaevich (1893–1937), the youngest Marshal in the USSR, was executed June 12, 1937. Wieczynski, *The Modern Encyclopedia of Russian and Soviet History*, vol. 40 (1985), 79–82.

shouting. But he looked like Tom Thumb, and I yelled back, Why are you talking to me like that? I'm not deaf! The investigator was so angry, he jumped out of his chair, and so did I! We glared at each other, shaking with rage, when, at that very moment, a giant of a man burst into the office. He was about 25 and built like a buffalo. He came at me, eyes glaring beneath a protruding brow, arms as big as my waist, and giant mitts wanting to knuckle me. You're a provocateur! I couldn't restrain myself and bark, Who the hell is a spy? You are! Who's a provocateur? You are! He snatched my arm, and I grabbed a stool and whacked him on the head! The investigator snarled at me, I'm going to put a straitjacket on you, and you can rot in the Gulag!"

Suddenly, we heard a guard yell from outside. "Shut the hell up in the cell or else!"

The sailor shouted back, "You shut the hell up!"

The student shoved his way to the door and joined the sailor's taunt. "Go catch some innocent people; better yet, arrest your parents!"

The guard yelled, "You'll be going to the punishment cell!"

"Ha!" the student sneered. "Idiot, your cells are all punishment cells, and they're full!"

A key rattled in the lock. The guard burst through the door, and the student melted into the crowd. The guard called out the sailor's name: Dybenko. The sailor lit a cigarette. He did not move. More guards appeared and approached Dybenko. He pulled off his uniform jacket and folded it on the bench. Guards grabbed his arms and yanked him out of the cell. When we heard Dybenko's famous name, we were astonished. The consensus was he was brave for creating a stir. In hushed voices, we discussed the unjust investigators, the flaunting of Soviet laws and power-grab.

Pruss kept repeating, "You know, Dybenko's right!"

Fourteen days and nights passed. Dybenko's merciless beatings persisted. His handsome face became a bloody pulp of bruises, puffed lips and swollen eyelids nearly shut. His uniform degenerated into dirty, bloody rags, and scraps of underwear hung out holes in his once fine pants. His legs and feet, swollen to the size of logs, were too bloated for shoes and his filthy toes poked through holes in his ragged socks. He was exhausted and emaciated. His once broad shoulders had wasted away beneath his rags and looked like tatters draped on a coat-tree. I couldn't look at him.

And still, investigators burst into the cell, grabbed Dybenko in death grips, and screamed that he had betrayed the motherland. But the sailor bravely fought back. His beatings continued. His heroic behavior gave us courage, and every time he was dumped in the cell, we attended him.

Once when we heard the bell ring and the door unlocks, the sailor appeared so beaten and bloody that when the guards pushed him into the cell, he dropped in a heap like a sack of potatoes. He tried to stand but could only get to his knees. He couldn't breathe due to his flattened nose. We lifted him onto a bench. He couldn't lift his head from his shoulder. Pruss and Aleksandrov sat next to him, whispering.

Everyone wanted to know if he had signed the accusation, but the sailor remained silent. Our questions continued. He gasped mightily, raised his swollen arms, and clenched his fists as his eyes swam. The cell turned deathly silent. Prisoners squeezed in closer.

The captain lifted his wobbly head, forced his eyes open, and stared at us. "I signed nothing," he said. Then he clenched his feeble fists in defiance. His head was so heavy it fell to his chest. After a long minute, he moaned. "How insolent they are. They don't know anything other than doing their leaders' dirty work. I'm a true Communist! I must escape this madness!"

Dybenko wept. Aleksandrov offered him some of his tea, but Dybenko couldn't drink it. He laid his swollen arms on the table, dropped his wounded head on them, and slept.

"The investigators are beasts," someone whispered.

"Worse," the locomotive driver said.

"Shh, be quiet," hissed the Intourist worker.

Aleksandrov asked, "How much sugar can we collect for the captain?"

Somebody said, "Four small cubes."

"Not enough. The captain needs more."

I looked around at the prisoners' skeleton arms and frail bodies. "Take mine!" I said.

Others said, "Here, take mine too! And mine!"

Aleksandrov looked at our emaciated faces and collected the sugar. "Thank you, men! We've enough to help him! Now step back and let him sleep."

Brevda, a medical doctor at the Military Medical Academy, rolled a cigarette and said ironically, "Well, the captain would be happy to enjoy this cigarette—if he could inhale!"[4]

The door opened. Guards stepped in. We glanced at their fat, pink faces: *Who'd be next?* But they pushed through us purposefully. One guard eyeballed the sailor, and, stretching out vowels in his name, howled, "Doo-beenkooo! What's your full name?"

Someone groaned, "Oh, no, not the sailor again!"

The locomotive driver whispered, "These scoundrels are real bastards, damn machines!"

The sailor was slumped over the table, asleep. The entire cell was furi-

---

4. Brevda, Isaak Solomonovich (1892–1984), spent ten years in Kolyma. http://arch.iofe.center.

Five. The Sailor

ous. We mumbled curses and glared threateningly, but there was nothing we could do. We were in limbo.

The sailor had declared, "Tears won't help; fight for your lives! Never sign fake confessions."

The young men realized that they must follow that truth during questioning, suffer beatings, and await the court's decision. Only the Soviet court investigates facts and determines the truth.

I was worried about the sailor and wanted to pace, but there was no room, so I stood and pushed men aside. They shoved back. I stepped around some and over others, still trying to walk and think. One man, a typesetter, had worked at an underground newspaper during the Tsar's reign. The typesetter acted as if the cell were his home. Recently beaten, he had a line of sore-looking knots across his forehead that looked like red beads.

He offered, "There are three sets of investigators; they work in eight-hour shifts."

At the table, the guard glared at the captain and snarled, "Stand up, sailor!"

Every head in the cell turned and stared, faces red with fury. The sailor had just begun to sleep. Men helped him stand. Aleksandrov carefully raised the sailor's head, and a professor started to speak. The old man shook his head, and his long beard swayed as he looked at the sailor with sad eyes. He reached over, and tenderly raised his chin to let him sip sweet tea.

"Drink, Dybenko! Drink!" the men around him chimed.

The captain did not open the eyes. He sipped tea and choked.

The guard grew angry and screamed, "Dybenko, tell us your full name! Now!"

The sailor swallowed the tea, inhaled deeply, opened his eyes, and raised his eyebrows at the guard barking, "Come on Dybenko move! If you don't move, I'm going to punish the entire cell. You there—" he addressed Aleksandrov—"help him up!"

With help, the sailor stood, slowly straightened his back, and stood rigidly erect as if ready to address a fleet. He staggered, stepping back from the table, his bloated legs barely functioning. He waddled to the door like a crippled penguin. Then unexpectedly, he stopped and turned to face us. The cell hushed. He rasped, "My brothers," and then he lost his train of thought. He peered at his swollen feet and tattered socks. He said, "My socks are in shreds."

His mind was not functioning. He stared with a vacant look in his eyes.

Someone cautioned, "Don't sign any false documents, Captain!"

The captain turned to face the cell. His puffy eye-slits opened. He mustered the resolve to stand erect, as if to march, and cried out, "They have no right to intimidate people! Does the Party want that? NO! My treatment is a provocation!"

The guard screamed, "Shut up and move! Arms behind you! Out!" and shoved him.

From where I stood, I saw the wide corridor and cells to the left and right. The captain appeared resolute; his bearing portrayed the conviction to continue fighting. He lurched out of sight. The hushed cell, in awe and respect for him, heard him say, "Even if they kill me, I'll remain a Bolshevik. Who knows? Maybe I'll survive."

After his departure, our cell came alive with chatter. Aleksandrov groaned, "The captain will never sign their stupid lies! My heart weeps for him; they'll beat him senseless."

A metalworker, who I'd never heard speak, said, "It's a case of diamonds cutting diamonds."

Words flew from the lips of men: "Damn investigators!"

Pruss slumped on his plank in gloomy silence. I weaved through the men and sat next to him. "The captain believes in his innocence. They may crush his body, but they'll never crush his spirit," he said.

Beside the captain's remarkable stamina, I remember Tyrkov. He was a short, frail man. Tyrkov, too, like the captain, returned to the cell his face and body welted with scars and bruises. He, too, had refused to admit Chudov was a spy.[5]

---

5. Chudov, Mikhail Semenovich (1893–1937), Chairman of the All-Union Cooperative Organization, was executed October 29,1937. Vol'skii, E.V., et al. *Leningradskii martyrolog: 1937–1938*, t.5 (2002), 203.

Six

The Pilot

Shpalernaia Prison, Cell 20
Wednesday, July 28–Saturday, July 31, 1937

In our cell, the throng of prisoners was frail, thin, and filthy with scruffy beards and grimy, tattered clothes. One man stood out. He was a new, tall, handsome student-pilot of 26 wearing a crisp army uniform. For a month, he maintained a proud, silent gloom. He watched us from under a heavy brow fringed with thick eyelashes. He avoided contact. We gave him little concern, for all of us had experienced shattered hopes, growing fears, and the need for silence.

Surprisingly, one day, he spoke. He was sitting next to older men, which frightened them. They thought him a spy. "I signed their damn accusations," the pilot admitted. "And for my confession, they gave me a package from my parents as a reward."

Prisoners ignored his admission, for at that very instant the bell rang for lunch. Guards carried in a small barrel of *balanda*. Prisoners with bowls quickly snatched them from their pockets, held them out for a scoop of watery soup, and ate. Those without bowls waited for others to lick out their bowls like dogs. There were never enough bowls to go around. Men slurped *balanda*, licked their bowls clean, and passed them to the next in line.

Unlike us, the pilot did not get in the chow line. Under his arm, he carried a wooden box. While we slurped and lapped and waited, he opened the box, removed a starched, white napkin and spread it out over one end of the table. He removed a loaf of golden *challah* bread and a chunk of smoked salami. He lifted out a bottle of sweet tea, a package of Northern Palmira cigarettes, and laid them neatly on the napkin. Other prisoners' eyes gaped in disbelief as the pilot tore off a chunk of bread, a hunk of salami, and ate.

We drooled. I was still awaiting a bowl for my *balanda* when the pilot burped. He wiped his lips with his crisp napkin and started smoking. Prisoners had had enough and started mumbling curses. One man, a former grocery bagboy, still spooning his *balanda*, yelled, "The pilot doesn't eat our food. Why do guards treat him better than us?"

Two students, awaiting bowls, asked the pilot, "Why did you sign their confession?"

He sidestepped the question. "You guys yak too much."

"Don't dodge the question!" exploded a student. "Tell us the truth!"

"There's nothing to tell!"

The students glared at the pilot. Pruss, who'd heard the conversation, calmly asked the pilot, "Why did you sign their accusation?"

"It was all bullshit!"

"Tell us about it," Pruss continued. "Don't dance around, and we'll treat you better."

Angry prisoners jammed around him, waiting to hear the pilot's story of betrayal. Still sitting at the table, the pilot sighed and shuddered. He glanced at the menacing men and appeared frightened. His body turned as rigid as a stone; muscles in his neck quaked.

"I signed their document about Marshal Tukhachevskii," the pilot confessed.

"What did it accuse him of doing?" Pruss asked.

"Ordering me to cross the Chinese border as if I was the Marshal's spy."

"Is that the truth?"

"Of course not. I'd never seen Tukhachevskii. Only pictures of him after his execution last month."

Men pushed in closer and asked, "Then why did you do it?" several asked.

In a cold sweat, the pilot wiped his brow on his uniform sleeve. He took a deep breath to summon his courage and looked at Pruss. "I told them I was a kid, too young to fly over our border with China when he said I had. I told him I was in high school when I was ordered to fly over the border on Tukhachevskii command. And that's the truth. Four years later I graduated from the Balashov Air Force School in Saratov Province and became a pilot."[1] But the investigator insisted, "Your age doesn't matter—only your pilot skill is important. It proves Marshal's denunciation. We'll keep your timing quiet."

The frightened pilot's uniform was sweat soaked. Prisoners studying him thought of their youth. Pruss, again cited the penal code:

---

1. The National Air Force School was founded in 1930. Wieczynski, ed., *Supplement*, 1988, vol. 47, 52.

Six. The Pilot

"In case of flight across the border by a military member, the adult members of his family, if they in any way aided the preparation or carrying-out of treason, or only knew about it and failed to report it to authorities, shall be punishable by deprivation of liberty for a term of five to 10 years, with confiscation of all property."[2]

Most understood his need to confess, stimulated by his story. It could have happened to any of them. The cell remained quiet, men filled with gloom, guilt, and horror. And then gradually, men whispered to one another. I couldn't make out their words; they were careful of being overheard. Only a wave of soft grumbles spread through the cell.

"Cell number 20, quiet!" yelled a guard from outside the lockup.

The men crowded close to the pilot. He remained sitting. In low voices, they whispered about his case. Then, after being repeatedly asked, he retold his story.

A peasant had heard enough. "You, pilot, are a slanderer who licks the gates of hell!"

That did it. The mood in the cell changed from understanding to disgust. The pilot's eyes swept the room, taking in the men glaring at him as a coward.

"Hey," he protested. "Screw it, I'm dead anyway!"

"Ahh, come on!" shouts rose. "You're a rotter! A monster!"

"Yes, you ruin the memory of an innocent man, son," Pruss said and turned away.

"I didn't want to," the pilot whined. "I had no reason to ruin Tukhachevskii. You know how investigators *talk* to people, with arms and clubs."

"Stop bellyaching," someone shouted. "We know firsthand how investigators *talk*."

Although a few prisoners remained silent, most were upset. "Are you a warrior or a coward?!" "Why didn't you bare your teeth?" "Don't you know how much the investigators cost all of us?"

From the corridor, a jailer barked, "Cell 20, shut up!"

The pilot became frightened. He tousled his hair, wiped his brow, and scratched his armpits.

Aleksandrov stepped over to the pilot and asked, "What *do you* know about Marshal Tukhachevskii?" He sounded hostile.

"Only good things," the pilot replied.

"Okay, I understand you had no purpose for ruining him. But do you understand what you did? Why betrayed him again?"

The army marshal's comrades were troubled and began relating fond

---

2. Kaple, *Gulag Boss*, 190.

memories of him. Tukhachevskii's soldiers smashed the White Army led by Kolchak in southwestern Siberia.[3] Others recalled how his Army smashed Denikin's forces[4] in the Caucasus Mountains and then destroyed the rebellion in Kronstadt in 1921.[5]

As the conversation went on: *How the pilot could have possibly agreed to declare Tukhachevskii a spy. The investigators must have beaten him to confession.*

"What now?" the pilot cried, his body limp with fear.

"Get the hell out, Judas, that's what!" someone yelled.

The former manager of the political department said, "My dear, young friend, they'll shoot you twice. First as a spy! Then as a betrayer!"

The pilot wept. "Sure, but they'll shoot you as well."

"You're not a real pilot!" someone yelled. "You're our executioner!"

The pilot laid his head on the table and sobbed.

Aleksandrov stepped over to him, running his hand through his hair in frustration, and stared at the pilot with disdain. Then he tapped the pilot's shoulder. "You've forgotten that truth is brighter than the sun." Aleksandrov looked around. "Am I right, men?"

"Yes!" the men cried. "The pilot's a liar!"

Aleksandrov retold the pilot of Tukhachevskii achievements: How he fought the White Army, how he drove White officers and soldiers from Russian cities. "He freed Samara, Syzran, and even Simbirsk, Lenin's city. They forced your denunciations, but that didn't give you permission to slander Tukhachevskii. You're out of the Party!" Aleksandrov stopped speaking and smoothed his hair. We were mesmerized, staring at him: *What he'd do next.* The long scar across his face twitched as he asked the pilot, "Have you ever flown to China?"

"Of course not," the pilot explained hopefully. "I was a kid."

"Then how could you have delivered Tukhachevskii's orders? You couldn't, so retract your confession!" Aleksandrov growled, his arm making a circle above his head.

The pilot gazed up then stared at the floor in dejected silence.

"Look at these people, pilot. They're dirty, their clothes are rags,

---

3. Kolchak, Aleksandr Vasil'evich (1874–1920), a polar explorer and commander in the Imperial Russian Navy, fought in the Russo-Japanese War (1904–1905) and in World War I. He was recognized as the "Supreme Ruler and Commander-in-Chief of All Russian Land and Sea Forces" by the leaders of the White movement. Wieczynski, *The Modern Encyclopedia of Russian and Soviet History*, vol. 17 (1980), 110–113.

4. Denikin, Anton Ivanovich (1872–1947), was a lieutenant general in the Imperial Russian Army (1916) and, later, one of the White generals in the Civil War. Wieczynski, *The Modern Encyclopedia of Russian and Soviet History*, vol. 9 (1978), 64–67.

5. The Kronstadt uprising was a major unsuccessful uprising against the Bolsheviks in March 1921. Wieczynski, *The Modern Encyclopedia of Russian and Soviet History*, vol. 18 (1980), 94–97.

Six. The Pilot

they're starving, yet they have betrayed no one. Now, *retract your words!*"

Just as Aleksandrov spoke, we heard the heavy tread of guards approaching. The cell door squeaked open and, astonishingly, the guards called the pilot's name. He pushed off the table and walked to the door. Pruss took his arm and said, "Son, believe in the truth."

The pilot left with his box of food and us: *What would happen to him?*

Naturally, the men started talking. Some were frank and talked loudly. Others whispered. It was stuffy in the cell, and I went to the broken window and sat on a plank with the engineer from the Kirovski Plant. An artist sat at my feet wearing a dirty, torn, dress-shirt. His head looked huge, crowned by a helmet of black curls. He was around 35 and acted like a puffed-up Tom Turkey, sitting on his suit coat in the Turkish manner. When he spoke, his deep voice soothed like a cat's purr. One man, a famous mathematician, said, "People have been living in hell. In desperation, the intellectuals shape makeshift chessmen out of bread, charcoal, and spit, avoiding the future with games. We all respond to cruelty differently."

The engineer and I were tired of talking about the pilot. He asked me, "Where did you grow up? Was your young life happy?"

I responded, "Yes, I grew up in Saratov on the Volga River."

We never saw the pilot again.

Seven

I'm Held in Captivity

Nikolaevskii District, Saratov Province
Reflections on the Summer of 1919

Inside our cell, storytelling helped shorten our days. When it was my turn, I decided to tell the tale of my father and my capture by the Cossacks. It began: In the summer of 1919, Dad was secretary of the Volzhskii Party District, member of the Board of Consumer's Society, delivering food and goods across Saratov, and member of the Revolutionary Tribunal and Committee for Registration of Bourgeoisie of the Red Guard. His boss asked him to propagandize revolutionary ideas among peasants.

Before that summer, I'd never left Saratov. My parents were poor, and I often dreamed of leaving the dusty city to gallop across Saratov's broad steppes. Our Nikolaevskii District consisted of 1700 square miles and contained a diverse population of Bashkirs, Germans, Jews, Russians, and Tatars. That summer, my father was sent to the Nikolaevskii District to confiscate grain from local peasants. The Saratov newspapers had declared a bread shortage in Russian cities, and Lenin's government barely survived that disaster.

Lenin's decree resulted in a four-year struggle in Saratov. In 1918, Cossacks abolished the Bolshevik's Council of Workers and Peasants in the Ural Province and formed a military government. They vowed to sweep Bolsheviks from power. Every day we read accounts of the Cossacks' and peasants' rebellions breaking out across the province. They claimed, the development of the success of our enemy in the Nikolaevskii District troubled a lot of people. Accurate information about this district was missing; for example, the district's military strength was wrong, and we were told to reveal all the drastic measures.

Despite these worrisome events, I asked father to take me with him to collect grain. Early one summer morning, I heard hoof beats and looked out the window. Father appeared at our house with a horse and wagon loaded with hay. My heart leaped. For the first time in my 12 years, I'd ride in a horse-drawn wagon and be free to see the countryside and explore.

I jumped out of bed and yelled, "Bye, Mommy," and ran out to see the chocolate brown horse with white stockings legs and a long black tail. I named her *Belonozhka*; Dad hid the rifle and papers under the hay; we climbed into the wagon and left home.

Soon our sprawling city disappeared as we drove east into the vast steppes, alive with fresh air and swooping birds, rolling out in front of us. Our first day was 15 hours long. But the ride filled with chirping birds and drinking streams' fresh water in the hot, spaciousness was delightful. Father relayed tales of the Volga River and Stepan Razin[1] and told me of native birds and the vast sky and barge haulers, along with tales of Scythians. These mental threads still stretch across my mind, linking my family's past to my present, and I still feel their presence in my soul. I understood my motherland's heart for the first time; here was its blood and flesh. At that moment, I teared up in happiness and wanted to kiss every grain of sand, every blade of grass, and every soaring bird. I felt any grief befalling the steppes would be my grief, any happiness my happiness.

As the sun climbed, we grew thirsty and hungry. The sky was cloudless, the land parched. The arid steppes stretched out endlessly. Finally, father stopped for a rest and lunch beside a stream. I jumped down, gave *Belonozhka* hay, and we enjoyed bread and honey and water from a babbling stream. I caught grasshoppers while listening to Dad's stories how birds taught their babies to fly the same route for thousands of years. He laughed and called me his Gosling.

The first day was long, and we finally stopped beside another stream, fed and watered *Belonozhka*, ate more bread with honey, and bathed in the cool waters. Dad smoked as the sky turned pitch-black and a dome of stars popped out, sprinkling the heavens to the horizon. I felt peace, listening to the soft coos of nesting birds and snuggling deep into the wagon's prickly hay for a good night's sleep.

At dawn, we rose, washed our faces, ate, fed the horse, and drove on to the next village where father asked the same questions: Who collects the grain for the government? Where is he? And how much is for the government, and when will it arrive in Saratov? With his duties discharged, Dad always made notes, and we'd leave for the next village. We'd been on our trip a week. It didn't rain, and the grass turned yellow as the hot south

---

1. Razin, Stepan Timofeevich (1630?–1671), led a Don Cossack rebellion against the nobility in southern Russia in 1670–1671. Wieczynski, *The Modern Encyclopedia of Russian and Soviet History*, vol. 52 (1990), 56–62.

winds burned our faces beet red and layered the road with thick dust. Father's face looked as brown as a gypsy's beard.

On the tenth day, we stopped at a large village, and, after Dad met with the Bolsheviks, he became nervous. People hurriedly gave us milk and loaves of freshly baked bread, still warm, for lunch. We ate quickly, and father's voice turned dire. We must flee for Saratov *immediately*, he exclaimed, never explaining why. We jumped into the wagon, and Dad slapped the reins on *Belonozhka*. We galloped at breakneck speed for home and only stopped minutes in villages for food, water, and hay. As the hours dragged on, Dad urged *Belonozhka* to trot. I felt something evil was about to happen.

Night came, yet under its starry blanket, we pushed westward. I slumped against Dad and closed my eyes. When I opened them again, the stars had disappeared, and there was a faint glow behind us of pink clouds floating on the horizon. With building anxiety, I asked, Dad, why did you drive all night? Dad yawned and said, "Go back to sleep."

Well, I couldn't go back to sleep. Soon the sky turned scarlet, and a big red ball of sun popped out of the steppes. My sweaty hands itched, and I looked at them, covered with red splotches, like chickenpox, from the prickly hay. Then Dad interrupted my concerns with real ones.

He tapped my leg and said Cossacks entered the village we were in last night. They're coming this way to attack. Petrov is our new name, if anyone asks. Soon we saw a dust plume rising behind us, and we shouted at *Belonozhka* to run. Dad and I put our ears to the road and soon watched a huge dust plume rise higher and higher. It grew closer every second. With resignation at our upcoming capture, we remounted the wagon, Dad took the reins, slapped *Belonozhkas'* flank, and clucked. Within 10 minutes, a gang of 20 riders swooped down upon us. Dad yanked the reins. *Belonozhka* reared and stopped. He did not expect that we will meet Cossacks fast.

I was so scared my tongue froze numb in the day's stifling heat. I wanted answers, but one look at father's face told me to be quiet. His red face grew pale; his eyebrows jumped like panicked caterpillars.

The riders reined in their horses. Dust settled. The men carried rifles and long curved sabers. A sunburned Cossack thundered, "Where're you two going?"

Dad replied calmly that we want to see his weak father.

The Cossacks grinned broadly, revealing crooked teeth, and sneered, "let's see your papers! Where do you live and who controls your village?"

Dad was unfazed and said, "I don't have papers. Sometimes Bolsheviks, sometimes Whites, sometimes nobody."

"And who are you, kid?" asked another Cossack.

Seven. I'm Held in Captivity

"My name's Sanka Petrov, and I'm going to visit my grandfather," I replied.

A stern looking Cossack ordered, "You two out of the wagon; stand over there!" He pointed his rifle to one side, and we stepped to the spot indicated. All the Cossacks dismounted and stomped up to us. They searched father and the wagon. I was frightened they'd find his gun and papers and knew they'd behead us. But the Cossacks didn't find anything on him or in the wagon. I was overjoyed: What had Dad done with his papers and rifle? My courage fled, and I clung to Dad. People said Cossacks beheaded kids with sabers. I prayed it wouldn't happen to me!

A Cossack ordered Dad to strip to his long johns; then it was my turn. The Cossacks searched me. I didn't own underwear, and after I was naked, they let me pull my pants back on.

One Cossack took *Belonozhka* by the bridle; two others rode beside us to the next town as we walked barefoot behind the wagon. The others galloped ahead at full speed.

I felt sorry for *Belonozhka* and hated the Cossacks and their fast horses. Two hours later, we saw a fork in the road and a sprawl of men. The Cossacks had driven them out of the next town; they ordered us to join this throng. Then, we walked on, and Cossacks added clusters of men, fellow Bolsheviks, all hungry and thirsty, but we were denied food and water. One Cossack with a deep voice shouted, "Ask again, and you'll get a bullet in the head!"

We walked all that day, slept in a field that night and, exhausted, on the second day were driven into a town and locked in a pen of high wooden fence encircling the enclosure. A house stood on one side. Hundreds of us were trapped there. The Cossacks took father and me to a corner and ordered us not to speak to anyone.

Soon an officer came to the porch, wearing a clean uniform with a white badge on his hat and bright shoulder boards. His eyes swept over the crowd. His face distorted. He fondled his saber. I worried he'd lob off heads. But he stepped off the porch into the crowd and shouted, in a nasal tone, "We're only shooting Communists. We'll let the rest of you go! But if you hide the truth, we'll kill everyone without trial!"

We froze. The officer's piercing eyes swept over us. Now, who are the Bolsheviks?

Every man bit his tongue.

He shouted, "We'll shoot every tenth man, then!"

The Cossacks counted the prisoners in groups of 10 and took them away for interrogation. Afterwards, the Cossacks threw men out of the house covered with blood, their bodies black and blue and bleeding from lashing. One in 10 men never came out. Two burly Cossacks approached us in the far corner and took Dad away. I remained rooted to the spot, awaiting his return. An hour later, Dad was shoved out of the house, his back deeply lashed.

For three days the Cossacks' torture continued, without food or water. Our lips were cracked open and bled. Some men fell into heaps; a few died of thirst. But on the fourth day, three big farmers appeared, and our agony increased. They'd probably been wealthy landowners before the Bolsheviks rose to power. They recognized and identified local Communists from the crowd, prodding them with sticks, like cattle, screaming, "He's a Bolshevik! He's a Commissar!" Then the Cossacks took those men away.

Dad said, "These guys know the local Bolsheviks; they've lived here a long time."

I watched the Cossacks bustling about all that afternoon. They formed columns of prisoners, lashing them into rows. When I ran to Dad's side, a Cossack grabbed me and hauled me inside the house, asking, "Why are you here, boy?"

"I was on the way to grandpa's home," I replied.

"Well, get out of here! Your grandpa will find you!"

"I can't go without him!" I started to cry uncontrollably and shake with fear. When I stopped sobbing, I begged the Cossack to let grandpa go with me!

At that very moment, another Cossack stomped on my bare foot, breaking my left big toe. Decades later, it still looks awful and crooked, and it reminds me of those horrors. But that day, I screamed and hopped up and down in one-legged agony. The nail on my big toe cracked open. Blood spurt. While I was hopping, a phone rang. I heard half the conversation. Someone had ordered the officer to march all the prisoners east as quickly as possible.

The officer with the mustache questioned me, and I stuck to my story. Frustrated, he finally booted me out the door and whipped me as I stumbled. His last blow sent me stumbling across the yard. I limped to father's side.

Then, in great confusion, the Cossacks, ordered the men into two columns, yelling, "All Bolsheviks are going east!" Quickly the columns shuffled out of the pen and headed in the direction we'd come. Despite my broken toe and lame foot, I hobbled as fast as I could, clinging to father's hand. I scrubbed tears from my eyes with the back of my hand, looked up, and saw fear and sympathy in father's eyes as we fell in at the end of the line. He moaned and gently raised my bare foot to examine the toe. He tore off a corner of his long johns and tenderly tied the dirty fabric around my big toe. Later, as we walked in the dust, Dad spotted, and picked, the elliptical leaf of green plantain, opened the bandage, and tied it against my big toe.

Hours later, we entered a village, and residents flooded out their

Seven. I'm Held in Captivity

wooden homes to stare at us. They pointed at different prisoners and screamed. "They're Bolsheviks!"

Cossacks shot them on the spot. With every new village, the length of our column dwindled as Cossacks shot identified men. Simultaneously, the column buzzed like a beehive with men debating their fate and certain execution in Uralsk.[2] By the time we made it to the last village that first day, it was dark. Guards herded us into a yard surrounded by a dilapidated wooden fence. One Cossack stood posted at the gate; another patrolled the perimeter; the balance of them galloped off on another mission. Exhausted, we collapsed to the ground. Dad immediately fell asleep, but hunger kept me awake.

Glancing around, I timed my jump over the fence, and soon scrounged about the village. It was deathly quiet. There was a sliver of moon. A dog growled. Frightened, I gave up and started back. But then I spotted the silhouette of a woman standing in her fenced yard. I heard a gate squeak as she opened it. She wore a kerchief and long dress. Closer, she was old, probably mother's age, 38. I dug my broken toe in the dirt to flee, but she called me softly. She seemed friendly and smiled. "What are you doing here, son? I bet you're hungry." I nodded and stepped closer. Bending down, the woman wrapped me in soft arms and pulled me into the warmth of her big, soft breasts. I prayed for food as she went inside. She came out with a glass of milk and a loaf of bread. I stuffed bread into my mouth and gulped milk. She gave me a packet of tobacco and two papers. Then she said that the leader of the Cossacks is staying in the next village. "He's cruel to Bolsheviks. But there aren't any Cossacks in our village, just a couple of guards. If you flee, the steppes are vast and ripe with sunflowers and wheat to fill your belly."

I nodded understandingly, finished the bread and thanked her. She hugged me, and I left.

I slipped through the village, scampered over the fence, and crept to father's side like a three-legged colt, holding the big loaf of bread in one hand. I tried not to wake him, but he was already awake, waiting for me, worried. I gave him the bread and tobacco, and he asked me to tell him what happened.

I told him the story, how I jumped the fence and hid under red, thick, high bushes. Knowing that the only one Cossack was here guarding us, Dad said we should escape.

And, in the darkness, father, two of our comrades, and I crawled across the yard, jumped over the fence, and slunk to the big red bush. By

---

2. Uralsk, a Ural River city, is in western Kazakhstan. Wieczynski, *The Modern Encyclopedia of Russian and Soviet History*, vol. 41 (1986), 99–106.

the time the sun rose, we were buried deep in the bush. We heard sounds of the captives moving, but we didn't move or speak.

Men ran. Hooves clattered. Guards cursed. And then everything grew silent. The muffled sounds faded. We remained hidden for a long time. Later, we peeked through gaps in the red bush to see dust rise from the long column of prisoners marching east. Cossacks on horseback circled the column, lashing stragglers like stray cattle. Once at the edge of the village, they took the southeast fork, toward the Urals. We remained hidden, barely breathing for a long, long time. When we ceased seeing dust, one of Dad's comrades pulled tobacco from his pocket and started to roll it in the paper.

Dad grabbed his hand and stopped his smoking. Cossacks might spot it. Tonight, we head west. And we hid in the red bush all that dreary long day. No one saw us. Around noon, I asked Dad's permission to visit the woman again, thinking she might offer us bread, but he refused. When the village finally slept, we crept out of the bushes and, bending low, left. We walked all that night, and every night after that through endless fields of ripe wheat and sunflowers. Dad navigated by the North Star. We slept during the days.

Wheat stubble cut our sore bare feet. I tore my shirt into bandages to wind around our feet. We were always thirsty and rarely found water. Once, we saw a draw-well but were at a loss at how we could get the water out of it. Then father took my pants, and, with me standing naked and he in his long johns, tore my pants into ribbons, knotted them together, and made a rope. He made water pouch with my shirt, tied a rock inside it, and lowered the cloth "rope and pail" into the well. My shirt came up wet with a little water, and we drank thirstily, squeezing water out of my shirt into our mouths. We repeated the process until we satisfied our thirst, then I covered my nudity with my wet shirt, and we slept until dark.

On the seventh night our legs gave out. But father pushed on. As night fell on the eighth day, out of nowhere riders appeared in the near distance. We needed to hide, but we lacked the time or place.

"Are they Whites or Reds?" Dad thought aloud as four riders approached, and we looked at them carefully for indications. Two looked like Cossacks, two, with red ribbons on their chests, looked like Bolsheviks.

"What are you doing here?" the riders yelled, and despite his weakness and fatigue, Dad stood tall and replied calmly." Comrades, please take us to your commanding officer. We're Bolsheviks who have escaped Cossacks."

The rider pointed in the distance. "You're among friends. I'll take you to my commander."

With that, I looked around and said, "That is the end of my story. Who's turn is it next?"

Eight

The Hundredth Prisoner

Shpalernaia Prison, Cell 20
Monday, August 9, 1937, 8:00 a.m.

As questions about my story waned, the electric bell buzzed. Night brought its usual darkness and endless interrogations: *Whose turn would it be next?*

Prisoners pushed and shoved and argued for planks and a haven far from the door. The newer, weaker men flopped to the cement floor, grumbling, "Don't take my corner! Don't squeeze me! Shove over! You're taking too much room! Get your elbow out of my face!"

Though weak and dejected, prisoners soon drifted into restless sleep. Since I'd been in jail two months, I was no longer the *new man* and had moved from the cold cell door area to the warmer center of the room. Squeezed in between two others, I pulled on my Boston suit jacket, pulled off my shoes, and laid my hat atop them for a pillow.

Sleep eluded me, and I laid awake, dreading what was to come, worried about my family. Men snored and coughed. Night's relative quite ended when the guards screeched open the door and yelled names.

The prisoner beside me whispered, "They always come. Whose turn tonight?"

The guards grabbed someone, for I heard, "Let's go! Let's go! Now!" It was closet dark; I couldn't see the men taken. Then the cell became silent again.

"Let's sleep," the man lying on my left arm said.

I agreed but could not. I dwelled on this horror and thought of my family. I heard an investigator swearing followed by howls of pain and the thumps of his pummel leaching through the thick walls.

The guy lying on my right arm whispered, "Why do they question us every night, all night?"

"Because they're thieves doing the devil's work," a nearby voice answered.

The man lying on my other arm said, "Shut up; I want to sleep."

"Okay, fine, let's," I said. "Let's all turn in unison onto our right side and sleep." And, like conjoined triplets, we turned, spooned together to dream—or have nightmares.

My bare feet rested on a man's head. He started sneezing. Men hissed, "Stop it!" "Cut it out." "Hold your nose." But the Sneezer couldn't stop. He'd caught a cold, or pneumonia, and he kept it up all night, keeping half of us awake and the chorus of gripes continuing. "Damn it, be careful!" "Your heel's in my face!" "There's nothing I can do. We don't have enough room." "Move your arm." "Move your leg." "For Christ sake, shut up; I'm exhausted." "I can't sleep on cement." "Shut up and let the devil do his work," a voice wailed. Silence reigned for a few minutes. The voice of a young man whisper, "When will they let us go?"

"Soon," a second youthful voice snapped. "The investigators are promoting their careers by arresting the innocent."

"In the interrogation cell, I showed the guard my fist."

"And what did he say?"

"We're kind to prisoners and patted me on the back. I didn't believe him."

From outside the cell, a guard yelled, "Shut up; no more talking!"

After some hours, near dawn, the interrogated prisoners began returning. Sobbing and crying in pain; the cell door constantly squeaked open to let them in. We were anxious to hear their stories and find out what was happening. But the wake-up bell soon rang, and guards shouted, "Everybody up!"

I had hardly slept. In my heart, I felt something was wrong, and not just the endless noise, complaints, and interrogations. Evil lurked. At morning headcount, guards counted 99 men. They always maintained 100 men in the cell. "Who died?"

"Who'll be the hundredth now?" someone asked. That prompted guesses to pass the time.

The cell door opened, guards shoved in a freshly shaven, cleanly-dressed fellow.

He introduced himself: "I'm Leon Eliashberg, an economist at the Asbestos Factory."[1]

"What's it like in Leningrad?" a man asked anxiously.

---

1. Eliashberg, Leon Natanovich (Leon Mordukhovich) (1907–1937), was executed November 29, 1937. Vol'skii, E.V., et al. *Leningradskii martyrolog: 1937–1938*, t.3 (1998), 466.

Eight. The Hundredth Prisoner

"Life's tough. Since January, Soviet brass arrested all managers in charge of large factories. Now agents are arresting the next tier, supervisors, shift bosses, and economists, like me. The government is destroying our military, culture, trade unions, and party organizations. What's ridiculous is they charged me with the crime of forming and leading a new terrorist organization of a thousand people." He spouted out well-known names: Vasil'ev, Kodatskii, Chudov, and Alekseev.[2]

Aleksandrov set his hand on Leon's shoulder. "You're now our hundredth prisoner."

At that moment, the cell door opened, and the pilot entered, which created heartfelt stares. With a swollen nose and eyes puffed shut, his uniform was in more tatters, and we hoped the investigators had freed him at last. Our hopes died when he said, "The investigators were frustrated. I refused again to sign their lies, and they showed me a long list of my 'alleged crimes.' But what more could they do? Nothing. So eventually, nothing came of it."

Prisoners moved so the pilot could slump on the table. Someone made him hot tea. Famished, he stuffed down a rye crust. I squeezed past other men to stand beside the former party secretary, talking to a student. "Why did agents arrest you?" he asked.

The student seemed dumbstruck and said, "I was studying at the Pedagogical Institution, honored by Nadezhda Krupskaia, and when we celebrated New Year, we were with the family of a Bolshevik.[3] The old man had voted for something or other 20 years ago, and they arrested us all because of it, calling us a terrorist organization."

The party secretary studied him and went on, "Know why they arrested me?"

The student looked at him desperately. The typesetter scoffed, "Look at him! A worker or a peasant doesn't ask stupid questions. Only a kid thinks there's a straight answer to his arrest."

"Guys, take it easy," the old man said, taking his pipe made of bread from his mouth. "Who gets arrested and who gets shot are planned by the government beforehand. Their goal is to liquidate us, the whole country if need be."

The engineer from the Electroseela Plant looked at the old man and nodded. "Even Stalin doesn't know how his investigators administer *justice and punishment*."

---

2. Alekseev, Petr Alekseevich (1893–1937), Chairman of the Leningrad Professional Union, was executed September 6, 1937. Vol'skii, E.V., et al. *Leningradskii martyrolog: 1937–1938*, t.4 (1999), 18.

3. Krupskaia, Nadezhda Konstantinovna (1869–1939), Vladimir Lenin's wife. Wieszynski, *The Modern Encyclopedia of Russian and Soviet History*, vol. 18 (1980), 111–115.

The old blacksmith rapped out words as fast as a ball-peen hammer striking an anvil. "I don't know a thing about Stalin or the Party, but I do know that without the approval of Stalin's higher-ups, no one would be doing these crazy things!"

Those simple words settled down on our broken hearts like a black silk shroud.

The student looked at the blacksmith. "What do you mean?"

The old blacksmith's face saddened. Wrinkles etched his forehead. "I've had a long life, son; I've been a party member for 30 years and had the right to think this way. This cell and men"—his arm circled the room—"is not the party I joined." His words rang with conviction and courage. "I recently read an article in our newspapers that claimed 1937 is exactly like 1917. Investigators liquidated the enemies of the people and political directions came from above."

"But the article wrote of enemies of the people, and we're not enemies of anyone!" a man shouted from the corner.

"True," the blacksmith said. "But here's the rub. People, our friends, coworkers, and neighbors, think we *are* enemies of the people because we're here. Remember, they believe the state's propaganda: *We never arrest people for doing nothing wrong. And we will jail you if you claim we held you unjustly.*"

"But I *was* wrongly arrested," the student wailed. "I had a friend, Pashka. I went to school with him. I remember his parents. We graduated from the same Technological Institution. The investigators told me his parents had become capitalists, but they were merchants. That absurdity makes Pashka a saboteur. I yelled at the investigators and said, I know Pashka's parents like the peeling knows the orange. His parents are simple, honest people."

A group gathered around us, nodding agreement but remaining silent. None of us ever thought we were enemies of the people. We could not understand the madness going on. *Why is 1937 exactly like 1917? We liquidated the White Army 20 years ago. Who wants to destroy them again? Who now decides justice? The investigators have finished their interrogations. What more do they need?*

"Listen!" someone said. "We'll have a court appearance. It will be fair to all of us."

"Ah, don't yak to me about Soviet judges' fairness," scoffed a man. "The court will produce mechanical sentences. Your party is over, friend; you'll die in jail."

Two of our friends sat on the floor, near us, talking. One, a peasant,

Eight. The Hundredth Prisoner

wore pants made of devil's leather, gray shirt, and bare feet[4]; the other looked like city man. The peasant said, "The sailor's skin had turned green from repeated beatings; I spoke with investigators once."

"You mean you signed their interrogation?" asked the city man.

"What?" The peasant was puzzled.

"His question's clear," the city man explained. "Did you sign their confession?"

"I signed some record," the peasant said, frowning.

"What exactly did it say?"

The peasant scratched his head and screwed up his face. "The investigator read it to me. He said I am a member of a tractor organization. But I never saw a tractor; I'm a stable hand."

"I think you confused the word *tractorist* with *terrorist,* or *Trotskyist*," the city man said. "The words sound similar. You signed a document saying you were a *terrorist* or *Trotskyist* not a *tractorist*." He threw up his hands. "What a mess!"

"Why did you sign that record?" another man asked indignantly.

"The investigator ordered me to. His eyes opened wide, he waved his arms at me, and then he hurled me to the floor. What could I do?" He glanced around. "What'll they do to me?"

The city man said, "Wait and see."

And this is how the days and nights dragged on. Endless talks, endless investigations, endless swearing, endless beatings, endless fear, endless doubts.

---

4. Devil's leather, or moleskin, is a heavy cotton fabric, woven and sheared to create a short, soft pile on one side. Its nap feels like chamois. Kirsanova, R.M., et al., *Kostium v russkoi khudozhestvennoi kul'ture 18*, 176.

Nine

My 60th Day in Prison

*The Investigator's Office
Monday, August 16, 1937, 1:00 a.m.*

 Two months passed since the ill-fated night of my arrest and still no changes. I'd grown accustomed to my cellmates' complaining and investigators' threats: *Sign this confession, or I'll destroy you! I'll mutilate you!*
 Prisoners always screamed: "Bandits! You can cut me to pieces, but I don't know anything and will never sign your confession!" *That might end up a lie.*
 This night, I heard keys rattle; the lock clicked; the cell door squeaked open. A husky voice growled, "Bolotov!"
 I had nowhere to hide. "Okay, stooge," a guard snarled, squinting at wasted faces until his eyes rested on mine. "Time for your questioning!"
 I hated the sadistic man but had no choice. I summoned my strength. My legs and feet ached from beatings. My damp pants clung to my stick-legs like compression stocking. I bent over enough to jam on and lace my shoes. My feet were so swollen I had had to ram them on. The laces were too short to tie. I pulled on my Boston suit coat and cloth hat, then wove through the throng to the door.
 When passing the cell's new hundredth man, he touched my arm. "Friend," he said, "be steady! Stand firm! They'll leave you alone after a while!"
 It was my tenth straight night with Baryshnikov. He never let me sit. I craved sleep. The identical questions were fired prompting the identical replies. Over and over. Finally, my legs gave way. I crumbled to the floor, too weak to stand: *Should I sign the document? If I do, they'll let me sleep. What will my future be if I don't sign?*
 They beat me until I stood and slumped against the wall in the fetal

position. Then Baryshnikov whispered in my ear. "If you sign, I'll let you sleep! Otherwise, I'll beat your face to a pulp!"

His soft words struck like a hammer. I didn't move. He swore and beat me savagely.

I did not sign. I don't remember much, but I knew Baryshnikov was my bitter enemy. I'll always remember his eyes, how they opened wider when he screamed, his pupils looking like black dots on white eggs. I remember shaking my head clear and vowing, "I'm not signing your false confession."

Stories flashed through my mind, relief from Baryshnikov's beatings.

Dr. Plotnikov, an elderly professor at the Military Political Academy, had said after he confessed to honoring Tolmachev, the investigators let him sleep.[1] He admitted he revered the man they called a terrorist, signed the record, and they did not disturb him for two days. But then the investigators asked him to sign another record: that he had made a bomb. He fretted about confessing to that but finally gave in and wrote he had an explosive. They let him rest some nights. Then they demanded he admits terrorists had given him the bomb. One admission led to another and another. Allegations never stopped. When the broken, old man realized what had happened, it was too late. He had signed his death warrant.

When the investigator asked him, "Tell us, dear Professor Plotnikov, how you found the bomb," he replied, "My dear fellow, I never had a bomb! I don't know what one looks like!"

As if jabbed with a needle, the investigator leaped from his chair and started stomping and shouting. "Why do you lie? You signed our record! You had a bomb! That's all there is to it! Who gave you a bomb?"

"Nobody!"

"But you admitted to having a bomb!"

"You told me to!"

"Don't take me for a ride you stupid old fool!"

"I have no idea what you're talking about!" the old man cried.

"You don't recall who gave it to you; how it disappeared? Did you throw it in the Neva?"

Through humiliation and mockery, the investigator tried and tried to obtain another false confession, but the old man refused. "I'm not going to sign anything more! I'll stay here forever and never lie again and use my last ounce of strength to do it!"

---

1. Plotnikov, Isaac Solomonovich (1888–1936), in 1918 became one of the many commissars in the Military Control Center in Petrograd, and he was relieved for selling confiscated belongings. Batulin, P.V., Voitikov, S.S. "Zloupotrebleniia vlastiu v organakh Voennogo kontrolia. 1918–1919." *Voprosy istorii*, No. 8 (2010): 46–55.

Plotnikov's story persisted, fixed in my mind, soothing the torments of Baryshnikov, whose face was red with anger. He yelled, "Are you going to answer my questions, creature?! Stand in the corner! Don't look out the window. Stay right here until you die!"

Despite the tempest in the interrogation room, outside, the prison was a quiet, white night, the Neva's waters ruffling in August's gentle breezes.

Baryshnikov eventually tired of badgering, and he left the room. Sapozhnikov, another investigator, replaced him. He did not shout. Sapozhnikov looked at me strangely and picked up a newspaper. While he read, his intent look mystified me. For the first time in my interrogations with Baryshnikov, Sapozhnikov allowed me to sit for 10 minutes. *I must withstand their test.* My throat was dry. I craved sleep and water. There was a bottle of water on his table. I was so thirsty all I could think of was water.

I decided to risk a beating and asked, "Comrade Sapozhnikov, may I have a drink please?"

"It is not for you, Bolotov," Sapozhnikov said. He did not ask me to sign the record, and for that I was thankful. Suddenly, he ducked his head at the bottle and said, "Drink!"

I gulped greedily then looked out the window at the Liteinii Bridge over the Neva. People with bouncy steps walked over it in dawn's early light. How happy they seemed. And here I sat, drowsy, aching, and sleepless.

Sapozhnikov began, "Have you ever had a gun, Bolotov?"

"I had a Browning when I served in *CHON*."[2]

"Ever used it?"

"No. I guarded a warehouse in 1922 and 1923. The Cossacks were in our area. Life was dangerous."

"Why were you alone?"

"I was ordered to guard the warehouse. It was 1922; I was a commissar in a camp working with young men in construction training and had to carry a Browning."

"Did you ever shoot after that?"

"In 1927 with the Twentieth Division while at the university."

"When else?"

"Maybe three or four times a year afterward at local shooting ranges. But I haven't shot in five years." I looked out the window at the sidewalk,

---

2. CHON, or *Chasti Osobogo Naznacheniia,* refers to the local police who guarded the industrial and economic sites and suppressed rebellions, 1917–1925. Wieszynski, *The Modern Encyclopedia of Russian and Soviet History*, vol. 30 (1982), 223–228.

Nine. My 60th Day in Prison

now full of people. Traffic was heavy. A tram rumbled past. Life flowed. How I missed it.

It was about six o'clock. I was exhausted and collapsed onto a chair. My head rested on the windowsill in the cooling breeze. I lifted my eyes and watched the people strolling beside the burgundy-dark waters of the Neva. A tugboat chugged past; its droning bass rattled the windows; its black smoke belched into the clear blue sky. Sunrays mirrored off the Neva danced on rooftops and reflected off the investigator's table.

The rays were so bright they hurt my eyes. I turned to face Sapozhnikov and watched him doodling small, strange figures on paper. When he noticed me watching him, he stared at me intently and wrote: *Don't sign the record; it will save your life.*

I froze. Thoughts flashed through my head. *Why they had tormented me so if I were to live? What more do they need? Why do they continue to beat me?*

The interrogation stopped. A silent hour past. *What and why was I saved?* A storm brewed. Light faded. The Neva's waters darkened and turned choppy. With the night's interrogation ended, hope, energy, and dreams filled my soul. It was time for investigators to send me back to my cell. But at that very instant, the door opened wide, and Baryshnikov fell upon me like a hurricane.

"Well, Bolotov!" he screamed. "Did you sign the accusation?"

I shook my head.

"No? You're a villain! We've wasted too much time with you. You think you're a devoted member of the Party, but the NKVD wants you to sign the record. Do you know you've been expelled from the Party for two months as an enemy of people? Go ahead, sign the record, and that'll be it!"

"No. I refuse to sign your outrageous lies," I said.

"If you don't sign the Party will shoot you like an incorrigible enemy. If you do sign, you'll receive a jail term and good recommendations to a labor camp."

"I don't understand your logic. I won't sign dishonesty."

"You're lying!" he screamed. "You *will* sign!"

"No, I won't. The Young Communist League and the Party have taught me to live and fight for honesty and pure Communism. Why don't you understand that? Why am I here? Why do you demand I sign lies? Keeping me here is cruel and absurd!"

Baryshnikov slammed his hand on the table. "There's no purpose in this. We should have crushed you like a bug, you're a swindler."

I let that slide off my back and yelled, "Tell me, what's going on! You can do what you want, but I'll never go against the truth and the Party!"

Baryshnikov yelled, "Shut up! I'll show you what a 'lie' means! You're going to Kresty Prison with no food!"

While he swore, trying to intimidate and humiliate me, prisoners' faces flashed across my mind. Truth will prevail. Finally, I returned to cell 20. *My final interrogation had ended.*

Ten

My Stay in Two Prisons

Arsenalnaia Naberezhnaia, Building 7
Tuesday, August 24–Thursday, September 2, 1937

A Black Raven drove me from Shpalernaia Prison to the Kresty Prison, directly across the Neva River. Its cell doors of thin wood reverberated whenever guards screamed, and guards allowed me to lay down and sleep anytime. There were several narrow trestle-beds in the cell; I pushed two together and covered them with straw for a mattress. Four men occupied the cell; two came from the Okhtenski Plant, an engineer from the Kirovski Plant, and me.

Our food was rotten, rancid buckwheat in salt water, known as *Kresty Balanda*.

As the end of August 1937 approached, it poured nightly. Rain hammered barred windows, leaving me harassed by insomnia. Investigators never called me for questioning. I knew nothing of my family and spent agonizing hours worrying about them.

Once I heard the familiar voices of two guards, and I pressed an ear to the door to hear their gossip. The upstairs guard asked the downstairs guard, "Heard the news?"

"What news?" the downstairs guard replied.

"A radio announced a few minutes ago; we are shooting to death enemies of the people."

"We gun them down daily. Stalin never forgives people's weaknesses. He's killing all terrorists…"

After I overheard that news, we began to listen carefully to guards' corridor chatter. We also heard a radio blasting throughout the day from loudspeakers of Kresty Prison's endless lists of executed enemies, all claimed to be White Army officers, bandits, and saboteurs. Our hair stood on end whenever we heard names of people we knew or prominent party members.

On August 25, loudspeakers announced the NKVD had arrested enemies of the people and saboteurs at my former factory. It took 10 days to shoot them all. One man, Sedov-Nevolin, had been a member of the Party since 1904; he had just started working at Red Triangle in 1937. The NKVD prosecuted him and the others as counterrevolutionaries and saboteurs. Soviet henchmen wanted to rid the country of young engineers, old workers of 60, all hard-working professionals, and all old Bolsheviks. NKVD agents organized groups in the factory, asked old Bolsheviks to lead them, and then arrested them for refusing to pay salaries and poisoning workers with gasoline. Their lies continued, "If the enemies of people weren't saboteurs you'd make more money."

Another night, during guards gossiping, one said, "You're lucky."

The other guard said, "Why?"

"Because you deal with counter-revolutionaries."

"What are you suggesting? These men are quiet."

"But remember, they're clever engineers, scientists, and chemists. They can make bombs here in Kresty Prison!"

"My prisoners only break the glass and tear up mattresses to throw out windows."

"Investigators told me with such enemies of people I need to be on guard constantly."

"If you're on guard now, you better check because your criminals are making a row, shouting and banging tables."

We heard one of the guards walk away, muttering, "Yeah, yeah! You're an idiot."

I had no idea why the investigators moved me to Kresty Prison, for within five days, guards shoved me into a Black Raven and drove me back to Shpalernaia Prison. This time, though, they opened a heavy iron door and shoved me into a narrow, windowless, one-person, first-floor cell, a wet stall with wooly-mold walls. There was enough ambient light around the door from a weak overhead bulb to see an iron bed, tiny table, and a three-legged stool chained to the floor near a toilet. There was no mattress, and the bare metal frame hurt when I laid down. Guards slid porridge through a slit in the door. The dim bulb never turned off.

Guards controlled everything in my life: "Stand until you're tired." "Sit and place your arms on the cold iron table." "Don't sleep or doze." "You must stand or sit during the day!" "You may walk in your cell during the day but not sleep. Sleep at night."

The "sleep at night" directive was a sick joke. Renewed interrogations filled every night.

Ten. My Stay in Two Prisons

I pulled my cloth cap down over my eyes and walked back and forth 10 feet like a blind man whenever I started to doze. The iron-covered Judas Hole clicked every 10 minutes, swinging up for spying. I was no longer a rational man but a new Soviet prisoner, cursed at if I tried to sleep. Sometimes I sat; guards peeked through the judas hole and hissed, "Get up!"

My thoughts focused on the possible trial. I wanted to tell the judges the truth about myself and their "creative" confessions. But what good would it do? They'd think I was trying to ingratiate myself.

On day two at Shpalernaia, a cellmate appeared named Lepekhin.[1] He'd been the Director of Leningrad Intourist Hotel Europe, the state agency that controls foreigners' visitor and their money. We commiserated. Since there was only one bed in the cell and I was younger than Lepekhin by 20 years, I lay on the cold, bare, asphalt floor. As usual, I arranged my shoes and cloth cap as a pillow and closed my eyes and grew physically and mentally sick, thus beginning my third month in prison without a trial or even the hint of one.

The investigation began again with the loutish Baryshnikov. "Sign the record—*basta*—period!" he demanded in all-night interrogations.

"I'll never sign it," I insisted. The questioning and my refusal continued for hours. Later, in the cell, I said to Lepekhin, "Maybe they'll finally let me go!"

"I don't think so," the tall, gaunt, shadow of a man said.

"But why not? I'm innocent."

Lepekhin looked at me. "They'll send you to the other side of the earth."

"Why?" I insisted, indignantly. "It's all a mistake." I stared at the emaciated man. "Do you think they'll ever let me go?"

He rose with sad eyes. "Never. I signed their accusation. It said I'd connections with foreigners." He smiled sickly. "That's what Intourist Managers do, work with tourists."

"Why did you sign it?"

"I feared tortured, and when they slapped my face, I gave up," he lamented. "But you didn't sign their accusation; that's why they'll send you to Siberia."

The judas hole opened. An eye peered in. Lepekhin and I remained silent, watching and waiting. Keys clattered. The lock clicked. The iron door screeched open. An officer stepped in, his leather heels clicking crisply. Unlike Kresty Prison, Shpalernaia had carpets on the stairs and

---

1. Mikhail Pavlovich Lepekhin is mentioned in *The List of Convicts of the Second Category by the Military Board of the Supreme Court of the USSR* on July 13, 1937 (AP RF, opis'24, delo 410, list 58), http://stalin.memo.ru/spiski.

halls that muffled steps and muted screams. "My name's Korolev," the man said. "I'm Secretary of the Military Board of the Supreme Court. These are the charges against you two."

He passed us papers. I held mine up to the bulb's weak light and read the charge. The first words made my heart race: Resolution approved by Vyshinskii and Zakovskii.[2] My hands tremble as I flipped to the last page and saw my interrogators, Baryshnikov's and Sapozhnikov's signatures. I went back and read it; it left me feeling hopeless and heartbroken. As I read, our small, smelly cell seemed to shrink in the profusion of lies. I began to realize the insurmountability of my problems. I stiffened my arms and held the paper closer to the feeble light: *Are these people out of their minds? Where are the facts supporting the charges? These words distort my life. They're not me; they describe some scoundrel, not me!* Oh, they'd written down my first and last names accurately. But the bitter words claimed *I was a member of the Trotskyist-Zinov'ev's terrorist group, that I'd killed Sergei Mironovich Kirov and prepared an attempt on the lives of Stalin, Voroshilov, and Molotov.*[3]

And the slander continued: *I was a kulak's son, exploited peasants, refused to give grain to the Bolsheviks, and damaged collective farms' tools. I wanted to bring capitalism back to the Soviet Union and had a prosperous life.*[4]

I finished reading The Resolution. I'd never read such ridiculousness but was at a loss as to how to reply. I stared at Korolev. He stood there, smugly looking at me. I wanted to scream: *You're wrong! Stop this madness and tell the truth! Know that I am a real Communist, an engineer, the son of a Bolshevik from Lenin's times!* But I could only threaten him with thoughts. He, like all the investigators, feared facts and distorted reality to make shambles of all our lives.

---

2. Vyshinskii, Andrei Januarievich (1883–1954), Chancellor of Moscow State University 1925–1928, in 1935–1939 became the main prosecutor in Stalin's Great Purge. Wieszynski, *The Modern Encyclopedia of Russian and Soviet History*, vol. 43 (1986), 129–133. Zakovskii, Leonid Mikhailovich (Stubis, Henrich Ernestovich) (1894–1938), head of the Leningrad Province NKVD and the Commissar of State Security, was executed August 1938. Vol'skii, E.V., et al. *Leningradskii martyrolog: 1937–1938*, t.1 (1995), 677–678.

3. Voroshilov, Kliment Efremovich (1881–1969), military and navy commissar and one of the most active members of the Great Purge. Wieszynski, *The Modern Encyclopedia of Russian and Soviet History*, vol. 43 (1986), 67–69. Molotov (Scriabin), Viacheslav Mikhailovich (1890–1986), commissar of the Ministry of Foreign Affairs. Wieszynski, *The Modern Encyclopedia of Russian and Soviet History*, vol. 50 (1989), 127–132.

4. On July 30, 1937, the NKVD issued Secret Order No. 00447 *About repressions of former kulaks, criminals, and other anti-Soviet elements*; it was enforced to November 1938. Batsaev, I.D., Kozlov A.G. *Dalstroy Trust Sevvostlag OGPU-NKVD of the USSR as Presented by Documents and in Numbers (2 parts). Part 1 (1931–1941)* (Magadan: NEISRI FEB RAS, 2002), 216–218.

Eleven

The Night Before the Trial

Shpalernaia Prison's One-Man Cell
Saturday, September 4, 1937

The charge I was *a kulak's* son was absurd, but it reminded me of my youth and those poor but happy days in Saratov.[1] I remembered the hot summer of 1910. With five kids to feed, father worked as a stove-setter in the Schmidt Brothers Steam Mill that stood on the banks of the Volga at Bol'shaia Sergievskaia Street. During spring and summer, he put in overtime evenings and weekends at a second job, making fireplaces and stoves for people lucky enough to own homes. But even with his double wages, Mom had to sew blankets from rags.

Though my parents worked long hours, we often lacked money to pay rent on our basement apartment and were thrown into the street. Landlords never liked kids, and they often reported that father was a Bolshevik.

After many years of struggling to save, my parents' dream of owning a home became a reality. They'd gone without to save and had borrowed money from my mother's relatives, until, at last, they had 140 silver rubles stashed under their bed. With that money, they bought a little hunter's cabin, 15 by 13 feet, with a low ceiling and windows on three walls, located on the edge of the city, close to the Volga, at 16 Kamyshinskaia Street.

How well I recall our arrival that hot summer day. With Boris in her arms, mother opened the cabin door, and we followed her into the tiny, stifling room. The north wall was solid boards, but the other walls had small, frameless windows with the upper halves opened, held up with sticks. A breeze carrying bird songs floated in, stirring dust off ceiling crossbeams.

---

1. The term *kulak* designates a grain speculator who resales grain for substantial profits and opposes programs to collectivize the countryside. Wieszynski, *The Modern Encyclopedia of Russian and Soviet History*, vol. 18 (1980), 18, 151.

Mother beamed. She made a circle with her hand, indicating for us to sit down in a circle, and she placed a bowl of sunflower oil that sparkled in the sunrays. Then she gave each of us a bagel sprinkled with poppy seeds. We broke off chunks, dunked them in oil, and laughed and joked, loving our first meal in our new home.

Mother smiled. "Children, this is *your home*! We'll never have to look for another basement to live in." We sang songs, and the day was as bright as our hearts. We had always lived in tiny, wet, basements—usually occupying only half—with holes in the walls where huge rats darted in-and-out. Because I was four, Mom sat me in a chair beside the cradle to guard baby Boris against rat attacks. When they scurried out of the walls, Boris would cry, and I'd swat the rodents with a stick. Once, Mom told me, rats gnawed the side of a boy's belly, so I never took my eyes off Boris. He was a handsome baby with golden curls and big, blue eyes. We all loved Boris, but my sisters and brothers never wanted to watch him.

Mother's joy at having a home was infectious. We filled our bellies, and when finished, jumped up and ran around the tiny space, yelling, "And are we going to live here forever?"

"Yes," Mom said. "But don't leave the yard. Listen to your older sister, Anna. Father and I must shop for furniture and bring things back by horse and wagon."

That summer, father built an addition to the cabin, doubling its size to 400 square feet and raising the ceiling. He framed the windows to make the house warmer in winter, and later, during times of troubles, the dwelling provided our sanctuary.

Our nest stayed bright and cheerful all that summer. The sun shone through the windows, east, south, and west as the earth turned. Every day the sun warmed us, and I remember well my parents saying, "After 10 years of married life, we finally bought a home! No one will ever yell again, 'You're Stenka's Razin rags!'"[2]

Now investigators charged me with being a *kulak's* son. Does my life sound like that of a rich man's son? No! My grandparents were also destitute.

As I looked around the cell, reality returned. Top Soviet officials had signed these terrible charges, labeling me a terrorist. I felt abandoned, and yet I tried to reassure myself: *You're not going to your grave. You'll have a trial. The tribunal will reveal the truth.* But I remained nervous and soul sick. Again, and again, I read the charges; they drenched me in cold sweat. I threw myself on the floor and chanted, "The charges are bogus!" I swore

---

2. Stenka is the diminutive of Stepan. Translator's note.

Eleven. The Night Before the Trial

and dashed back-and-forth, screaming at Lepekhin, "Look at these ridiculous charges! How could they think I planned to kill Stalin, Molotov, and others? These accusations will kill me!"

Lepekhin never replied. I stayed torn, one-minute confident, unsure the next. Most of the time, I could not convince myself of the seriousness of the charges; they were *that* preposterous! But indignation was useless. *The trial will save me.*

Lepekhin, sat on the bed, staring at me. "What're you talking about, Dreamer? Their charges sound fine. Be thankful they didn't kill you, Bolotov. The law of January 12, 1934, stated we all were terrorists, and they'd confiscate all we owned and arrest your family. That law came about after Kirov's murder by Nikolaev. The law stated that authorities must carry out sentences, verdicts, and executions quickly."[3]

"Look, I understand that, but those directives were against enemies of people," I said. I reflected. *"I'm not one of them!"*

"Leonid, they're arresting you for what you represent."

"For God's sake, shut up, Lepekhin! Do you think they're right?"

"Not at all!" he countered. "But they're cunning. Once ink hits paper, nothing will change their charges; they'll stick!"

We didn't sleep that night, talking about our trials. Lepekhin seemed to accept his situation and lacked the will to fight. For once, the guards didn't bother us as the hours dragged on. Slowly, I realized what would happen to me. I vowed to remain honest, not slander myself or others, and to tell the truth. Finally, as night became day, I slid the charges into my Boston suit pocket.

The next night, we stayed awake. The Judas hole opened repeatedly. Guards whispered, "Lay down; sleep."

Are you an idiot? I said to myself. *Why are you whispering?*

All that night as I felt the charges press against my heart, Lepekhin and I remained in silent misery. What more could be said? Thoughts haunted me so much that I finally muttered to Lepekhin, "Do you know, I never expected to see these charges? I figured they'd see their mistake and let me go. I know they've shot other communists, am I no better?"

Lepekhin remained silent, and a thought flashed through my head. "If the trial supports such lies, maybe I shouldn't fight them. Maybe the party needs falsehoods to prove a point, and I'm too stubborn to understand." I

---

3. Nikolaev, Leonid Vasil'evich (1904–1937), shot Sergei Kirov December 1, 1934, at the Smol'nyi Institute where he was a history instructor. Stalin made a rare overnight trip to Leningrad and ordered the execution of Nikolaev, his wife, and mother. These assassinations launched the Great Purge of 1937. Lenoe, Matthew E. *The Kirov Murder and Soviet History* (New Haven: Yale University Press, 2010), 252.

began to think like an investigator. Should I tell them the truth or lie about myself? Should I risk my family's honor?

I sprawled out on the floor and wrestled with these thoughts. My father appeared in a dream and said, "Be steady!" His words filled my heart. Still dreaming, I assured father, "They'll not break me." Father nodded, and his vision disappeared. I awoke: *What just happened? Was I dreaming?* In any case, I knew what I must do: be unwavering and resolute. Like father during his grueling years, I remembered the socialists' revolt in Saratov and his struggle.

The Bolsheviks wanted to proceed faster and form a military division with large districts throughout the city. They took over a building in Ilinskaia Square for use as an artillery barracks. Their guards controlled nearby streets, including the corner of Ilinskaia and Bol'shaia Kostryzhnaia Streets. Father worked under Red Guard leader, Sergei Zagumennii,[4] and I often served as their night messenger.

A revolt occurred on Kamyshinskaia Street, our way; another on Shelkovichnaia Street. Dad worked all night, and I often cat-napped on the couch in his office, watching him at his desk, writing, or speaking to people on the phone. Sometimes he'd wake me, and we'd walk to check guard posts. I'd walked ahead, stopping to peek around corners to assure they were clear before he'd follow. At his request, I memorized the names of all the guards, the Mensheviks,[5] and gave him news I overheard.

One night, walking on Ilinskaia Street, it became eerily quiet near the deserted alleys and adjacent streets. Then, crossing Ugodnikovskaia Street, I saw a Red Army soldier. He swore at me, "Get the hell out of here, kid! NOW! They're coming!"

I whipped around. Armed rebels were rushing down the street. My eyes darted left and right. I spotted a wicker gate. I ran and slipped through. Behind it were two more gates. Locked. I saw a third gate—open—and ran in, right into Red Guards, waiting with pistols drawn and rifles ready. They were not amused at my stumbling into their lookout. I fled.

Two days before the rebellion, Antonov-Saratovskii, Secretary of the Saratov Executive Committee, drove past our street in his truck, waving.[6]

---

4. Zagumennii, Sergei Ivanovich (1897–1937), head of the Saratov Peasants' Committee and commander of the Saratov Eastern Army. Gokhlerner, V. M., Medvedev, V.K. *Istoriia Saratovskogo kraia 1917–1965* (Saratov: Saratovskii gosudarstvennii universitet, 1967), 60.

5. The Mensheviks are an anti-Bolshevik Party, 1903–1925. Wieszynski, *The Modern Encyclopedia of Russian and Soviet History*, vol. 50 (1989), 57–65.

6. Antonov-Saratovskii, Vladimir Pavlovich (1884–1965), suppressed numerous anti-Soviet revolts from 1917 to 1922; he was a member of the Supreme Court 1923 to 1938. Wieszynski, *The Modern Encyclopedia of Russian and Soviet History*, vol. 2 (1976), 53–54.

Eleven. The Night Before the Trial

He'd always visited Bolsheviks' meetings; now tough rebels yelled for his death, "Let's shoot him, we have the rifles!"

Two evenings later, I was walking down a street and saw a young White guard posted. As dusk fell, boys gathered around him to see his rifle. Women approached.

"Who do you support?" a woman asked the guard.

"I don't know," the White guard replied.

"Are you for workers or the bourgeoisie?" another asked.

"A White officer ordered me to stand guard here, so I stand here."

"It's after 9 o'clock and getting dark, you can be shot."

The next evening when Dad appeared, Mom was unusually worried, "White officers could arrest you."

Dad agreed. "Stay off the streets tomorrow. The Bolsheviks will attack and reclaim their barracks. Strays can kill you!"

The next day dawned sunny and hot. Mother and we kids stayed home, but I soon tired of sitting around the house and left, shoeless— shoes saved for school—and headed for the streets in a short-sleeve-shirt and pants. The streets were ghostly quiet. White Revolters slept behind houses in the bushes. I spotted a three-inch cannon on the corner at Kamyshinskaia and Shelkovichnaia Streets aimed at the Red Guards' barracks. It stood out among shorter buildings. Men started firing cannons and rifles. Bullets whistled. A stream of rat-a-tat-tats were heard.

I was so scared I ran home, stumbling and sprawling and breaking my toenails. After that, I couldn't walk barefoot for weeks. From inside, I saw Red soldiers rushing to their cannon, but they did not shoot. Mother boxed my ears. "Stay inside! On the floor!" Bullets zinged through the walls of our house. We panicked. I worried about Dad, and if a shell might destroy our house with us inside. As the sun finally dropped below the horizon, that day's rifle and cannon fire ceased. The streets filled with survivors shouting, "Hurray! Hurray!"

I peeked out and watched Red Guards and Bolsheviks overrun the White's barracks and arrest them. We observed the Reds parading Revolters in a forced march through the streets. The leader of the White Army, Viktorov, had arrived from Samara, but he had escaped.[7]

We lived in a district where families sympathized with the Revolters. Only three families, ours being one, supported the Bolsheviks. When the Revolters arrived in Saratov to spread their rebellion, many asked mother

---

7. Viktorov, N. led the socialist-revolutionary revolt against the Bolsheviks in 1918. Babushkin, V.F. *Dni velikikh sobytii* (Saratov: Privolzhskoye knizhnoye izdatel'stvo, 1984), 168–191.

maliciously, "Well, Varvara Ivanovna, where is your Petr Antonovich? Why doesn't he join us?"

"He's working," mother always replied.

Sympathizers were quiet. Red Guards had annihilated the White Revolters, and families flooded the streets in celebration like forest mushrooms springing up after a summer rain.

Yampolskii, our neighbor, and a *Menshevik*, spoke to Mom, his intonation was sweet. I called these political flip-floppers KWD—*Kuda weter duet*.[8]

That day the counter-revolution came to an end in Saratov. Communism prevailed!

---

8. KWD: *Kuda weter duet*, or where the wind blows.

Twelve

The Trial

Shpalernaia Prison Basement
Sunday, September 5, 1937, 6:00 p.m.

"Enough of reverie! I must live in the present," I told myself. After a restless night, I awoke to the dreaded sound of keys jangling in the cell's lock, a sound that filled us with fear.

A guard shoved opened the door. "Bolotov! Your turn! Grab your things; let's go!"

His words implied that I'd not be returning. I smiled grimly at his reference to my "things." My only things were a pair of underwear mother gave me the night of my arrest, which I still wore though they had turned to rags.

I rose, shook Lepekhin's hand, and said goodbye. I walked ahead of the two guards with my heart beating so hard it might break. Still, I stepped resolutely and held my head high as guards barked, "Turn left, turn right, downstairs to the basement."

I told myself that my trial would reveal the truth and the trial would set me free. The court would express its regret and acknowledge it: *You're not an enemy of the people, Bolotov, go home!* Oh, how I hoped and prayed and believed in Soviet justice! I encouraged myself muttering, "Remember, you're a member of the Party!" And yet I didn't believe it as we walked down the long, dim halls.

"The door on the right," a guard said, unlocking it.

I entered a huge room filled with 10 or 15 chairs neatly arranged. Another guard stood beside a small table with a paper and a list of names. On it, I saw strange scribbles. An idea crossed my mind: *The scrawl means a death sentence.* There were no other men present. *We're waiting for witnesses and investigators; surely they'll give me the chance to defend myself.*

"Sit!" a guard ordered.

I sat on the edge of the last chair in the first row, trembling. Two

64   Part I—Defeat of the Working Family

guards stood behind me; a third remained posted at the door. My right leg started shaking uncontrollably. I couldn't stop it. I looked around. There was a long table cover with red fabric, *the Revolution's color. Red symbolizes Soviet justice.* Behind the table were two doors. We waited. *Where were my witnesses?*

Suddenly, the guards proclaimed, "Stand! This trial's beginning!"

I stood, shaking. Where were my witnesses? But I told myself: *Proclaim your innocence.*

Four, well-known judges entered the hall. I'd heard their speeches on the radio and seen their pictures in *Pravda*: Kostiushko, Korolev, Matulevich, and Rychkov.[1] They looked exhausted, as if having worked all night. Matulevich wore the uniform with four stars on his shoulder board, emphasizing his lofty status in the Communist hierarchy. Kostiushko, a general, had the most ribbons, and Korolev had the three bars of a colonel on his shoulders.

Korolev glared at Matulevich, lit a cigarette, scowled, and began reading the accusations. When he finished, he demanded, "Do you recognize your crimes, Bolotov?"

"No, comrade, I don't."

He looked up, shocked. "Then why did Kochergin give this convincing evidence?"[2]

"I've no idea. Ask him."

"Kochergin cited Gushchinskii, the engineer of your factory."

"Gushchinskii knows I never participated in any counter-revolutionary organization. But the investigators never confirmed this with Gushchinskii."[3]

Matulevich inhaled deeply and mumbled, again, "Do you recognize your crime?" He banged the table so hard the ashtray jumped.

I was disgusted. The judges acted like children and hid behind lies. "Those charges you read have my biography wrong," I declared. "They claim I'm the son of a wealthy *kulak*. The truth is my father worked in a steam plant. The charges claim I joined the Party in 1931, but I joined the Party while at Saratov University in 1931. It says I killed Kirov and planned

---

1. Matulevich, Ivan Osipovich (1895–1960), Vice Chairman of the Military Board of the Soviet Supreme Court. Conquest, Robert. *The Great Terror. A Reassessment* (New York: Oxford University Press, 1990), 624. Rychkov, Nikolai Mikhailovich (1897–1959), Chief Prosecutor of the RSFSR after 1931. Zalesskii, K.A. *Imperia Stalina* (Moskva: Veche, 2000), 397–398.

2. Kochergin, Evgenii Emelianovich (1884–1937), Manager of metallurgy at the Red Triangle Factory until executed August 24, 1937. Vol'skii, E.V., et al. *Leningradskii martyrolog: 1937–1938*, t.4 (1999), 229.

3. Gushchinskii, Pavel Filipovich (1903–1937), Chair of the mechanical branch of the Red Triangle Factory until executed August 24, 1937. *Leningradskii martyrolog: 1937–1938*, t.4 (1999), 131.

to kill Stalin and Molotov. That's slander! They claim I wanted to bring capitalism back. Absurd!"

Matulevich studied his cigarette and said casually, "The charges don't play a significant role."

"They don't?!" I asked, bewildered. "Then exactly why am I here, comrade?"

He whispered his colleagues and then said, "So you deny Kochergin's statements?"

"Yes, he probably had been *ordered to say that*."

"What do you mean by that?" Matulevich fired back.

"The investigators are cruel. You said Kochergin gave testimony against me and Gushchinskii, but I couldn't confront Gushchinskii either."

My head churned with their madness. What more could I say?

"Well, defendant Bolotov?" Matulevich said. "Why are you silent?"

"I've told you the truth. How can I convince you?"

"You can't." Matulevich stood and fixed me with prickly eyes.

I couldn't understand what more he needed to hear: repentance, a plea for my life? I trusted fairness would prevail. I hadn't signed their false accusations. Did the judges want me guilty to shoot me? I stared at their indifferent faces and remained clueless as to how to prove my innocence. And then, as if to protect its overload, my mind switched from this lunacy to the happy days of my childhood, skipping stones on the Volga and rolling old tires down dusty roads with pals. I saw mother sewing at the bedspread frame stretched out in our little home, making rags into blankets to feed us.

Those days of childhood were floating through my mind when, suddenly, I blurted aloud, "I swear, I'm innocent! I turned 11 in 1918 when Dad returned from the war. Neighbors called us Bolsheviks and now I am a *kulak's* son. Outrageous!"

From somewhere deep within me, I found the strength to continue. "Dear judges, I became a Bolshevik when someone tore down Communist posters plastering Saratov. Children splattered axial grease on slogans that said true Soviets don't vote for Bolsheviks since their leaders were German spies. I can't remember a time when I was not an active Communist and remain so to this day!"

The judges stared at me in silence. Then Matulevich stood, hands on hips, glowering at my impertinence; however, I continued, "I grew up with Soviet power! It's gibberish to label me the son of a *kulak*, a capitalist, or bourgeois. I beg you, start my real trial!"

The ground seemed to tremble beneath me. The judges were unable to believe my outburst. Shocked, I realized they'd already made their decision. My ranting was irrelevant.

They stood, filed out of the room, and I plunked down, defeated. *What now?*

Two minutes later, a guard barked, "Stand up! The proceeding will begin!"

The judges had left one door and returned through another. They sat.

Indifferently, Matulevich pronounced, "On behalf of the Union of Soviet Socialist Republics, we find you, Bolotov, Leonid Petrovich guilty of being a participant in a counter-revolutionary organization that killed Sergei Mironovich Kirov and made attempts on the lives of Stalin and Molotov. Our sentence is"—he glared at me—"death by firing squad!"

The judges stood and left.

While I sat stunned by the sentence, within minutes, they returned. *What now?*

Matulevich looked hurried. "There's been a new resolution by the Supreme Court of the USSR," he snapped, "Bolotov, you're lucky. You're to be imprisoned 10 years instead!"

I'd expected justice. Now the judges used the excuse of some committee for sparing my life! But locking me up for a decade? I looked at the judges and wanted to scream: *Don't shame Soviet power.* The judges hurried from the hall.

A guard prodded me with his automatic rifle. "Up Bolotov!"

With a broken heart, I left for my sentence.

Thirteen

I Meet My Convicted Friends

Shpalernaia Prison
Sunday, September 5–Wednesday, September 8, 1937

From the basement courtroom, two guards prodded me upstairs to a maze of halls and squashed me into a murky cell crammed with men, their gloomy faces gaunt, vitality drained. They looked humbled, crushed, and defeated. Each man "knew" he was innocent and remained hopeful for the future. The 37 men—I counted—had endured sham trials, too. I recognized men from the Red Triangle Factory, among them: Nikolai Dobronravov, Anatolii Kulikov, Fedor Suvorov, Vasilii Serebriannikov, Andrei Orlov, Lazar Alymenko, Isaac Brevda, Maks Skoblo, Ivan Balakin, Gavriil Eroshkin, Petr Cherniak, and other engineers and doctors.[1]

Over the next days, I met Aleksandrov, Kuleshov, Grigorii Zheelov, Mikhail Bogdanov, and Aleksandr Evdokimov.[2] All were grief-stricken for being found guilty in mock trials and awaited a terrifying future. And yet, to a man, they remained loyal to the tenets of Communism, convinced that Soviet officials would grasp the injustices doled out in Leningrad.

---

1. Their names are listed in *The List of the Second Category of Convicted People, July 31, 1937* (AP RF, opis' 24, delo 410, list 148), http://stalin.memo.ru/spiski. Skoblo, Maks Solomonovich (1893–1963), Director of Leningrad Neuro-Surgical Center, was released early from the Kolyma camps and lectured in Tomskii Medical Institution from 1946 to 1949. Kozlov, A.G. *Iz istorii zdravookhraneniia Kolymy i Chukotki* (1941–1954) (Magadan: Magadanskoie knizhnoye izdatel'stvo, 1991), 92–93. Balakin, Ivan Prokhorovich, editor of *The Party Life. Ves' Leningrad: adresnaia i spravochnaia kniga*, 25. Cherniak, Petr Vasil'evich (1904–1937), an assistant mechanical engineer at the Red Triangle Factory, was executed. Vol'skii, E.V., et al. *Leningradskii martyrolog: 1937–1938*, t.4 (1999), 522.

2. Zheelov, Grigorii Zakharovich, Director of Vyborgskii Palace of Culture: Bogdanov, Mikhail Vasil'evich, and Evdokimov, Aleksandr Maksimovich are recorded in *The List of the Second Category of Convicted People, August 31, 1937* (AP RF, opis' 24, delo 410, list 64; list 343), http://stalin.memo.ru/spiski.

The atmosphere in the cell hung grim and sinister—horrifying, really—yet combined with grief that united us, despite our fetid bodies, faces bleached as white as snow, and threadbare clothes. Some men, who had yet to endure sham trials, had no idea what to do or how to prepare for them, and we talked for hours. But as night fell, we grew silent, lost in misery and despair. A few men received packages and squirreled food and cigarettes into their pockets; few shared.

One prisoner, Vasilii Grossman, a rangy, thin man with eyes that sparkled, tried to lighten us with jokes. With rag scraps, he adorned his tattered coat with fake general's insignias. "My dear friends," he broadcast in fake British, "I say, today is our last ball at Shpalernaia Prison. You, sir, who'd like wine? Would you prefer, red, white, dry, or sweet?"

We laughed at the absurdity.

One guy yelled, "Vasilii, don't kid!"

"Well, *excuse* me!" Vasilii scoffed. "Just being here is bizarre and worthy of ridicule."

Then Evdokimov and Kuleshov stopped the gayety, announcing the arrest of Iosif Vaishlia.[3] When he had been ordered to sign accusations of members, he refused.

"They're enemies of people," investigators shouted. "You must sign the denunciations!"

But Vaishlia retorted, "Arrested men must be proved enemies. You must establish they're not genuine Soviets who don't believe in our ideals."

"So, you're as guilty as they are," the investigators avowed, and Vaishlia shook his head.

Grigorii Zheelov and Balakin relayed how investigators tortured Chudov and Kodatskii until they could barely move. They'd been healthy, handsome men, and their treatment was a savage reprisal against the old Bolsheviks who'd built the Party.

Nikolai Dobronravov was in Cell 18 with the executive director of the Red Triangle Factory, Naum Vasil'ev. Dobronravov claimed bruises and scars covered Vasil'ev. Investigators demanded he signs accusations against all the leaders and members of the People's Commissariat of Heavy Industry. He refused.

Years later, while writing this memoir, I always tried to be honest and factual. Neither Vasil'ev, Gushchinskii, nor Dobronravov gave evidence against me.

Suddenly an idea flashed across my mind: Someone controlled our

---

3. Vaishlia, Iosif Stanislavovich (1906–?), leader of Young Communist Committee in Leningrad, arrested November 1, 1937; there are no documents as to his verdict and death. Bohanov, P.P., et al., *Zhertvy politicheskikh repressii Irkutskoi oblasti: pamiat' i preduprezhdeniie budushchemu* (Irkutsk: Irkutskaia oblastnaia tipographiia No. 1, 1999), t.2, 49.

Thirteen. I Meet My Convicted Friends

trials. When I was in Cell 20 at Shpalernaia, I concluded officials compelled investigators to beat the truth out of us. Recalling those senseless beatings, they'd been directed to beat us and were indifferent to the truth. Even if they had wanted to help us, they couldn't. Their orders came from above.

Control by others was why two of my judges seemed sympathetic in their silence, and Matulevich had mumbled to me, "Be steady! Don't give in!"

Then I was sent to a transit prison to await my 10-year exile.

Fourteen

Second Transit Prison for Men

Konstantinogradskaia Street 6–8
Thursday, September 9–
 Monday, November 15, 1937

On September 9, 1937, we were transported by Black Raven to the men's second transit prison on Konstantinogradskaia Street. The cell was on the fourth floor and held 1,300 men. Across the way, a similar cell was full of men. We witnessed this log whenever we marched to the yard for exercise. The holding cells were so large because, in the 1930s, the NKVD liquidated the mechanical and metal workers' workshops and replaced them with vacant floors lined with three-tiered, wooden bunks. The abandoned machine-tools rusted outdoors just as men rotted in the cells. We laid on plank beds, crawled beneath them, and sat wherever we could find a spot. My group was labeled "the most dangerous" and quartered close to the cell door.

By the autumn equinox, Thursday, September 23, 1937, fall arrived with a vengeance. Frigid gusts of bone-chilling wind whistled through open windows. Many of us had been arrested during the summer and slept on the cement floor with caps laid on shoes for pillows without blankets against the biting cold. Shiveringly, the prison-issued my first warm clothes, replacing the tattered rags I'd worn since arrested, June 17.

At the beginning of October, the administration announced we'd be allowed relatives' visits. For entire days, guards screamed names, their voices hoarse from calling. When we heard guards approaching, we pushed to the cell door, but no one called our names. Twilight fells. Dusk settled. And finally, when we'd given up hope, a guard shouted, "Dobronravov and Skoblo *come!*" The two happy prisoners elbowed out of the cell.

Fourteen. Second Transit Prison for Men 71

We waited impatiently for their return. Nikolai Dobronravov and Maks Skoblo returned 30 minutes later, sad and dejected.

"What's the matter?" I asked.

Nikolai and Maks cried bitterly. "They said secret agents had arrested our wives. Our kids were sent to orphanages or will stay with relatives; our apartments are locked and sealed."

"They shot Chaplin,"[1] Nikolai said.

We grew quiet. For the first time, I saw strong men weep.

It was in the second transit jail I learned through arrestees that my mother had fled with our children to Saratov. Elena Pamfilovna took her grandsons to Moscow, as many grandparents had, saving their grandchildren from being renamed and living in orphanages.

A few prisoners received food parcels whose relatives visited Skoblo, Mikhailov, Brevda, and others. From these visits, we learned the terrible news that NKVD agents crammed our wives into animal wagons guarded by German shepherds and banished to unknown places.

I still remember how six children had visited Bogdanov with their shattering new. The youngest child was four, and they all complained about being hungry. They cried and said their mother had been arrested, leaving them alone.

None of us expected this painful news: *What prison terms had our wives got? Why were they arrested? We soon realized our wives had been deemed enemies of the people.*

Much later, I learned women hid letters in the train wagons, figuring if wise people found them they would be able to determine the route taken and send their mail to the families indicated. Sometimes these letters were received, revealing their itineraries and locations. The usual stamps were Leningrad, Vologda,[2] Murmansk,[3] or Tomsk.[4]

We interpreted their letters and figured their trains spent days and nights on rail sidings. It was November. With no family connections, most wives simply disappeared without a trace.

Meanwhile, we husbands were in a transit jail and permitted to exercise twice a week. Half the prisoners could manage to walk down the steps

---

1. Chaplin, Nikolai Pavlovich (1902–1938), led the political branch of the Kirov Railroad until executed September 22, 1938. Vol'skii, E.V., et al. *Leningradskii martyrolog: 1937–1938*, t.10 (2010), 520.

2. Vologda is a vital transport junction in Northwestern Russia, 407 miles from Saint Petersburg. Pushkareva, M.I. *Atlas shem zheleznykh dorog SSSR*. 2nd ed. (Moskva: Glavnoe upravleniie geodesii i kartografii pri Sovete Ministrov SSSR, 1980), 70–71.

3. Murmansk is the world's largest city above the Arctic Circle, 829 miles from Saint Petersburg. Pushkareva, *Atlas shem zheleznykh dorog SSSR*, 22–23.

4. Tomsk, an old city in Siberia, is located 2,261 miles from Moscow. Pushkareva, *Atlas shem zheleznykh dorog SSSR*, 58–59.

from the fourth floor; thousands never had enough time to go the stairs before guards commanded, "Stop walking and return!" The prisoners reluctantly returned to their cells.

In my cell, all the inmates had received infamous Article 58, designed for political prisoners. The investigators and guards wanted to hammer into our heads that we were "enemies of the people." One day, the singer, Muratov, expressed this thought when he stood, shoulders straight, head tilted back and sang: "Finally, their slander overflows and bursts, multiplying itself, and producing an explosion like the tremor of a cannon shot with its confusing thunder. We, the miserable slandered ones, vilified, trampled upon, and under public scourge, have been fated to destruction."[5]

Thirteen hundred men fell silent. Then there was loud and prolonged applause that alarmed the guards and brought them to our cell's door.

"What's going on in there?" guards yelled.

But there was no noise within the cell. We remained quiet and thought of the famous Soviet event: The day of the October Revolution, November 7, 1937. We saw red flags from our fourth-floor cell and admired the beauty of Leningrad. That Great October Day was the Greatest of Soviet holidays, and here we were in jail forever!

But another fate awaited us.

---

5. Fisher, Burton D., ed. "The Art of Slander" in *The Barber of Seville by Rossini* (Coral Gables, FL: Opera Journeys, 2002), 68–69.

Fifteen

The Train: Leningrad to Vladivostok

Sortirovochnaia Station
Tuesday, November 16–Friday, December 31, 1937

On November 16, 1937, without goodbyes, Black Raven trucks drove 32 of us to the Sortirovochnaia Train Station under cover of night. When we stopped next to the train's slatted-wagons, guards ordered us to join echelons of 1,300 men assembled by neighborhood and height that formed stair-step units. We muttered and complained and thought of our wives, convinced something horrible had happened to them.

The harsh snarls of German shepherds circled us, growling and straining to attack. What nonsense! Who did they think we were, bank robbers?

"*Attention*!" the captain of the guard yelled.

Instantly, silence replaced the grumbles of the skeletal mob.

He bellowed boarding instruction. Men moved past me. I recognized distinguished men, commanders in the Red Army, legendary party members, trade unions leaders, professors, doctors, teachers, engineers, students, writers, and artists—men the country badly needed. I boarded.

Loading dragged on far into the darkness. Finally, with feet as numb as stones, guards locked our wagon, coupled it to others, and a steam locomotive that huffed and strained, left the siding and chugged us onto the main track. Soon, wheels clunking slowly on rail-joints, then clicked faster as the train gathered speed and the freezing November wind whistled inside. My life flashed before me, the aching resentment, humiliation, and mortification; how could this have happened?

"Farewell, my Leningrad!" I grieved aloud. "When will I ever see you again?"

"Never," grunted a man squeezed in next to me.

The temperature plunged to bitter coldness in night's long shivering hours. After an eternity, we saw a glow in the frosty-haziness to our right, meaning we were heading northeast. Some men guessed we were going to the Solovetskii Islands. Other men guessed we had trained south to Moscow, detoured around it, and were destined for Siberia to the northeast. They were right. That morning we saw deep snow and nothing to eat.

Vasia Grossman, the jokester with the sparkling eyes, laughed and expounded, "Dear friends, you're about to discover you're 300 miles east of Leningrad in balmy Vologda!"

After 24 hours, the brakes howled, couplings banged, and the train squealed to a stop in the middle of a whiteout. Guards unlocked our wagon and yanked the door open. A thick frosty mist rolled across the flat white steppes. There was not a house in sight.

"Why did we stop here?" someone asked. "To sunbathe?"

"To throw out the dead, idiot!" a guard shouted. "Grab those corpses and toss them out!" We took the bodies of three men by their heels and shoulders and heaved them into a snowbank.

Then guards searched us, pawed through our scant belongings, and warned, "We'll be leaving you in Vologda. You'd better know, your new escorts hate jokesters!"

Grossman was right, we were in Vologda.

In Vologda, we had a half-portion of *balanda* and bread crusts. It grew colder as we chugged east. Every morning guards lugged armfuls of branches to the wagons for our *burzhuikas*, that radiated little warmth in the draftiness for the men able to squeeze next to it.

Nikolai Dobronravov and I bunked on a lower plank and were thankful to his mother-in-law for our warm coats; they saved our lives in the subzero wagon. Mornings, men complained of not being able to feel their legs and fingers. Some nights, men froze to death, their near-weightless corpses tossed in snowbanks after roll call, and short rations of *balanda* and bread.

But despite our hunger and chattering teeth, most of us survived the six weeks. We often stopped at rail sidings for passing trains and heard young people sing songs with mournful voices that touched our souls. They had no idea what was happening to us or in store for them. They lived in a cocoon woven by a Soviet hierarchy for naïve citizens.

In the second month aboard the icy wagons, the *burzhuika* branches stopped. "There are no more branches for your fires!" a guard announced, but our daily body searches continued. For what? Guards yanked open our wagon doors, the biting wind whipped in, the dead were tossed out, and head counts continued. Nothing changed. Win-

Fifteen. The Train: Leningrad to Vladivostok

ter sunset early, and we wrapped our baggy clothes tightly around our dwindling bodies, glad to be alive in the frigid dark. We had no energy to move or talk and could only huddle together like toothpicks for warmth. Our false verdicts may have fettered our minds and bodies in this miserable trap, but they never chained our souls, for it is impossible to stop human thought furious over injustices. Thoughts flow freely! I dwelled on my happy childhood.

One day, somebody announced, "My friends, today is December 31, 1937! All respectable Soviets celebrate the coming New Year!"

"Even scoundrels like us?" someone snarled.

"Of course! The New Year will bring changes!" Vasia Grossman, the eternal optimist, agreed, serving up a winning smile.

Grigorii seconded Vasia pronouncement. "Yes, let's celebrate it!"

"Maybe they'll release us!" someone cried. "Oh sure!" others derided.

They were wrong. Most of us found 1938 was life's final year.

Cold darkness shrouded Siberia, and the train rumbled on. Bored men lamented, "We are driving east," but others sang folk songs to pass the time to the Pacific coast. Tales of secret romances and jokes spun by Vasia Grossman, our beloved master of ceremonies, filled our hours. At 30, Vasia had the energy to performed theatrical scenes to our delight. They might freeze him to death, but they'd never crush his infectious obstinacy!

During the first night of 1938, we congratulated each other filled with New Year hopes for release. "Our truth is the collective truth! It will triumph over these lies!"

How mistaken we were!

Everything had long ago frozen solid in the wagons. Whenever the train stopped, NKVD guards beat the icy doors with hammers to loosen them enough to open and begin rollcall and toss out corpses. Wearing thick, fur coats and *valenki,* winter boots, guards felt inside our pockets and clothes with their warm bare hands, warming our bodies as they searched for contraband.

"Close the door! We're freezing to death!" prisoners screamed at them.

"Shut up!" guards yelled. "We know what we're doing! We'll close them when through!"

"Give us firewood, we beg you!" a prisoner pleaded.

"You burned it all!" the guards replied. "There's no more."

Short winter days stayed gray and cold. Frost built at night. My body felt frozen solid, but my thoughts pushed on. In my mind's eye, I saw sunny Saratov, my parents, Nina, our kids, and our first meeting with Nikolai Dobronravov's family in Leningrad. Those long-ago reminiscences captivated me, and I felt 20 again, full of youthful enthusiasm. I was a student at

Saratov State University with a meager scholarship of 17 rubles a month. My parents couldn't help, and I found a job at a local school. Nina was the top student in Saratov's high school 13 and editor of the *Young Pioneer's Journal*. I admired her care in fulfilling her duties.[1] Nina also volunteered, teaching illiterate women to read. Her Young Pioneers vowed to the ruling Bolsheviks they would end illiteracy by the tenth anniversary of the October Revolution.

At 16, Nina cared for her home as her mother was bed-ridden. Her father was a tailor, and evenings, Nina did her homework, read extensively, made clothes, and cooked.

Our shared respect and devotion flourished. Love's first feelings emerged during our work together. And, because of her parents' wariness of young men, we attended movies, or, once, attended Vladimir Maiakovskii's poetry reading in a Bolshevik Club.[2]

Three years later, in December 1928, Nina and I were married. After graduation from the university, my advisors sent me to Moscow for engineering courses, and Nina became a student at Saratov Pedagogical College. During her school break in December 1930, she visited me in Moscow. I met her at the Paveletskii Railroad Station, and we took a tram to my apartment on the corner of the Arbat and the Smolenskii market. Moscow impressed us with its towering buildings, streets, and squares. Nina, laughing as we entered my small room, sat on the bed, stretched her legs, and said, "Leonid, I'm happy being with you!" We hung her clothes, and I showed her my kitchen with running water. In Saratov, she still carried water from the well.

At that time, the new economic politics flourished. It was the new state capitalism policy proposed by Lenin that crammed farmers' markets and stores with groceries and goodies. Nina loved the Okhotnii market, near the Kremlin and Manezhnaia Square, where, in addition to a plethora of local foods, vendors sold an array of live birds.

During those joyous days, I attended courses from 9 to 2. I joined the Party Committee at my institution, and with great passion examined Marx's *Capital*[3] in Lenin's interpretations, Bukharin's *ABC of Commu-*

---

1. Vladimir Lenin's All-Union Young Pioneer organization was founded for children 10–14 and existed from 1922 to 1991. All Young Pioneers wore red neckties and pins with the slogan *Always Ready!* Translator's note; I was a Pioneer from 1975 to 1980.
2. Maiakovskii, Vladimir Vladimirovich (1893–1930), admired Bolsheviks' ideas and glorified them in his poetry. Students and families, including mine, memorized his poetry as if it was the Bible. Translator's note.
3. Marx, Karl (1818–1873), author of *Capital: Critique of Political Economy*, focuses on surplus value and exploitation of workers; it became the central doctrine of Bolshevism and Marxism. Wieszynski, *The Modern Encyclopedia of Russian and Soviet History*, vol. 19 (1981), 183–188.

Fifteen. The Train: Leningrad to Vladivostok

nism, and Lenin's work, *The State and Revolution*.[4] When someone called me: comrade, I stood proudly. Comrade Bolotov, here is your new ID; comrade Bolotov, lock the door; comrade Bolotov, turn the lights off! And our professors and students declared the old morality was dead!

At that time, I earned 120 rubles a month, enough for us to shop for elegant shoes and clothes in GUM, the foremost department store in Red Square. One winter day, we bought a stylish outfit for Nina with matching high, laced, leather shoes. Another day we bought my first Boston suit. Sometimes Nina and I regaled ourselves in small restaurants at tables draped with elegant, white table-cloths bearing China, and silverware. We enjoyed tasty appetizers and red and white wine poured into crystal goblets.

We celebrated New Year's Eve, 1930, with the Red Square throng below the bright ruby stars shining on Spasskaia Tower, the main tower of the Kremlin. After the January 6 holiday, Nina reluctantly returned to Saratov and her studies. Two months later, in March 1930, Nina left Saratov, and joined me moving to Leningrad for my new work as an engineer at the Red Triangle Factory. My days started at seven a.m. and ended at 10 p.m. In addition to my work, I lectured at the Leningrad Automobile Institution. Nina cooked, washed our linen, and made our clothes.

Soon after that, I received a telegram from father: *Someone stole my wallet! Send 100 rubles to Stalingrad.*[5] *Money to be claimed at the post office*. I borrowed the sum from comrades at the Red Triangle and wired it to him. That summer, Nina and I visited my parents at their home in the Kalmykian steppes, in Bashanta, where father managed a procurement center.[6]

The train ride to Stalingrad was long and dusty, and it was stifling-hot when we arrived in Salsk, Rostov-on-Don. Since we had to wait 10 hours for the next train, Nina and I swam in the Volga and enjoyed the beach. We rented a small boat; I paddled; Nina tended the rudder.

"How lovely and hot!" Nina exclaimed. "It's like a sauna!"

"Yeah, not like the icy Neva!" I echoed lovingly.

Once bathed, we rowed back to Stalingrad, returned the boat, and sent a telegram to my parents: *Meet us in Salsk*. Unfortunately, no one

---

4. Lenin, Vladimir Il'ich (1870–1924), founder of the Bolshevik Party and the Soviet Union. His work *State and Revolution* (1917) is dedicated to the dictatorship of proletariat, which must fight its inner enemies with the army. Wieszynski, *The Modern Encyclopedia of Russian and Soviet History*, vol. 19 (1981), 161–170.

5. Stalingrad, aka Volgograd between 1925 and 1961, is a river, rail, and port on the Volga River. Wieszynski, *The Modern Encyclopedia of Russian and Soviet History*, vol. 54 (1990), 206–208.

6. Bashanta, settled in 1872, was renamed in 1971 for the Soviet hero Oka Ivanovich Gorodovikov (1879–1960). Wieszynski, *The Modern Encyclopedia of Russian and Soviet History*, vol. 13 (1979), 66–67.

met us upon our arrival, and we looked for transportation to Bashanta 40 miles away. While eating lunch, our waitress mentioned a man owning a horse and wagon who could help us. We met him, and he agreed to drive us, leaving at twilight. The setting sun left us in darkness, and within 12 miles, the horse collapsed, and Nina and I settled onto the grass under the wagon to sleep. Steppe birds chirped their good nights, and I soon drifted off. But Nina said she did not sleep, worried about the trip.

At sunrise, the horse refused to walk. We pleaded with the horse, and it finally plotted a few yards and stopped. We realized our wagon trip was over.

Then, an unforgettable mirage appeared like a cinema depiction. Out of a cloud of dust, two barefoot girls broke through behind us, in a wagon, pulled by a pair of burly oxen. Our horse barely moved aside, despite the driver slapping the reins against its skinny bones to keep up with the ox cart. No luck. Our nag stopped. The oxen passed. Our dashed hopes rekindled when the girl driver yanked back on the reins. Our driver yelled, "Do you have room for two passengers?"

"Sure! Join us," one yelled. "But we're going to Bashanta!"

"We are too," Nina cried and jabbed me in the ribs. "Come on!"

We switched wagons, and Nina and I soon sat as proudly as a king and queen beside the girls. The taller girl took a switch and struck the hind quarter of the lead ox, shouting, "Shoulder on!" And soon we were moving forward at an oxen's pace. It was the first and last time we ever enjoyed an ox cart ride.

During the trip, the girls answered our questions happily and we theirs. They said there was a Cossack town, Sandata, 20 miles from Salsk, on our way, with no men! No one knew why. The Sandata women had rebelled, demanding the authorities return their men. A military division from Rostov-on-Don[7] attempted to restrain the women but was unsuccessful, but it left the women without their banished men.

The four of us talked, shared food, watered and fed the oxen, enjoying the abundance of wildlife in the steppes as we drove through grain fields southwest of the Bashanta River. By late afternoon, we spotted Bashanta's onion domes on the horizon. At that time, the town had 2,000 homes sprawled along the river flanked by steppes, golden with ripening grain waving in the breeze. Closer, we saw fields bordered by tall feather grass and wormwood, a wild perennial in the daisy family that emitted a sharp odor.

---

7. Rostov-on-Don, a Don River port city, is the largest city in southeast Russia and the administrative center of Rostov Province. Wieszynski, *The Modern Encyclopedia of Russian and Soviet History*, vol. 52 (1990), 147–149. The girls told Leonid and Nina about the first Soviet repressions in their town in 1930.

Fifteen. The Train: Leningrad to Vladivostok

Leonid and Nina, 1930 (Collection of Lana Bourret).

Left: Dmitrii Narkisovich Doroshevskii, father of Elena Dmitrievna (Doroshevskaia) Dobronravova, circa 1918. *Right:* Elena Dmitrievna (Doroshevskaia) Dobronravova, circa 1928 (Arzamas Museum of History and Art).

Clouds of dust plume rose from our ox-drawn-wagon and twisted into the afternoon heat before settling to dust a flour-white layer over the parched land and us. The sharp, weedy smell of wormwood was nearly nauseating in the oppressive heat, and we covered our head with our jackets. My sleeves were rolled up, but the sides of the wagon were too hot to rest my arms upon, and we drove through town looking as white as ghosts. I noticed that the cinema hadn't arrived in Bashanta. No one swam in the hot river either.

After brushing off dust and making a few friendly inquiries, we found my parents.

We spent 10 joyous days with them and their friends. On the last day, Dad harnessed his horse and drove us back to Salsk. Father's horse was well-fed and well-trained, and I'll never forget Dad's pleasant mood on our return. We'd discussed them joining us in Leningrad, and, on the way, Dad sang songs from a Broadway musical, *Rose-Marie*.

Our vacation ended; we trained back to our little apartment in Leningrad. I resumed work at the Red Triangle Factory, and for the next two years, life continued with long hours and

Elena Pamfilovna Doroshevskaia, mother of Elena Dmitrievna (Doroshevskaia) Dobronravova, circa 1918 (Arzamas Museum of History and Art).

Nikolai Petrovich Dobronravov, husband of Elena Dmitrievna (Doroshevskaia) Dobronravova, both Gulag victims, circa 1929 (Arzamas Museum of History and Art).

Fifteen. The Train: Leningrad to Vladivostok

fun days off. We called my parents and insisted they come and live with us.

Soon after our son was born in 1932, we began renting summer homes with Nikolai Dobronravov's family south of Leningrad. Taking trains to the suburbs of Leningrad: Tolmachevo, Dudergoff, Martyshkino, and Siverskaia, we walked to the piney woods on lush hillsides above rivers known as "Northern Crimea." We fried potatoes with mushrooms, picked berries, and swam in the rivers. One day we'd devoured all our meat, and I rode a bike to the farmer's market in Luga through thick, green field stretching to the shaded woods. When I got to the market, I bought a live rooster, put it in my leather bag, and hooked it to the bike frame. How little Gena laughed as he watched it being pulled out of my bag, flapping and crowing.

How lucky we were with my friend's family! Elena Pamfilovna graduated from Smol'nyi Institute.[8] From her, Nina learned to make Napoleon torts. Elena also was an excellent advisor about cultural life in Leningrad.

Left to right: Nikolai Ivanovich Poliakov, Leo Poliakov, Natalia Petrovna Poliakova-Golikova, 1931 (Arzamas Gaidar Museum).

---

8. Smol'nyi Institute was the first school of women's education, 1764–1919. Wieszynski, *The Modern Encyclopedia of Russian and Soviet History*, vol. 36 (1984), 61–63.

Thanks to her, we visited the ballet at Aleksandrinskii and Mariinskii Theaters, listened to voices of the gifted artists Leonid Utesov, Ivan Kozlovskii, and Sergei Lemeshev.[9] I remember on March 26, 1932, Nina and I heard Bukharin's and Lunacharskii's speeches dedicated to the centennial of Johann Wolfgang von Goethe's death.[10]

How we celebrated the end of 1934 with the Dobronravov's family on Vasil'evskii Island![11] Elena Pamfilovna and her daughter, Lelia, played the piano and we danced to waltzes, polkas, tangos, and foxtrots. At their apartment, we met Natalia Poliakova-Golikova, a sister of the famous author, Arkadii Gaidar.[12] She told us of her brother's youth and how his children's books were well-known abroad. Natalia's husband, Nikolai, who had attended Tolmachev Military Political Academy, suppressed Antonov's gangs in Tambov Province with Marshal Tukhachevskii, and, after the Civil War, served in the Moscow military district.[13]

We enjoyed the last night of 1934, never sleeping until almost the tardy winter's sunrise at 10:00 a.m. Coming home, Nina and I missed our first tram to the Obvodnii Canal, and we crossed the Neva River on the ice. We were close to Narvskii Gates, and the day was cold but stimulating as the snow crunched under our feet. Gena never awoke but breathed slowly and noisily. We arrived home after hours of walking, delighted with our holiday, and happily flopped into bed. After that long night of celebrating, we rested all day and invited the Dobronravovs to visit us on January 2, 1935. Nina awoke that morning, worried.

She asked, "Leonid, how will we ever entertain the Dobronravovs? We have neither glasses nor decanters or any of the things we need."

"Leave it to me, Nina," I replied. At 9, I dressed warmly and hurried to the tram. The streets were empty. People had celebrated the end of 1934 and were still resting on New Year's Day. I saw an empty tram, jumped

---

9. Utesov, Leonid Osipovich (1895–1982), was the conductor of the first jazz orchestra. Zalesskii, *Imperia Stalina*, 455–456. Kozlovskii, Ivan Semenovich (1900–1993), was an opera singer in the Bolshoi Theater. Keldysh, Iu. V. *Muzykal'naia entsiklopediia* (Moskva: Izdatel'stvo "Sovetskaia entsiklopediia," 1974), t.2, 861. Lemeshev, Sergei Iakovlevich (1902–1977), was an opera singer in the Bolshoi Theater. Keldysh, *Muzykal'naia entsiklopediia*, t.3 (1976), 226.

10. Lunacharskii, Anatolii Vasil'evich (1875–1933), was the first Commissar of Education. *Ibid.*, 1981, vol. 20, 188–194. Also see his speech, "Goete i ego vremia," in *Literaturnoie nasledstvo* (Moskva: Zhurnal'no-gazetnoe ob'edinenie, t.4 [1932]: 5–20).

11. According to a notation from November 29, 2000, in *Bolotov's Memoir*, Dobronravovs lived on Vasil'evskii Island at building 1/25, on the corner of Lieutenant Schmidt Street and Fourteenth Line.

12. Gaidar, Arkadii Petrovich (1904–1941), was killed during World War II. Gaidar, T.A. *Golikov Arkadii iz Arzamasa* (Moskva: Politicheskaia literatura, 1988).

13. Poliakova-Golikova, Natalia Petrovna (1905–1967), married Nikolai Ivanovich Poliakov (1900–1943) in 1925. He was the military commissar of the 16th Regiment and arrested in 1937; his place of death is unknown. The Arzamas Museum of History.

Fifteen. The Train: Leningrad to Vladivostok

aboard, and rode it into the central city. Jumping off at an antique shop on Narvskii Prospect, I bought six elegant glasses, a decanter, and three wines: Cahors, a Port 54, and a fine Tokay.

When I returned, Nina was overjoyed. She cooked all day in our little kitchen, filling the apartment with scrumptious aromas.

"Oh, Leonid," she worried, "We don't have enough time to get everything ready!"

"Don't worry," I comforted her. "We'll have plenty of time!"

She gave me a list of more groceries, and I ran to the store. In 1935, grocery stores were always opened and full of mouthwatering foods during the holidays. There was an array of different types of salami, bologna, cheese, beluga, sturgeon, oranges, pears, lemons, tomatoes, pickles, all readily available and ready for selection.

That evening, when the Dobronravovs and Petrazhitskie arrived, our table was heaped high with delicious goodies! During breaks from eating, we sang and danced. With my mandolin, which I bought at a Saratov market at 14, I played Russian folk songs. Our friends asked me to play more, and little Kolia Dobronravov and Gena held hands and danced. Elena Pamfilovna complimented Nina on her delicious meals and my playing. An unforgettable atmosphere of kindness and friendship reigned!

Some months later, my parents arrived to live with us. Nina got on well with my parents, and my father loved her like a daughter. Nina learned Dad preferred fish, and she always cooked it for him. Mother helped Nina and watched Gena whenever Nina visited downtown.

In winters, we visited a skating rink as I loved skating. Nina watched me, counting my laps, worrying I'd get hurt. Her image is still fixed in my memory: ruby lips, pink cheeks, and tender blue eyes. Nina always looked elegant and natural, and we ordered several silk dresses and shoes for her.

When our brothers and sisters visited, we brought them to theaters and museums and bought them clothes. Once Nina's sister, Olga, stayed with us for two years, and I helped her find work in my factory. Evenings, she attended courses as she wanted to become a student at one of the Leningrad institutions. Our life was enjoyable and bright. These reflections remained with me for decades as the prisoners' train continued to Vladivostok, as distant to me as Timbuktu.

I heard the sharp thumping of the train's steel wheels on track joints as I said farewell to 1937. What would 1938 bring? In Krasnoiarsk our train stopped.[14] An escort ordered us to tie our clothes in knots and fol-

---

14. Krasnoiarsk, a large city east of the Urals, is a leading industrial and commercial center, located 2,841 miles east of Saint Petersburg. Wieszynski, *The Modern Encyclopedia of Russian and Soviet History*, vol. 49 (1988), 168–171.

low him to the *banya*, sauna. The frost was fierce as he counted us. We wore summer clothes, and I put on rubber galoshes. My feet were frozen. After our hot *banya*, we re-boarded the train and continued east. We broke plank beds to burn for heat.

Finally, on January 15, 1938, a strange warm breeze filled the wagon. Vasia Grossman said to us, "My dear friends! Look, there's no snow! Siberia has ended. This is Vladivostok, on the Pacific's rim."

Sixteen

Vladivostok Transit Camp

Knolls of Vladivostok
Sunday, January 16, 1938

At the end of our 60-day, Leningrad-to-Vladivostok odyssey, we banged to a stop at the railroad station and guards shouted, "All of you, grab your things and get out!"

Two months of confinement in the cramped dark wagons, left us barely able to open our eyes in the bright sunshine or walk as our unused muscles had atrophied. And yet, the guards, straining to hold leased dogs, threatened, "Get down now or we'll shoot you!"

We Leningradians supported each other and climbed down from the wagon to squat on the ground in rows of five as directed while nipped by snarling dogs, slobbering with wet tongues and bared fangs. Once the wagon was empty, guards counted us and ordered us to march from the station to the transit camp. More guards rechecked the wagons, seizing our cups, plates, and spoons given us by Leningrad relatives.

What a sorry sight we must have been: tattered, unshaven, filthy men, trying to march in a column like cadets dressed in rags that even criminals wouldn't steal. We prisoners, students, commissars, Red Army and Navy commanders, Party leaders, trade unions managers, and factory workers were a hodgepodge of old and young, professors and students, doctors and engineers, artists and teachers, thieves and rapists, NKVD agents and highly skilled specialists. As we trudged through the streets, I felt sorry for the young prisoners who'd never had the chance to experience life, marriage, and work.

Along the streets, Vladivostokians stared at us in astonishment. Their eyes told us we had touched their hearts. Some walked beside us and asked, "What happened to you?" "Why are the secret police with you?"

I heard the same replies over and over, "We have no idea. It's a mistake."

After an hour's march we climbed a knoll and approached the gate of the vast, barbed-wired Vladivostok transit camp. Over the gate, a sign warned: WE WILL RULE YOU WITH AN IRON ROD! Inside, there were wooden barracks, water tanks, and a mess hall. Near the gate, there was a small column of women. After seven months in prison, this was the first time I'd seen women. *Would Nina be among them?*

It was our first time in a transit camp, and we witnessed how secret police stored enemies of the people from across Russia awaiting icebreakers north to Kolyma mines.

Inside the gate, zones divided the camp. The first held prisoners of domestic crimes; those men worked for the guards. My column continued through it and a large latrine, reeking with toilet-chlorine, to a larger, more secure area, separated by more barbed wire.

A tall, sinewy man met us by the narrow gate and began reading names and shouting in a thick German accent. Using obscene language, he demanded we each state our Article of Conviction and length of confinement. "*Shriek* it out so I can hear!"

When our turns came, we Leningradians, to a man, protested, "We've all been convicted by the same military in sham trials." The German, trying to intimidate us, swore and shouted back at us.

We replied in kind. "Who are you? What's a German doing counting Russian heads? Why are you so insolent toward innocent men?"

Our revolt succeeded a little. The German stopped swearing, took our files, and started calling us by name, "Aleemenka!" he yelled.

"It's not Aleemenka; it's *Olemenko!*" a man shouted. "I have no Article of Conviction or prison term! I'm innocent! Your flaky files are fabrications!"

"Shut up!" the German yelled back.

"Why don't you learn to scream in Russian?" we shouted at him.

"You're all guilty bastards!" he barked, so angry and frustrated his face turned purple. "You'll learn who the hell I am in this zone!"

The German did not allow Alymenko to walk into the area and called out several more names from the Leningrad column. No one replied.

We crowded close to him near the gate. The German was infuriated. But neither his blind fury nor his threatens helped him, and he screeched, "Balakin! What's your Article?"

"I don't know!" someone replied. "I don't know anything!"

"Shut up! You're counterrevolutionaries! We'll force you to speak!"

"Don't even try, you sick, German dog!" men roared.

No one admitted his guilt, and a scuffle took place near the gate. Guards fired rifles into the crowd. The German gave up, cursing, and we walked into the zone, marking only our last names as we passed in front

Sixteen. Vladivostok Transit Camp

of him. At the same time, he ordered his men to slice off the officers' military overcoats, now ankle-length, at the knees. This humiliated them even more.

The German shrieked, "You may have been brass in the Red Army, but now you're here! There's no escape!"

Once inside this zone, we gathered in small groups and said why had the government let Germans humiliate us honest Soviets. Our consensus was they must have arrived in the Soviet Union before 1937 and been ordered by the German government to become spies and penetrate Soviet camps. But was this true or rumor?

At dinner time, we were allotted one loaf of bread for every 10 men and fish *balanda* in washbasins that we had used to bathe in earlier. With neither spoons nor cups, 10 heads slurped from the tub! Later, as we made ourselves at home in the prison yard, men in other zones tossed over the barbed wire empty cans for us to use. We threw back small chunks of bread in payment.

Around us, some criminals became Gulag *rich*. They always had the essentials of prison currency: bread and tobacco. They found us political prisoners soft and told us we had no idea how to survive in camp but insisted they did. Use their service or else. Fortunately, our group had been thrown cans and not had to make payment in bread, and we never had to use criminals for the nicety of our tables.

Seventeen

Behind Barbed Wire

The Transit Camp
Monday, January 17–Sunday, May 15, 1938

The transit camp stood atop the city's highest knoll overlooking Golden Horn Bay to the east and, west, to the city of Vladivostok. Looking landward, I could see the end of the city, and, seaward, the endless Pacific. Often, I stood outside the barrack, staring at its boundlessness for hours, recalling my past, present, and trying to see the future. Here, 7,000 miles from home, I was cut off from a family with no idea I'd continue this odyssey to Arctic Kolyma, another world away.

It was often below zero in late January in Vladivostok, and when cold I went inside to reclaim my space on a third-level plank. Body heat helped keep us warm. Our column had been lucky since we took over an empty barrack soon after the December 1937 departure of the last ship for Kolyma. Now we must wait for Arctic ice to break.

Leekhtner, an old, sick Bolshevik, laid next to me. He ran his fingers through his long, gray, matted beard, trying to untangle it, and he said he'd been a member of the Ukrainian government and manager of the Bank of Ukraine. *Why he'd been arrested and banished to Kolyma. Surely, he'd die there.* He lay weakened and had missed his turn for a chunk of bread. His kidneys troubled him, and doctors advised him to drink lots of water to irrigate them. But guards only assigned a cup of water, per man, per day. I felt sorry for him, my father's age, and brought him bread and *balanda*. A few days later, he grew strong enough to climb down from our shared plank.

One day, Leekhtner received a package from Kiev. Excited, he tore it open and found an elegant suit his wife mailed. I read her letter: *You're working with top people and need to look your best every day! It is not good to look dirty.* Leekhtner's eyes watered at her unsullied words; he broke down, sobbing, "Officials lied to her."

When the criminals heard of the suit, they stole it; no exceptions in the transit camp, old or young suffered thievery. A few days later, Leekhtner told me why the NKVD had arrested him. Investigators detained Stanislav Kosior.[1]

"What was his crime?" I asked.

"Planning the murder of Stalin and Molotov."

"Just like me and hundreds of others."

Leekhtner nodded. "Right. Lubyanka investigators demanded Grin'ko sign accusations to confirm Kosior's counter-revolutionary activities.[2] Then they pressed Grin'ko, saying they knew he'd spoken poorly of Stalin and Molotov, brutally beat him, and began to work on their verisimilar documents to project the 'truth' that thoroughly discredited him. Later, the NKVD arrested me and ordered me to sign the denunciation of Grin'ko, which, in writing, claimed he was a counterrevolutionary. I refused to sign this lie. The investigator then pronounced his sentence on Kosior, Grin'ko, and Leekhtner. That's why I'm here."

And that's how life went on…

New columns of convicts arrived daily in our transit camp from Moscow, Georgia, Armenia, Ukraine, Belorussia, Kazakhstan, and Siberia. When Uzbeks, Tajiks, and Turks entered, their dark skin, big turban knots, and ethnic clothes stood out, and guards confiscated their turbans to which they protested. Space shrank as prisoners wedged into areas behind the barracks, living and sleeping outdoors. Guards ordered us to fence off holding areas, and on the grassy knolls closest to us, prisoners slept under the sky despite cold nights. Fortunately, I stayed dry and mostly warm. During the waning days of April, it turned hot. We waited impatiently to escape and leave for Kolyma. Unfortunately, the Okhotsk Sea's winter raged on, and its northern shore was solid ice.

Some days prisoners could not hide from the sun's bright sting, and still more prisoners came, told unheard stories and news. The Plenary Session of January 1938 documented the illegal actions of the NKVD. Hearing that Party news, I immediately, wrote a letter and mailed it to Stalin with copies to Vyshinskii and Kalinin.[3]

No one replied. And yet, to a man, we hoped and prayed for release.

---

1. Kosior, Stanislav Vikentievich (1889–1939?), Ukrainian Communist Party leader, 1934–1938. Wieszynski, *The Modern Encyclopedia of Russian and Soviet History* vol. 17 (1980), 221–223.

2. Grin'ko, Grigorii Fedorovich (1890–1938), the third People's Commissar of Finances, 1930–1937. His signature appeared on the bank note. Wieszynski, *The Modern Encyclopedia of Russian and Soviet History*, vol. 13 (1979), 161–162.

3. Kalinin, Mikhail Ivanovich (1875–1946), President of the Russian Soviet Federative Socialist Republic, supported forced collectivization and industrialization. Wieszynski, *The Modern Encyclopedia of Russian and Soviet History*, vol. 15 (1980), 187–191.

Most of us believed that the truth would set us free and restore our lives. "We *will* see our families in May!" some exclaimed wide-eyed.

But May of what year? One man commented on the Plenary Session of 1938, "Top officials want to stop this bloody tire from rolling, no one will let us go."

The Khabarovsk prosecutor echoed this. "The government lies to the Party, and the Party lies to the people." Every corner of the camp buzzed with rumors as we awaited what might happen.

My friend, Nikolai Dobronravov, assured us, "My dear comrades, our relatives will greet us with flowers!" A Muscovite declared, "Comrades! You're acting like kindergarteners! We face a huge and terrible business so large only the government can be responsible for it as it is *not* a simple matter of releasing so many people." A dark-skinned Georgian shouted, "Are you saying the Central Committee didn't know what's going on in the NKVD? HA! Ezhov[4] and Yagoda[5] had to have been ordered to arrest us."

We talked and argued and guessed, blindly drawing fallacious conclusions. A few prisoners were glad to be arrested and looked forward to a new life with work.

One Georgian waved his arms and asked these colorfully clad prisoners to be quiet. "You're from different places, but Stalin is one of ours, he's from Georgia. Look at what he's doing to us Georgians!"

Georgians argued and yelled how the investigators had treated them. "Agents put me in a cage with shit on the floor" one complained. Another cried, "They didn't let me sleep!" A third shouted, "The guards whipped my wife and me!"

One day, a man from Khabarovsk began talking back to a guard standing at the watchtower, and the guard ordered him to be silent. The man refused. In seconds, a shot rang out. The Khabarovsk prisoner fell, dead. Isaac Brevda looked at the corpse and thought the bullet hit the man's belly. The shooting was usual. Every hour shots rang out, reminding us of our tenuous place in the transit camp.

Balakin lamented, "Young people today believe official orders, deaf and blind to the truth. When we criticize our comrades, we use the theory of class contradictions, class struggle, and class enemy. We're now paying for our failures to teach them this."

---

4. Ezhov, Nikolai Ivanovich (1895–1939), NKVD head 1936–1938 and enforcer of the Reign of Terror, or "Ezhovshchina," which climaxed in the period of mass liquidations. Wieszynski, *The Modern Encyclopedia of Russian and Soviet History*, vol. 11 (1979), 34–39.

5. Yagoda, Genrikh Grigorievich (1891–1938), one of Stalin's instruments for implementing the Reign of Terror. On March 2, 1938, Yagoda was charged with plotting the "Right-Oppositionists" and executed. Wieszynski, *The Modern Encyclopedia of Russian and Soviet History*, vol. 44 (1987), 137–140.

Seventeen. Behind Barbed Wire

One day, guards ordered four of us to dig a cellar and privy holes for a new little wooden house. The spot's icy, heavy dirt made excavation slow as big hunks broke into small pieces. I was frozen and knew I'd die of pneumonia from wet feet in city shoes. Soon we heard that the head of the transit camp was going to live there. He hated the camp's true criminals, and he asked enemies of people to do the digging.

An old woman lived in the house with the warden. She was always cleaning and sweeping and bustling here and there. She would often step out on the porch, look at us shivering, and invite us in to get warm. We took turns inside and watched the old woman cook and whiffed smells of borsch, hamburgers, and bread. The smells floated around us and made our mouths water. Naturally, the guard assigned to watch the four of us, sat inside all day, staying cozy. Neither the warden nor the old woman offered us food; they just watched us with sour smiles as we worked. Despite it being the warden's home, we were delighted to see family life again. When we rested, we enjoyed brief relief from suffocating boredom with his family.

Leekhtner grew sicker and constantly asked for water. Once a day, I took a large bucket to the edge of camp—guards allowed us to fetch water from a huge copper tank. I guessed the water was sterile, for it was still warm, and I drank a little, returned and gave the rest to Leekhtner. Some wives of enemies of people, who'd followed their husbands, would appear at the copper tank for a chance to see them. One day, a husband, a farmer, met his wife by the tank. He said authorities arrested her for campaigning against Soviet power and talking too much.

The farmer objected vehemently. "Why do intelligent men listen to her nonsense? She's been at home every day of her life and never bothered any Soviet officials. And even if she had, she'd complain about the bread being too hard or herring too salty. She doesn't understand anything and mumbles all day like a radio." He laughed.

The investigator sprang at the word *radio*, grabbed the farmer, and said, "Three-year sentence." We weren't allowed to mention radios.

As April waned, we still waited in Vladivostok. Lucky prisoners hid in the barracks' shade. Most men scorched in merciless sun. Torture continued. We craved escape to Kolyma. Anything place was better than this.

On May Day 1938, a few men celebrated. We honest Soviets, trusting and believing in Communism, were gloomy looking at festively decorated columns behind the barbed wire.

Eighteen

Kulu

The Okhotsk Sea
Wednesday, May 18, 1938

On a balmy May 18, 1938, the transport ship *Kulu* docked at Vladivostok harbor.[1] After a hurried skilly breakfast, thousands of us marched down the hill overlooking the blue Pacific for the shipyard. As we boarded, the men grew silent. The pleasant expectations of work vanished in the rumors of Kolyma's bitter cold nights and days, even in May.

Boarding was slow. It took several days for 6,000 captives to climb the ladders and find sleeping spaces. As my group stepped aboard, guards hurled fistfuls of dry, rye croutons into our hats, screaming, "That's your food for the next week; stretch it!"

I carefully emptied my hat into my pocket and wound into the ship's dark hole crowded with rows of three-high plank-beds and, everywhere, men sprawled on the steel floor. My group had entered last, and we got quarters at the rear of the hole on the slippery floor. We flopped down and tried to sleep. I felt the propellers roar to life, and the ship reverse. The engines groaned, the massive ship shook, and I sensed movement backward. It turned and nosed into the channel on the high tide. The day was 70 degrees, and guards soon let us topside. I stood on the fantail and watched Vladivostok disappear. To our port side passed towering cliffs pocked with a million bird nests. Parents soared nearby, filling their beaks with bugs for hungry hatchlings. Soon, I worked my way to the stern and watched Russia's easternmost villages and headlands sink into the ocean as we entered the Sea of Japan. Gentle swells grew deep, and eight-foot rollers slapped us broadside. When the ship turned north, heading for the Nevel'skoi Strait, the narrows between Siberia and the Sakhalin Islands, the weather changed.

---

1. The *Kulu* ferried 3,800 passengers on each voyage to Kolyma. Bollinger, M.J. *Stalin's Slave Ships: Kolyma, the Gulag Fleet, and the Role of the West* (Westport, CT: Praeger, 2003), 80.

Eighteen. Kulu

Despite the total darkness in the ship's belly, sleep was impossible with bodies packed onto the cold, wet steel, the clamor of engines, and the tossing of turbulent seas that jarred us and frightened us to death. We struck ice floes the fifth day in the northern reaches of the Okhotsk Sea, which is icebound November through the June. Rough seas flipped over the *parasha*, and we had no way to shovel the waste, which soaked the area—and us!

Aboard the *Kulu*, criminals worked the hold for "treasures." Guards didn't care that their gangs beat us unmercifully to steal our clothes and shoes. Fortunately, Leningradians had stuck together, and the crooks avoided us. They remembered an occasion at the transit camp when Eroshkin had received a parcel. Criminals had approached him and demanded his tobacco. Eroshkin gave them some.

"We want all of it!" a criminal screamed. "Give it, or we'll tear off your arms!"

Criminals snatched the parcel from Eroshkin's hands, and suddenly, unexpectedly, a bunch of our sailors jumped from their planks, yelling, "Stand where you are!" They retrieved the stolen tobacco and chased the criminals out of our barrack joined by a dozen Leningrad workers. Our combined threat kept them away.

After that, Aleksandrov, our leader, said, "Now boys, don't misbehave!" And the criminal snarled, "We won't touch Leningradians!"

"That's wise! If you do, we'll kill you!" Aleksandrov vowed. "That's a promise!"

Most of us quickly ate our croutons by the second day; water ended day three. During the nights, criminals stole whatever men couldn't hide; but they avoided us. By day five, far north of Vladivostok, we left the Sea of Japan and entered the Okhotsk Sea. The day was gray, and the roar of big waves was endless, breaking over the bow and leaving us gasping for air in the foul hole. Despite the Okhotsk Sea terribly roughness, I made my way through a hatchway, always opened in daytime for men needing the Okhotsk Sea's toilet. At night, guards locked it up, and we used any available corner as if we were dogs.

The *Kulu* looked like a giant matchbox, but it confidently plowed through towering waves crashing through whitecaps curling over the bow. I worried she might go down, but it didn't … for now. That catastrophe came later. She pressed on, slicing through the waves while groaning under the stress of waves poundings like a hydraulic ram.

Usually, prisoners did not remain on deck long, only to relieve themselves. One day I watched an old fellow approach; he looked interesting, and I spoke to him. But he ignored me and clung to the handrail. I tried again, but he remained deathly quiet, staring into the sea. A wind blast pulled opened his overcoat. His pants were rags. His cap flew off. Sleet beat his face.

"Maybe you've had enough fresh air and should go in," I suggested.

He gave me a vacant look and returned his gaze to the turbulent sea. Then he held his head high and stiffened, proud to be staring at eternity, forgetting this nightmare and ignoring reality! A second later, the old man swung his frail body over the handrail and plunged into the icy depths. I clutched the handrail and leaned far out over the *Kulu*'s side, eyes fixed on the dark, frothy waves as ice pelted my face. Whether anyone else saw him, I can't say. But the ship never slowed. The sea swallowed him. He had stood beside me one minute, and then he ceased to exist. With no signal bell or life rings, the *Kulu* pounded on. I returned to the hole, wondering if the old man had done the right thing. Drowning in the Okhotsk Sea was faster than freezing to death in the Arctic. I never blamed him, and yet, I could not condone his taking his life.[2]

Seven days and 1,550 miles later, we arrived at Magadan's Nagaev Pier on the evening of May 25. When the steel doors opened, guards shoved us down a ramp and marched us across the frozen sea to the pier. A cutting wind blew down snow-covered hills. Elephant-sized boulders lined the shore and cast foreboding shadows in the sinking, but never setting, sun. Once on land, roll call began. The names of men who had died of disease or starvation in route and whose bodies unceremoniously flung into the sea were left unnoted. With rags for clothes and worn-out shoes, we asked for replacements.

The commander promised us, "You'll get them in camp."

I would never have dreamed I'd be in Kolyma from then until 1957! But I was.

Nagaev Bay, 1937 (Dal'stroi Territories Photo Album of 1942–1943, Ministry of Inner Affairs, State Archive, Russian Federation, Moscow).

---

2. The Dalstroy Administration cleansed Kolyma of the disabled, sending them by ship to Vladivostok. It sank. All passengers drowned.

Part II

My Stay and Work in Kolyma

Nineteen

From Magadan to the Taiga

Kolyma Roads
Wednesday, May 25–Thursday, May 26, 1938

Kolyma introduced us to harsh climatic conditions. Leaden clouds shrouded the sun, buried hill-tops, and cast its frozen desolation over everything. On this unforgiving edge of the earth, we shivered while guards wore thick, raglan overcoats. They herded us into a pair of columns and marched us from Nagaev Bay to Magadan. In places, the road hugged the sea, squeezed tightly against near-vertical cliffs. Despite nights of daylight, we disheartened men ignored guards' shouts to be quiet, calling out, "Are any of you Muscovites, Leningradians, Ukrainians or from the Volga River region?"

Men replied, "I'm from Pskov."[1] A dark-skinned man shouted, "I'm from the Khakassia."[2] Someone asked, "You guys got long terms?" And someone replied, "Twenty years!" "Ah," someone else yelled, "Stalin loves me more, I've got 25, just as his top aides, Molotov and Ezhov, did!"

As we approached Magadan, local appeared to stare at us. Some moved closer, but the guards struck them with their rifle butts. Despite the blows, locals persisted in asking, "What was happening in Russia before you left?"

A voice shouted, "Only the Devil knows what's happening to our people."

Our columns stretched out several miles from Nagaev Bay. Men leading the column entered Magadan while some still waded along the muddy shore. In 1938, Magadan was shabby and poor. There were a few

---

1. The distance from Pskov to Magadan is 3,745 miles. Translator's note.
2. Khakassia is in eastern Siberia, 4002 miles from Magadan. Wieczynski, *The Modern Encyclopedia of Russian and Soviet History*, vol. 16 (1980), 117–118.

streets and fewer one- and two-story brick homes widely separated by large empty lots overgrown with brush and strewn with debris. Dandelions, juniper, honeysuckle, and willow-herbs grew everywhere.

At a barn-like building on the edge of town, guards ordered us to line up for showers. The sky was the color of cement. Wet snow fell, but, thankfully, it melted fast, and soon turned to rain that came down hard and cold, whipped by blasts of a nor'easter off the Okhotsk Sea. Starving and shivering, I looked around at the emaciated men: *What else can these poor souls endure? Is this their end? These men will never confront the guards and bureaucrats.*

The men looked sad but accepted they were marking time in this frozen hell. So far, they had dodged fate. Aleksandrov tried to explain things to Bogdanov. Leekhtner lowered his head and plunked down on his sodden backpack. Brevda and Skoblo carried on a quiet conversation. A group from my factory, including Nikolai Dobronravov, Anatolii Kulikov, Fedor Suvorov, Lazar Alymenko, and Vasilii Serebrennikov, huddled together, seeking warmth and sidestepping puddles. Before their impris-

The narrow, curvy road along the Kolyma River (Dal'stroi Territories Photo Album of 1942–1943, Ministry of Inner Affairs, State Archive, Russian Federation, Moscow).

onment, they looked healthy, hearty, and ruddy-cheeked. Now, they were bent, skin and bones. Aleksandr Evdokimov jumped from foot-to-foot, trying to get warm.

Finally, 16 hours after arrival, we handed our backpacks and knots of clothes to the criminals for safe keeping and stripped. One hundred naked men at a time entered the old wooden barn with one showerhead and 10 washbasins. Ten men at a time shoved under the shower, wet and lathered themselves before rising off. Much too soon we were ordered out of the bathhouse, and an attendant shut off the water, screaming, "Fly out of here, fast!"

We were still dirty and naked and covered with soap, but he chased us out, stumbling as soap burned our eyes. Men squeezed me from both sides. I managed to grab my cloth knot only to discover criminals had stolen my shoes. Skoblo complained, they stole his sheepskin coat.

Someone yelled, "Trust no one in Magadan!"

After that show I ran barefoot through the freezing mud, looking for any shoes. Finally, after a futile search, a guy handed me a piece of wire and a pair of size 11 galoshes; I wore nines. Without a choice, I wired them to my feet and joined the column, barely able to walk. Prisoners stepped on my heels, and I felt them bleed. I asked for a pair of shoes, but a guard said, "You'll get new ones in a camp," so I tightened the wires and plodded on.

A half-hour later, the column stopped and split into groups. Every day, trucks left for the taiga. Political prisoners craved work. As relieved as I was for an assignment, my soul was indignant when I had to part with my best friend, Nikolai Dobronravov, when ordered aboard a different truck and whisked away. I never heard from him again.

Guards ordered us to squeeze in tightly. We pushed and shoved and made room until not one more body could be jammed in aboard the truck. The truck jerked off. Lazar Alymenko sat on my galoshes, warming my feet, and leaning against my legs. I squeezed between Bogdanov and another man. There was only one road north from Magadan, the Kolyma Auto Road.

Sporadically, along road, wooden buildings of prison camps laid out in huge squares encased with barbed-wire sprawled out with watchtowers. Guards parroted orders through loudspeakers at men and sometimes women.

One memory stayed with me, a hauntingly sad scene of young, barefoot women in light summer dresses pushing wheelbarrows of tailings from a gold mine to a residue dump. Guards as strong and nibble as elks watched them, and our escort explained that wives of enemies of people must work for their crime of marriage.

Nineteen. From Magadan to the Taiga

The driver pushes on as fast as he could over the pot-holed, dirt road. Every six hours he stopped for a one-hour break at roadside cafeterias. He ate. We didn't.

Bogdanov muttered nonstop, "Guards eat well; we starve."

For the next 24 hours, our truck sped over mountains' twisting road, rising and falling, U-turning, gunning up switchbacks beneath towering cliffs, leaving me feeling like I was on a merry-go-round. Prisoners screamed, *"Driver, we aren't logs to be tossed around!"*

Soon, the truck ahead of us on a pass flew off the edge of a hairpin curve. Our driver slammed on the breaks. Trucks behind us skidded to a stop. We clamored out and peered down the sheer face 1,000 feet. No survivors.

"Deep precipice," the driver said casually. "Let's go! We're late! *Reload!*"

We climbed aboard, and the truck sped off. One guard sat next to the driver; a second guard, in the back, faced us and leaned on his rifle. Though authorities banished hundreds of thousands of people to the vast taiga, there was never a fight with the guards over a rifle.

The next day our long ride ended. The trucks stopped on a sprawling plateau crowded with countless inmates and delivered pitiful-looking prisoners who huddled together for warmth, waiting for authorities. Now, a hundred miles north of Magadan, the weather changed abruptly; the taiga, dry and warm during the day, turned bitter cold during the nights of days.

A sailor from the battleship *Marat* said, "Guards, when are you going to feed us?"[3]

The guard shrugged. "When you get to camp."

"And how long will that be?" the sailor insisted. "Three or four days?"

"Depends on how fast you walk," the guard spit out.

"The law says you arrested us and must feed us."

"Oh-ho," the guard mocked. "So, you're a lawyer who can read and write?!"

"Hey, take my place and I'll watch you starve. Unlike you, I've visited England while aboard the *Marat* with Tukhachevskii.[4] I've sailed the Baltic

---

3. The battleship *Marat* (1914–1953) participated in the 1937 British sea parade for the coronation of George VI (1895–1952) positioned beside the German cruiser *Admiral Graf Spee*. Stephen, Martin, and Grove, Eric. *See Battles in Close-up: World War 2* (Annapolis, MD: Naval Institute Press, 1988), 11.

4. In 1936, Tukhachevskii attended the funeral of King George V of England. Stoecker, Sally W. *Forging Stalin's Tukhachevsky and the Politics of Military Innovations* (London: Taylor and Francis, 2018).

and know my value as a man. Last fall I should have returned home, but officers, like you, arrested and banished me to Kolyma. Now give us our damn bread!" The sailor howled.

"I owed you bread? Ha! No one owes anything here. March!" the guard shouted.

An hour later, guards with wolf-sized German shepherds joined us. We halted for document signing of newly added prisoners, bringing our company to 250. Guards ordered us to march to Nizhnii At-Uriah. On the long journey, we stopped at two towns, Atka and Palatka, for *balanda* and fish. It took three days over barely passable roads before we walked through deep valleys of bogs and icy streams following paths, really, animal trails, through the vast wilderness with the shepherds nipping at weak and falling prisoners. Some men collapsed in swamps, abandoned forever in the taiga. And still, we marched on, day and night…

Twenty

The New Power

Nizhnii At-Uriah
Srednekanskii District
Wednesday, June 1, 1938

In dawn's bright light, our hodge-podge of political and criminal prisoners arrived at a barren, hill-top-knoll in remote Nizhnii At-Uriah and collapsed in a compound surrounded by barbed-wire in three-acres of emptiness.[1] Two 65-by-20-foot canvas tents and a watchtower stood where we were to construct a barracks and staff buildings. The criminals took one tent. Enemies of people took the other. The camp's sleepy administration ordered guards to examine our bags and knots and take anything they wanted, which wasn't much.

The guard searching me was angry at my empty bundle. "Why don't you have anything? Where did you hide your clothes?" he screamed.

"I didn't hide anything," I replied quietly. "Criminals stole my things."

"Let me look again," he yelled with a Ukrainian accent and started digging. He found nothing and shoved me toward the watchtower, snatching the end of my red silk scarf that Nina had given me the night of my arrest. *Was he going to strangle me with it?* But he spun it into a ball and stuffed it in his pocket. Then he stomped off, eyeing bigger knots thicker with promise.

He shouted, "Everything out on the ground!"

When more new guards arrive, they'll be nothing left to steal?

As the morning sun rose high above the eastern knoll, former Red Army Commanders' stood barefoot alongside doctors, engineers, and

---

1. The At-Uriah mine was a part of the Northern Mountain Industrial Administration along with five other mines. Their administrative center was in Khatynnakh, located at 62.5° N latitude and 150° E longitude. Batsaev and Kozlov, *Dalstroy Trust Sevvostlag OGPU-NKVD of the USSR as Presented by Documents and in Numbers (2 parts). Part 1 (1931–1941)*, p. 1, 11.

college professors, holding their once-expensive clothes, now grimy rags, standing in their underwear. Those of us in work clothes were lucky: No one stole prison uniforms: dirty, cotton pants and shirts, and heavy, shapeless shoes known as *ChTZ* made of old tractor tires.[2] I tied on mine with a rope through slits in the rubber.

Once dressed, a big burly military-type appeared in "Heaven's Gate"; he cast about in insolence and waved his arms for attention, then he launched into an oration: "From this day on, forget your freedom!" A deadly silence fell over our company, and he raved on, "Our country needs gold! You don't need to be smart to mine it. All you need are biceps." He flexed his massive biceps.

A prisoner said, "Who's that guy?"

A team-leader and former criminal, replied, "He's King of Slave Camp Two, that's who!"

Then the King ordered us to enter the barbed-wire enclosure and sit beside the canvas tent. As we sat, we heard a ringing metallic sound: A guard banging a pipe on a steel-rail hanging beside the tent door—the signal to get up. The sound brought men out of the tent. Their eyes fell away from us indifferently. A few asked for tobacco. Never had I seen such dismal humanity.

After the King's oration and these poor men's appearance, team-leader set up a chow line. We each received a pound of bread and a scoop of *balanda*. While we ate, leaders divided us into six, fifty-man groups and announced we'd begin the night shift that evening. We scrambled into the tents and onto bare planks to sleep.

After sleeping all day in the hot, stuffy tent, the clanking of rails woke us. Guards armed with bludgeons burst into the tent. "Wake up! Rise, you scoundrels!"

I jumped off my plank and started to join men running outside. My broken galoshes flapped. I tripped and ducked a blow. Slow prisoners were beaten mercilessly for their tardiness. Old men suffered worse and deadly fates. But guard beatings were never resisted. I'd tripped when the wire holding my galoshes broke. I couldn't walk and tore my shirt into strips. Whoever was beating the rail kept it up. Its shrill was deafening. That same penetrating sound woke me every day for the next 10 years, a sound I've never forgotten. I was near the door, bent down, tossed the wire, and wrapped my galoshes to my feet. As luck would have it, two steps later the rags untied. I tripped and fell again. A guard beat me as I re-tied the rags and ran out.

---

2. *ChTZ* is an acronym for Cheliabinsk Tractorny Zavod. Margolin, *Puteshestvie v stranu Ze-ka*, 76–77.

Twenty. The New Power

When I stopped, I was in the back row next to a lanky man sticking out his tongue at the rail hung on a wire. Guards ordered us to string barbed wire and erect new tent poles to expand the camp in the afternoon heat. Two hours later, the leader yelled at us, "Time to eat and guzzle!" We followed him to a group of prisoners waiting in the chow line. Every man was supposed to receive a pound of bread and *balanda* that looked like green water. After eating, we lined up in a U-shape, facing the tent.

The King, dressed in a Youth League uniform, sat watchfully nearby. He was about 36 and admired himself while a prisoner polished his boots. Someone said he was in Kolyma because of his murders. Authorities assigned him to control us mining gold. *He looked like a coward, a weak man, who sold himself as executioner for a piece of silver.*

"We—" he stressed the word—"have been feeding and giving you water! *We* have given you life! If you don't earn enough gold, I'll strangle you with my bare hands and yank out your guts!" As he screamed those threats, King spread out his beefy arms. "And I *will not* give you bread unless you meet your quota!"³

I wondered where this man could have learned his abusiveness. Mamedov, an Uzbek, standing behind me muttered, "I'd like to ram a rock down his throat."

A former prisoner from the Solovetskii Islands Gulag whispered, "He'll annihilate us."

King's barking reminded me of the investigators' language in the Shpalernaia and Kresty prisons. *Did they attend the same school? Both hollered at us convicted under Article Fifty-Eight with the same sick expressions and vulgarities.* I tried to ignore King's rants by shrinking into my inner shell, which helped me survive.

On June 1, guards, under King's command, ordered us to work at five o'clock that sunny afternoon. Kostia Sidorkevich, our team leader, yelled in his powerful voice, "Form rows of five men across and 30 deep!"

As soon as we formed lines, guards searched us for weapons as if we were armed.

After the search, guards marched us to the barbed-wire gate where King took another headcount. Sidorkevich screamed, "March! No stepping left or right, or I *will* shoot you!"

"What if I jump up and not left or right!" someone mocked.

"Shut up! March!"

---

3. Geologists claimed that the gold yield was 0.5 ounces per cubic yard of sand. Batsaev and Kozlov, *Dalstroy Trust Sevvostlag OGPU-NKVD of the USSR as Presented by Documents and in Numbers (2 parts). Part 1 (1931–1941)*, p. 1, 11.

Twenty-One

Baptism of Fire

Camp 2
Thursday, June 2–Wednesday, June 15, 1938

As evening approached, the Arctic sun still blazed bright and high in the sky. It hadn't dipped since noon. Its rays blinded us as we march five abreast down a dirt road into a deep, winding valley between towering mountains. Beyond that gorge, we descended a knoll into a peatbog humped with island-mounds too high and too far apart to jump from one hummock to the next. When I planted one foot, my other sank knee-deep in cold peat slush. My *ChTZ* filled with its foul brown water.

Sloshing, we left the bog and entered the rocky basin of the At-Uriah River cascading down mountainsides. We followed Sidorkevich and clung to each other, crossing, as the river's brute force kept knocking us down. Tall, branchy, larch trees had fallen across the icy river, but the guards didn't allow us to use them to steady ourselves. I watched an old Ukrainian get hit by a wall of icy water so hard it sent him sprawling, swamping him. In seconds, his body thumped over rocks and under the torrent and out of sight. Our mood turned hopeless at his drowning.

Guards tried to train us like circus animals. "Dig in your heels! Stand tall! Quiet!"

Vania stabbed back, "What do you want me to do, walk on my ass?"

"Who the hell said that?"

"Your sham trial and sentence put me here; I'm innocent as Count Monte Cristo."[1]

"Shut up! I'll show you Count of Monte Cristo!"

"The water is icy; may we please walk on the larches," the sailor asked politely.

---

1. *The Count of Monte Cristo* is Alexandre Duma's novel (1846).

Twenty-One. Baptism of Fire

"What the hell kind of sailor are you?" the guard mocked. "Can't you walk on water?"

"Sure, he can," Mamedov countered. "Off with your boots at the stream. Show him."

Men laughed. "Not only take off your boots but yank off your underwear as well."

"Cut the crap! Follow directions and march in rank," the guard bellowed.

"Comrades, better do what he says, or the idiots will shoot you," an old man warned.

A Baltic Sea sailor, wearing a striped shirt, which miraculously escaped theft, was a stubborn man. When guards stole his sailor's cap and exchanged it for a prisoner's cap, he refused to wear it. Now he said, "We need to wring out our clothes."

"Who's yapping?" a guard screamed. "We hate jokes. Shut up and march!"

"If this the River Jordan, you're John the Baptist?" someone grumbled.

"The Soviet government canceled all references to religion!" a guard yelled.

There was no stopping. No wringing out of clothes. And soaking wet pants clung to our bodies and water sloshed in our shoes, and still, they drove us on.

Finally, we crossed another peat bog and spotted the gold mine. Newly released criminals who'd chosen to stay and work in the mine met us. They were a team leader, clerk of the works, and squad leaders walking without guards. One said, "You'll work with shovels and wheelbarrows. Line up for headcount!"

"Don't forget the old man drowning in the river!" someone seethed.

"Don't stir up trouble!" the guards shot back. "Shut up!"

Our guards didn't know what to do with us. No one had given them instructions. And so, we sat on the wet knoll in the long grass at the mine for two hours until, finally, an overseer arrived and assigned us tasks. "The gold is under the permafrost. Cut it up, dig up the dirt, and haul it to the slag dump over there." He pointed at a mound 60 yards off.

Every man received his order for a space to start clearing. We looked around for tools and saw day-shift prisoners pushing all the wheelbarrows. Since there were no others, the clerk of the works ordered us to begin by clearing rocks.

"May we remove our clothes to dry them?" a prisoner asked.

"Start working; they'll dry on you!" he replied. "And don't ask for a break! You may sing a happy song as you work, now, hurry!"

The sun-bright night of June 2 was the beginning of my first all-night work in Kolyma. The day shift soon ended its labors, and we took up their wheelbarrows, crowbars, pickaxes, and sledgehammers. Regrettably, most of the men had never used any of these tools, and it was hard for the older men to push wheelbarrows full of peat, stones, and dirt. Overfilled wheelbarrows, too heavy for most, couldn't make it up to the dump by withered old men. Although many tried, all failed. Other men tried to dig with shovels, crowbars, and pickaxes, but no one taught them how to use the tools. Soon, old men started dying. After discussing their tragic deaths, we began working in pairs; the weak loaded wheelbarrows; the young pushed them.

Through the night, team leaders stood at the top of the dump, spying for loafers and beating them with thick poles. Petr, a former student at the Saratov Medical Institution, said to his old, weak partner, "Father, I'll push it; you fill it."

"*Hatar!*"[2] Mamedov yelled as he pushed his loaded wheelbarrow to the dump. He left it and hurried back for another. Things were looking up! Our productivity increased, but the administration then foolishly forbid us from working in pairs.

Despite that warning, we worried; guards slashed old men's food norms. In the mornings, we received a pound of bread, nothing for lunch, and for dinner a ladle of warm water mixed with rye flour. Sometimes cooks tossed in an ounce or two of herring. As we grew weaker, to achieve our goals, the administration reduced our sleeping hours and increased our working hours. They also kept us in the gold mine three straight days and nights for not fulfilling quotas. Usually, we worked 15-hour shifts in the mine and another two to three hours cutting logs for barracks, watchtowers, isolation wards, a military depot, and a kitchen. Then we walked two hours to-and-from the mine, leaving less than five hours of sleep. Young men ran ahead to the tents; guards drove the rest of us weary stragglers.

There were no days off. And King continued with endless speeches. I never listened to him but dreamed of release and mentally wrote letters to the Party's Central Committee; I met Vyshinskii and denounced my investigators. Sometimes I gazed intently into the northern sky to escape King's threats to "pull out our guts and execute us." Sometimes he would describe a picture of his hell and told us how he would choke the life out of us with his hairy hands. I was lucky because I was in the fifth row and mentally drifted away from him.

Once, guards ordered me to stand in the first row. Previously, I'd pre-

---

2. In Uzbek, *hatar* means danger. Krippes, Karl A. *Uzbek-English Dictionary* (Kensington, MD: Dunwoody Press, 1996), 186.

Twenty-One. Baptism of Fire

tended to listen to King. Now I was so close to him I saw the emotion on his face. *I'm doing well, pretending to listen.* Suddenly King punched me in the belly so hard I fell. Men helped me up. When I was upright, King pointed a huge finger at me and snarled, "I'll teach you how to honor the NKVD secret agents! You'll gorge yourselves on grass before you starve!"

After that vow, I was extra sensitive around our handlers even though they made me want to vomit. Soon, the administrators decreed we could march to the pit without guards. They knew, as we did, the taiga was an icy prison.

Despite King's humiliations, once I felt brave and asked Vladimirov at the tool shop, "Why do political prisoners work more than criminal prisoners? Our production quotas look mediocre, but we fill them, and still, we never get enough food."

"You won't survive until the first frost of August. Guards will deliver new prisoners from all over the country. *Muzhichok*,[3] don't look for the truth in the taiga."

Silently I left him and went to the tool shop to speak with the carpenter and explain that our wheelbarrows were poorly designed and nearly impossible to push, causing men to slip and fall. I'd been issued a wheelbarrow from the tool shed, and, as an engineer, had thought of ways to improve it. I found six nails and pounded them through three, one-foot-wide, four-feet- longboards and onto the two six-foot handles. I built a six-inch lip above the eight-inch steel wheel to keep the gold sand from falling out. My wheelbarrow became an important part of me and raised my self-worth. I took great care of it, fixing the wheel when it wobbled on its axle, repairing the lip when it broke. It handled smoothly and felt rather light, even when pushing a heavy load. Likewise, I valued my shovel and pickaxe and handed them to my shift-reliever to use with care when he replaced me.

Despite improvements in my tools, my waning strength soon ended my gold mine labors. My pickaxe became too heavy to hoist, and the rocks too hard to break. I'd flop against a ledge to muster the strength for the next strike, and guards would beat me.

On the way back to camp, I thought of my conversation with Pashka: *Political prisoners don't know how to survive!* It put me on guard. In camp, Pashka met me with a penetrating stare. "You, *muzhichok*, are shrewd and so skilled! Did you get a 20-year prison term for naming a collective farm cow a whore?"

I was offended. I'd worked long and hard all my life, helping father

---

3. *Muzhichok* is a tender diminutive for *muzhik*, fellow, meaning small man. Translator's note.

make stoves, carrying clay, sand and bricks. Now, I felt my strength fading. Pashka didn't know I'd received a full Article 58.

"You believe we're all scoundrels," he continued. "Kolyma changed us. I've been here since I was 16. My father was a *kulak*. Authorities trained me for Kolyma. One hit me because I couldn't push a wheelbarrow. I spit blood, but there was nothing I could do. Now I am thrashing and flogging you because I'm the authority and you're my slave."

Twenty-Two

Panning Season

The At-Uriah Gold Mine
Thursday, June 16–Sunday, July 31, 1938

As my beating continued, I reflected on those endless days, and after 30 years, I can still see our gold-panning season's opening etched indelibly before me. King hoisted a red flag on a pole, erected by prisoners, at the top of the dump. Then he ordered us to start wheelbarrowing the gold-bearing sand to it.

In three weeks, the 150 prisoners we'd started with had perished to 36, replaced with new prisoners. The officers walked confidently around the site, wishing to show us how hard they worked, growing furious at our snail's pace. We worked nonstop. Their drive for productivity went on relentlessly. We never walked pushing wheelbarrows; we ran. The slave-drivers screamed at the top of their voices, "Fascists! Come on! Chop, chop!"

One clerk of the work, a convicted pedophile, often stated he would be sprung soon because of his excellent work and the government's granting him amnesty. He wasn't.

Officers smiled at our tongue-lashing, and our slave-driver did his utmost to add to our misery. They'd approach a weak worker, spit on him, mock, "Don't you eat on purpose?! Why don't you want to help the motherland? Don't loaf lazy bones, move!"

Another officer grabbed a skinny man, shook him, and hauled him off. At the tailing dump, an officer looked at a young, healthy Siberian working exceptionally well, even running with his wheelbarrow. *The officer would admire his work.* Wrong!

"You look robust boy. Are you wearing a costume?" he observed. "Take him away!"

Guards hauled the Siberian off. Later, while guards were reading orders, they announced, "Two men shot to death today." No reasons stated for their killings.

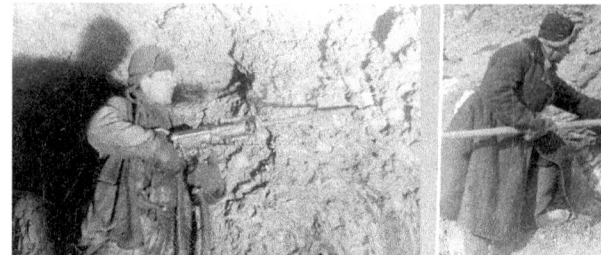

Extraction of gold from sand in Death Valley (Dal'stroi Territories Photo Album of 1942–1943, Ministry of Inner Affairs, State Archive, Russian Federation, Moscow).

Soon more officers climbed the tailing dump. The oldest one took a plywood blackboard from the clerk of the works and reviewed the number of wheelbarrows pushed up to dump. Through clenched teeth, he said, "Men, I don't see enough loads dumped! Don't you want to work?!" He rammed his fist into the face of the team leader. "You're a slovenly slob! You're covering up for enemies of the people! I'll kill you!" He flew into a rage, yelling at the workers like he was a tsar. Everywhere his cry was heard, "*Come on; come on!*" His behavior, intonation, and gestures reminded me of Vladimirov's and Sidorkevich's manners. I remembered Dante's hell was among the dead; *our hell was among the living.*

Compared to cutting peat, gold sand was hard work, and we labored with different types of rocks and their detritus. Often the small, geologic rocks looked like rooster combs, and our shovels were unfit to scoop them up in the sand. But cruelty continued. If officers didn't leave soon, no one would survive to the end of our shift. The officers, too, grew tired of beating and seeing workers collapsed like exhausted plow oxen.

One day a few small trucks appeared at the tailing dump. The mine boss was watching our dumping from afar, and the dump was slowly rising like a two-story house above the mine. Then they ordered us to shovel wheelbarrows full of dirt into the trucks, swearing at the workers, "Move your asses! If you're tired, wash rocks in the water tumbler."

When the overcoats all left, the mine grew silent. Workers dropped beside their wheelbarrows. I looked at the red flag flapping in the breeze, high above the slag dump, feeling despair.

"Do you see it?" a Muscovite asked, pointing at the flag.

"Yes, I see it," I replied with a fallen tone.

"Why did it have to happen under our flag?"

I had no answer, and, trying not to fall, I pushed my heavy wheel-

Twenty-Two. Panning Season

barrow again, thinking: *Prisoners have forgotten their families, even their mothers! In the Leningrad's prisons, we concluded that our investigators were mistaken; but no, the entire government had planned a systematic annihilation of innocent citizens.*

I remember well how Dmitrii, the Baltic Sea sailor, yelled at the guards, "Are you ever going to be human and leave the weak and sick in camp to rest! They're *dohodiagas* without the strength to tramp to the gold mine."

With glaring eyes, King snarled, "I'll send you to the isolation ward!"

The heated arguments with King ended with Dmitri's banishment to isolation from which no man returned. King accepted our fate and remained silent; the endless possession of horse carts hauling corpses from camp to a burial area near the mine continued. He turned to another problem one day and ordered Pashka, "Herd the sick into one big mob, and march them off!"

Pashka did as told and barked orders to a convoy of guards, "Round up all the weak men in one mass." These men's thin bodies and swollen faces had run with their wheelbarrows to fulfill their norms. Now, they tossed their tools and marched from the camp. No one returned.

In summer's white nights, our tents were visible from the gold mine. When mornings arrived, I'd watch men from the dayshift climb the knoll, hoist heavy logs, and carry them on their shoulders, often screaming in agony under their weight and think: *They're coming, they're coming! Soon it will be our turn in the logs.*

I'd worked hard during my 14-hour shift and dreaded having to carry logs again.

"Come on!" guards bawled. "Time to carry logs!"

"Who's going to shut his God damn mouth?" the sailor growled.

Finally, in morning's bright light, the air filled with the familiar metallic whacks of the banging rail, our call to stop mining. *I'd survived another night.*

Leaving the mine, the sailor yelled at King, "You're a scoundrel!" That launched King into a pompous speech.

"When will we behead him?" the sailor asked, not joking. "If he'd served in my fleet, he'd have been executed!"

"No one would take him in any Navy," a Leningrad professor of philosophy said. "The blood we shed here in Kolyma was for nothing and will never be forgiven."

"Why don't I see your wheelbarrow?" King mocked.

"When will his stentorian voice ever stop?" a Siberian roared.

We passed off our wheelbarrows, and then guards ordered us to deepen the drainage channel to the mine. After that, they herded us to the knoll and, later, to the tents for sleep. Today, eight frail men worked to their deaths. No one recorded it.

Next morning, after King's lecture, Sidorkevich and Vladimirov stomped around us, waving their bludgeons and ordering, "Enemies of the people, load those wheelbarrows full and get them to the dump! Come on, move!"

Before my eyes, Sidorkevich killed a frail, near-sighted, medical doctor because he couldn't push his heavy wheelbarrow to the dump. "You're a dwarf!" Sidorkevich howled. "Here you must work hard; this is not your clinic where you sit on your ass with assistants and write prescriptions all day." Then, Sidorkevich struck the doctor with his bludgeon and pushed his body off the path like a sack of sawdust.

Other criminals mocked the doctor, too. "He was a professor!"

Sasha Venstenostsev, a Moscow locomotive driver, yelled, "Leave him alone! He's dead."

Furious, Sidorkevich raised his pole and struck Sasha, knocking him down. We stopped at the top of the dump and watched Sasha roll down the slag hill.

One night, I watched in horror as Vladimirov killed the fifty-year-old engineer, Korovin, who'd been gasping and wheezing, trying to push his wheelbarrow. "Korovin, don't play the fool! I'll show you how to travel abroad!" And with his sledgehammer he struck Korovin, breaking his spine. Korovin fell like a tree and still Vladimirov raged on, "You'll soon be seeing France for betraying our motherland."

He grabbed the half-dead engineer and dragged his body to a pit with 10 corpses and dump him in. Most of us stood transfixed. In three weeks, we looked as if we were on our last legs, goners, skeletons—*dohodiagas*. We never washed our faces nor shed our dirty clothes and only begged for food at the kitchen window.

Meanwhile, Pozyvnoi Vasilii and Dul'tsev Semen, officials from Dalstroy, paced up-and-down on the path beside the mine. Dressed in military uniforms, they spoke quietly with Vladimirov and Sidorkevich near me. Pozyvnoi pointed at six men, barely able to push wheelbarrows, and asked, "What should I do with them?"

"Don't you know?" Pozyvnoi sing-songed rhetorically. "Take a wild guess!"

While they discussed our fate, I gazed, unwatched, at the sky. Small, puffy clouds hued pink in the east. A breeze ruffled tree leaves at the mine's edge. *The Kremlin said we were practicing socialism, but where was our grain?* Abruptly my thoughts stopped when Pozyvnoi yelled, "Don't you know what you should do with them? Darkness will take them, and

Twenty-Two. Panning Season

when the camp is empty, you'll bury them. New convicts will take their place, and we'll repeat the cycle over and over."[1]

Shackles rose on my neck. With a fearful heart, I pushed my wheelbarrow.

After three months of Kolyma's hell, men longed to return to Leningrad prisons.

"My dear friends," Grigorii Zheelov often said to us. "I'm at my end! Give me my *balanda*." After a few days, Grigorii couldn't hold his bowl, and I held it to his lips. But then his head dropped to his chest, and Grigorii fell into my lap, silently slipping into Kolyma's long, dark sleep.

Criminals derided Grigori's death. "Hurrah! A pal of Lenin has achieved socialism!"

In July, political prisoners made benches for mine criminals. Unlike them, political prisoners ate standing or sitting on rocks. What a crazy world! Criminals received full bowls of *balanda*, thick pieces of bread with sunflower oil, and half bowls of sweet tea with donuts. They never finished their meals and dumped leftovers on the ground before our bewildered eyes and always tramped on the food leaving us drooling.

Once, an old engineer looked at the criminals with tears in his eyes as they ate. They yelled at him, "Old Peckerhead, want a donut?"

"Yes, I'd love a donut," the old man replied.

"Then come to get it!" The criminal slid his bowl and donut toward him. But when the old man picked up the donut, the criminal threw his soup into his face and roared.

The old suffered constantly. But it is harder for me to describe how young men suffered from starvation as well. Youthful hunger was harder than it was for the older. One youth wanted an extra scoop of *balanda* and ran around, picking up empty bowls to lick before rinsing them. Suddenly, his camp leader entered the kitchen and struck him.

"What're doing? You received Article Fifty-Eight! Stop it, or I'll twist your arms off."

Only criminal prisoners could steal food without consequence. We weren't allowed to steal anything, even lick a bowl. Soon the line of political prisoners stretched to the rubbish pit. We dreamed of finding herrings' heads. Of course, they would do little to satisfy our hunger, but a drowning man clings to any lifesaver. If lucky in finding a small, salty fish head, after eating it we'd rush to a gutter to drink black water. Many men grew sick, and, with swollen stomachs, died. By such acts, the camp's administration effectively exterminated the last glimmer of hope for us.

Since we'd arrived in Kolyma a year ago, we'd not had a bath or issued

---

1. In 1939, Dul'tsev was awarded a Valor Labor medal, http://nkvd.memo.ru.

a change of rags. Lice feasted on our bodies 24 hours a day. The poor food turned our bodies hairless and as sleek and white as new-born mice.

The month of July took the lives of several thousand souls, but new convicts arrived to take their planks. It felt as if the entire country was resettling in Kolyma, the heart of Communist penal servitude.

Twenty-Three

Music While We Worked

The Valley of Death
Monday, August 1–Monday, October 31, 1938

My brigade continued to work the mine's night shift as August cooled and fall began. Colder temperatures brought frosts, and while we worked in light clothes, guards sat around campfires drinking *chifir*.[1] Camp lights shimmered in authorities' log cabins and glimmered off the snow. How we dreamt of warming ourselves in their toasty cottages. We'd built leaders' bungalows during our first two months in the Arctic while we slept in canvas tents.

On the knolls, pine trees ripen, cones opened, and the wind sowed delicious nuts, while underfoot fields blazed rose-colored with juicy, pink, wild lingo berries. But we weren't allowed to pick either, and the berries were trampled underfoot, turning our galoshes red. Between the clerks of the works and *VOKhR*,[2] they kept us starving while they reaped the benefits of our toil; new workers meant more gold and better salaries, and they remained indifferent to our drudgery.

We hadn't started pushing wheelbarrows again, when, surprisingly, the authorities appeared with a brass band. With drums beating, cymbals banging, flutes whistling, and trumpets blaring, we learned the musical delights of work to music. Guards usually drove us to the mines, hammering the tardy with rifle butts, but today, for the first time, they showed up to teach us how to march, to music, like soldiers. The musicians were criminals who usually slouched about all day on planks with nothing to do. Now they played music for us while the guards metaphorize into angry

---

1. *Chifir* is a black tea made with 1.8 ounces per cup. It acts like a narcotic. Rossi, *The Gulag Handbook*, 496.

2. The abbreviation *VOKhR*, or *voennizirovannaya okhrana*, refers to the NKVD guards who secured economic and industrial sites. Serokuzov, N.N. *Slovar' voshedshikh v obikhod sokrashchennykh nazvanii* (Vladivostok: Typo-Lithographiia. Iosif Korot,' 1924), 9.

German shepherds, barking at us to fulfill production goals. As the music played, we dug and shoveled gold sand into wheelbarrows, and cursed the brass band and authorities in their fine warm coats.

Sidorkevich came into our huddle of weak men and sprawled out to rest on a knoll. He started boasting that he'd many rubles stashed in the pillowcase he held up. "You'll be dead soon, and this knoll I'm sitting on will be your sepulcher. Whenever you see men dressed in uniforms like mine, start working and listen carefully! Unlike me, you attended universities, for all the good it did you." He stood, turned, and disappeared in the scrub pines, or *stlanik*.

When the music ended, the guards ordered us to dig graves. "Dig them poorly, and we'll toss you in while you're still alive." No one listened to his warnings. We could not work any harder without looking at dead prisoners piled up like cordwood. We laid them in graves with some dignity below numbered markers, not recorded, before winter arrived. *When will their families ever learn of their destinies?*

Meanwhile, some new political prisoners argued and fought with the guards to escape Kolyma's tyranny. Some committed suicide. Some chopped off their fingers, arms, hands, and legs. I remember well a 25-year-old laying his left wrist on a stump and chopping it off with an ax to avoid work!

Another tragedy happened early one morning near the river. Guards had herded us up to a knoll to carry logs to the camp before our mine work began. I was exhausted and barely able to drag myself behind the others. When I bent to grasp a log, my fingers were so sore they wouldn't function. Twenty men raised the heavy log, I pretended, and we plotted to the camp. There two men, Neil and Nikolai, who had hoisted the log, refused to carry it any further, dropped the log, and high-tailed it out of the camp. We stood for a long minute, unmoving but swaying under the massive log on our shoulders cutting into our necks. Our legs quivered. Men fell. The pair ran. Guards shot. The two fell, wounded and racked with pain.

The same day, three more men ran from the mine, escaping, including a top officer in the Red Army House.[3] Guards and criminals had often humiliated him for being physically weak and near-sighted. He knew the taiga would kill him as soon as winter arrived and formulated plans for escape. The trio never returned. Guards, aided by criminals, had shot them dead.

Escapees believed the miserable folly that they could hide and sur-

---

3. Its modern name is the Central House of the Russian Army named for Mikhail Vasil'evich Frunze (1885–1925), a commander in the Civil War. Wieszynski, *The Modern Encyclopedia of Russian and Soviet History*, vol. 6 (1978), 176.

Twenty-Three. Music While We Worked

vive in the taiga, an area of 1.5 million square miles stretching its vastness north to the barren tundra wilds. Everything in Kolyma, from its mountains, cliffs, rivers, and swamps to its wild beasts threatened life and guaranteed death. The long, bitter-cold winters and mosquito-laden summers added to the misery. *Damn you, Kolyma! Why did geologists ever discover gold here? Many prisoners dreamed of dying in the claws of bears or being stuck in a swamp, but never dying and being released from the agony of this hell.*

I felt deeply every knife stab and whiplash endured by my comrades, and my heart still aches from their injustices. In mid–August, my Leningrad friends, Ivan Balakin and Gavriil Eroshkin, died. God, bless them!

As August waned, winter arrived, and, in Kolyma, severe frosts and heavy snows appeared in late September and October. But guards herded us into the bathhouse and allowed us to scoop up handfuls of snow to carry inside. Each of us received two quarts of hot water. After the "bath," we looked like zebras; the snow and water only smeared dirt in stripes on our pale, skinny bodies. Afterward, guards took our worn-out rags and replaced them with "disinfected" wet clothes, crawling with lice, and we pulled these on. There were no warm overcoats, so we wound thin, cloth blankets around our shriveled bodies and hobbled the half-mile through the snow back to our tents.

The next day, guards returned our wet, disinfected overcoats and rushed us to the gold mine. They were oblivious to our having spent the night trying to sleep in wet clothes that froze to planks and bodies like glued gloves.

The fall season for panning gold was coming to an end, but, since the camp had not fulfilled its goal, authorities ordered us to build temporary, covered, heated enclosures by the mine. Using peat as fuel, we rigged two boilers with dual hoses to drive steam into the frozen earth. But there was never enough steam pressure generated to thaw the ground, and the idea failed miserably. We could have easily fulfilled our norms during the summer if the administration had changed its relationship by feeding us and letting us sleep eight hours, but now we were left to work in the bitter cold.

In the heavy snow, we laid 90 feet of planks for wheelbarrows pushing up the hill, trying to avoid getting stuck in mud or hitting rough, hard moguls. Our wheelbarrows grew heavier and harder to manage as the frozen earth clung to the small, front, steel wheels, freezing them like skids, unable to rotate. By comparison, in summer one gold miner could produce 50 to 80 wheelbarrows of gold-sand a day. By October, 30 miners produced a pitiful 30 wheelbarrows of sand.

One morning, before leaving my shift, I went into the hot, dark, steamy boiler-house to warm. I took off my wet peacoat and dropped it against the red-hot boiler to dry. Immediately, a stench of burning wool and steam billowed from my coat. I snatched it, but it stuck to the boiler and emitted a foul stench as I yanked it, I looked around. Hanging on pegs were dozens of peacoats, abandoned by prisoners killed on the job. Because a peacoat is not a man, it lived on; men only endured two or three months in this Valley of Death while peacoats lasted years.

Along with the peacoats there were shoes, boots, and ice-stiff clothes. Since only the friends of the administration—the criminals—were issued *valenki*, these, too, were lifesavers. Enemies of the people worked in lightweight summer shoes or *ChTZ* year-round. We wound them in cloth bags to keep our feet drier and warmer as our legs turned hairless from frostbite.

During the last week in October 1938, I worked with a sailor from the Black Sea Fleet from Sevastopol. We carried water to the temporarily covered and heated enclosure for a new building site. The sailor said secret agents had arrested him on his ship because his sister's husband was an enemy of the people. The sailor pleaded that he'd not seen his sister or her husband for three years as he had been serving in Sevastopol, 6,300 miles east of Vladivostok. But facts didn't matter to authorities.

The two of us carried barrels of water in cold, wet work. We lashed the barrel onto poles slung between our shoulders. Between the dangling

A Kolyma Gulag prisoner (Photo Album Report of 1938, State Archive, Russian Federation, Moscow).

Twenty-Three. Music While We Worked

lines and icy planks, we often slipped, slopping ourselves with icy water. The sailor was taller than me, and water sloshed onto me whenever I was behind him. When I took the front, water splashed down my back. At the end of our 12-hour shift, we looked like ice statues. We grew weaker every day and never had the time to deliver sufficient water to the heated enclosure. During the first all-night days of November, the river froze into solid ice, forcing us to hack it into blocks to carry. We never got wet again that winter.

One day the sailor asked, "Why do the guards beat us so often?"

"Because we're weak," I said, unsure where he was going with this question.

"I disagree with you. I was strong when I arrived here. I was neither far-sighted nor stupid when I served in the Navy. I learned my ship's functions and understood all coastal warning signs. Now, something in my life misfired. I never understood life's warnings about this coming storm. I was another man then, 32, strong and hardy; now I can barely walk."

"Pick up your end," I said, dismissively, "we've got ice to carry to Death Valley."

Twenty-Four

My Father's Letter

Camp 2
Monday, November 7, 1938

November 7 arrived, our favorite day of the year. Today, decades later, I still remember the splashy illuminations, posters, and banners waving brightly in Leningrad as we celebrated the 21st anniversary of the October Revolution. But there were no holiday celebrations in Kolyma in 1938.

After three hours of hauling ice with the sailor in day's total blackness, the clerk-of-the-works came to our tent and announced, "Bolotov, you've got a parcel and some letters from Leningrad! Go to the administration building for them!"

"Really?!" I exclaimed and rushed off, running in the trodden path cut into the deep snow, my heart leaping with joy. There, a guard gave me three letters postmarked in May, June, and July. He also gave me my parents' opened parcel. Of course, someone had ripped open the package and stolen the soap, toothbrush, and toothpaste. I didn't fault them. We never brushed our teeth, but I'd have liked to have washed my face with soap.

In the building's dim light, I was barely able to read my father words: *I trust you, son, because you joined the Party. I, too, remain a devoted real communist just like you.* I pressed father's letters to my heart and ran to the tent. A dull glimmer flickered from burning *stlanik* branches in the barrel stove, and a small oil lamp above it sputtered a trembling glow from its thin cotton wick. I wanted to read father's letters, but I couldn't get close enough to the lamp to read it with prisoners surrounding it, trying to dry their icy clothes. I waited. Finally, they rose and flopped exhausted onto their planks. As I waited, silence settled, but soon the lamp ran out of oil. My friend, Mark Sneetser, ran somewhere and brought back oil in a can. He pulled some cotton from his peacoat, stuff it in the lamp for a wick, and it cast a small, glimmering light.

He said to me, "Read all night, Leonid. Enjoy."

Twenty-Four. My Father's Letter

As the tent slept, I set under the oil lamp and read and reread my father's letter. His words resounded with a burdened soul. Dad vowed to do everything to seek my release: *My dear son, bureaucrats banished me from the Party in 1937 as if I were an enemy of the people. I resisted them. I said that you don't trust yourselves. I still maintained to them that my son is an honest and responsible man. You, dear comrades, have no evidence; you are destroying the Party that you built. When the new bureaucrats ordered me to push small carts in the factory yard, I said, do you know that I am a highly qualified worker who cast metal in a foundry? I couldn't do anything about the situation. I had to feed your children, my wife, and my step-granddaughter, Klara. You know well that I never did this kind of work when Nicholas the Second ruled Russia.[1] How vindictive these paltry people are! The Leningrad State Committee returned my Party membership card in 1938. I pleaded with the authorities that my son was innocent. But they had one response: If you think your son is innocent, send your petition to Moscow and intercede on his behalf. For as long as I'm alive, I'll fight for the truth as I fought for it in the Civil War. I've already visited Vyshiskii. His secretary told me that your file is in Leningrad and I should go to Leningrad again. I did. In Leningrad, more bureaucrats told I must go to Moscow. I made several trips from Leningrad to Moscow to appeal your case. The bureaucrats turned me into a soccer ball. I even tried to see the Party's Central Committee in the Kremlin, but no one permitted me an audience; no one allowed me to meet Stalin. I dared to and mailed him this letter below:*

> My Dear Father and Leader!
>
> I am asking you, like the wisest and fairest father to all citizens to trust me. I am an old Bolshevik and honest, hard-working man. My son, Leonid Petrovich Bolotov, is innocent of the charges leveled against him. The bureaucrats lied when they called him an enemy of the people. My son never signed the false verdict. The Party needs people like him. Please believe him, My Dear Father!

Further on in his letter, Dad asked me to be strong and firm: *Work as hard as you can for as long as you can. Be patient. Stalin will order an investigation, and you will be released soon. Your children, my dear grandchildren, are growing up fast and sometimes ask about you. Stand firm, my dear son! Also, Mom will write you. Here's a bear hug!*

I read and reread Dad's letter. It reminded me of all my yesterdays with my family and renewed my hope, meshing in my mind with dreams,

---

1. Nicholas II (1868–1918), was the last Russian Emperor in the three-hundred-year-old Romanov Dynasty. Wieszynski, *The Modern Encyclopedia of Russian and Soviet History*, vol. 24 (1981), 197–207.

traveling with father to Elan, Krasavka, and Rudnia to visit churches and salvage silver icons.[2]

Why didn't father write me anything about my children? Why was there only one line about them? I see my kids in my dream every night. Valeria throws her little arms around my neck as I close my eyes. I smelled breast milk on her lips. And then there was Gennadii, running to me, eyes sparkling with gold, cheeks flushing pink. I dare not stir as this picture would disappear. But I did. I flopped onto my plank and fell asleep, content for the first time in months.

The metallic whacks of pipe-on-rail echoed down the tent. "Wake up!" Guards kept banging the rail and yelling, "Get up, you lazy bums!"

Varvara Ivanovna (Cherntsova) Bolotova, Saratov, 1897 (Collection of Lana Bourret).

The tent stirred. Prisoners rushed outside for roll call in the bitter cold. After that, a skimpy meal and another long day at the gold mine. My friends, along with other prisoners, were astonished, for I acted like a spring robin! Prisoners joined me in excitement about my first letter. "Leonid, how lucky you are! Your father wrote Stalin; truth will find us!" they exclaimed.

The next day, Khmara, a guard said, "You'll all be released soon."

I agreed with Khmara and remained silent. Later, I sewed father's letters into my peacoat lining and carried them with me for months. How-

---

2. These towns are located 140 miles west of Saratov. Markova, N.T. *Atlas avtomobyl'nykh dorog SSSR*. 3rd ed. (Moskva: Glavnoye upravleniie geodesii i kartografii pri SM SSSR, 1971), 85.

Twenty-Four. My Father's Letter

ever, criminals thought I had hidden money, sliced open my peacoat, and stole my letters. But they could never steal those memories from my mind. His letter and the parcel gave me hope and saved me from an unavoidable death. I transformed from being a skeletal *dohodiaga* to a *rabotiaga*, or plodder, as the cook served me more *balanda* and oiled bread, and a medical doctor's assistant let me rest in camp during working hours when I gave him a box of *makhorka*, or coarse tobacco, from father's parcel.

Twenty-Five

My Search for Firewood

Taiga
Friday, December 2, 1938

Frozen mist hung over the Valley of Death. Truck engines sputtered and died. Rubber tires crumbled. Iron shattered. Thick layers of ice coated everything. With knives, we chopped ice off our peacoats. We knew when the temperature plunged to -58° work ceased, but the official camp thermometer never sank below -56.9°. Our teeth, lungs, and stomachs ached from the cold. When I saw a thermometer nailed to a window in a small log cabin, I shouted, "It reads minus fifty-two degrees!"

A clutch of men rushed to the office of the medical assistant and demanded he postpone roll call. While we shivered, guards burst in our tents checking for hiders who tried to avoid the cold. Then the medical assistant appeared beside me. "Men, go back to your tents!" he roared.

Men broke ranks and ran for the tents. Even the guards returned to their snug homes. No one went to the mine. Then the camp leader called the medical assistant who explained, "I told the Citizen Chief, the frost was minus fifty-two, and I've sent you to your tents. But he screamed, 'What are you talking about? Order the prisoners to the mine immediately!' Men, I insisted that it was impossible to work. We argued, but the leader insisted the thermometer showed minus 49 and ordered you to the gold-mine!"

The medical assistant turned and stared at the thermometer with Vladimirov and Sidorkevich. The mercury inside its narrow glass tube had contracted almost to the bottom and hung at fifty-four degrees below. We knew we were safe and returned to our tents. He would delay or cancel the roll call for the day. But I was wrong. Soon we were ordered, "Fall out!"

Every man left for the mine. Snow buried the sand-laden gold flecks under the permafrost frozen solid to a depth of 33 feet. Lacking technical equipment, we bored and drilled and chiseled. We set dynamite and

Twenty-Five. My Search for Firewood

blasted the earth and wrestled chunks of permafrost onto the sleds, and four or five men, harnessed like horses, pulled the sleds to the dump.

Prisoners worked 16 hours a day for months and knew well how to measure the temperature. They knew at -40° they could safely smoke; at -58° their fingers froze. On December 3, 1938, the temperature dropped to -76°, and we still wore *valenki* with foot-binding of rags from thin cloth blankets. And yet, every day, guards told their bosses, "The prisoners are well-fed. They're dressed for the season and healthy."

The chanting did no good. At the mine, my hands could not grasp tools. I had to get to someplace warm or I would suffer frostbite. I looked around. No one was watching. I crawled under a log house and snaked to a place beside the base of its fireplace and warmth.

After 14 hours, the guards ordered us to the taiga for firewood. "Freeze to death, but don't return to your tent without an armful of firewood!"

I dragged myself to the taiga. Although rested, it was nearly impossible for me to climb the knoll and dig in the snow for *stlanik* branches. I raked the snow with my hands and feet until I found a branch of *stlanik*. I snapped off its brittleness, breathing hard, crawled back to camp with the load. The guard on duty snarled at me like a dog, "Drop it here, prisoner, and go back! Hurry, or I'll send you to where the polar bears live!"

I left through the gate and stumbled into the darkness. After a few steps, I stopped and looked back at the dark camp. In its blackness, no lights shown, no stove-smoke rose. There was no moon or stars. What should I do? I didn't have the strength to return to the knoll for wood. My legs were so weak they would not move. I didn't dare sit; too many men froze to death, resting aching bodies in the snow. I pushed that desire aside and started climbing the knoll in a swirling blizzard. Razor-sharp flakes cut my cheeks and pricked my eyes. *Hurry, or you will die.* That command never left my mind. My legs moved like turtles. I often had to stop to punch a hole in the crust to tramp onward. I soon discovered that the ill-fated *stlanik* had been taken or hidden. *How skillful the stlanik is! It hides under snow-blankets when you need it for firewood.*

In the distance, I heard the roll call. I climbed and climbed in the chest-deep snow, looking for firewood and dreaming of stretching out on my plank. *Maybe it would be better to return to camp empty-handed. No! The watch guard would send me to the isolation ward, and I'd die from the cold. Why did you send me to the taiga again? Do you dream of getting a new award? I'd gladly smack your big fat mug.*

Suddenly, my right foot struck a thick branch. I bent down, pawed, and pulled up a *stlanik* limb. I held it into the howling wind, and ice shads flew off. "I have the wood," I said aloud. *Now I'll die here, isolated and alone on this damnable knoll.*

Barely able to lift my legs, I turned and aimed for the camp. But I was so exhausted I had to rest. My head dropped to my chest. My eyes closed. I talked to Kosarev: *Aleksandr! Save me from this injustice! Kosarev said, Leonid, I'll send your file to Stalin.*[1] But suddenly their images disappeared, and another mirage appeared. I was in the investigator's office in Leningrad. Baryshnikov demanded I sign the lies. *He yelled, Sign this paper. Period! He laughed at me.*

That broke my delirium. In control again, I hoisted the branch, shook off snow, and, rejoicing, continued to camp. I prodded with the blizzard whistling in my ears and my beard-ice chattering against my face like a rivet gun. I dragged myself into camp. But, shockingly, it wasn't my camp. They'd built it on the other side of the knoll: four camps with watch guards. I approached a log cabin. Inside stood an unfamiliar guard frying bread in lard.

"You've got a *stlanik* branch," he said. "Leave it here and have some bread. Roll-call will start in three hours."

How horrifically different guards are! One had sent me for wood knowing I'd die in the taiga; another gave me bread! I shook with fatigue, lacking the energy to remove my clothes and collapsed on the floor to eat fried bread. I muttered, "I've survived one year in Kolyma. Nineteen thirty-eight is about to end." The last thought I had, sprawled out on the floor: It's December 4, mother's birthday, and I'd survived certain death.

---

1. Kosarev, Aleksandr Vasil'evich (1903–1939), Communist Youth Organization leader, was executed in 1939. Wieszynski, *The Modern Encyclopedia of Russian and Soviet History*, vol. 17 (1980), 214–216.

Twenty-Six

My Broken Leg

The Dispensary
Monday, December 5, 1938–
 Wednesday, March 15, 1939

Next morning, I found my way to my tent. Sidorkevich ordered us to bust rocks in the mine. He always swore at my weak gang and didn't believe we were sick and unable to walk faster, mocking us because of our fragilities. As we stood in line shivering in -58° blackness, he shoved us; we fell, and I felt my leg snap. I tried to stand but couldn't. My leg had broken. The other miners stood with difficulty while I remained sprawled in the snow. They left me stranded there for four hours, thinking me dead. When they broke for lunch, several were astonished to see me alive and not frostbitten.

Still, in the snow, moisture on my lips had frozen. As ill luck would have it, I heard the guards' whistles warning of a dynamite explosion. Prisoners rushed out and scattered. A few rushed to me. Two wanted to carry me to shelter behind the tool shed. My leg throbbed.

"Run; hide behind the shelter!" I screamed. "They're dynamiting!" The miners took cover except for the criminal Sidorkevich who stayed, a bandit risking his life for me.

BOOM!!! A huge, rumble blackened the sky. A debris-cyclone of boulders, dirt, dust, and sand rained down on us. Blackness lingered. I knew this would be my last hour on earth. But, shockingly, Sidorkevich saved me.

He threw back his head and yelled, "Bolotov, I'm with you! Don't be afraid!"

Luckily, no rocks had smashed us. Much later, two nurses arrived on a low, wide sled pulled by a shaggy-haired, ice-covered horse. They loaded several sick prisoners and corpses onto the sled and then approached me. There was barely any room left, but they squeezed me in between a sick man and corpse and drove us to the dispensary.

The next day, a medical doctor and two assistances examined my broken leg. He said it hadn't penetrated the skin. He set the broken bones, squeezed my leg between two stout branches, and hoisted my leg with a pulley to a raised position. He ordered me to remain on my back until my leg healed. I was delighted to be confined for the next three months in the warm dispensary but saddened by the horrors I'd witnessed.

Guards and nurses carried in frozen corpses and exhausted men 24 hours a day. Those still alive were dropped beside two barrel-stoves. Sometimes the nurses gave them hot water, but usually, they didn't as they were too far gone. Only a few men recovered, and the guards quickly pushed them out of the dispensary and back to work.

Most weakened miners lacked the energy to speak and died in silent agony. I'll always remember Mamedov, who entered the dispensary and collapsed, closing his eyes forever.

While in the dispensary I met two men. One had his frozen leg amputated; the other suffered from tuberculosis, and metal straps held his body bolted to the iron bed frame. I was puzzled and asked myself, *Who, why, and how had he been banished to Kolyma?*

My one-legged neighbor stayed habitually cold and covered his head with a blanket. Once, a blizzard delayed the 10 men, pulling our firewood sled for days. The one-legged man yelled from beneath his blanket, "When will they heat our room? Say, what day is today? Is the sun bright?"

"A blizzard is raging, preventing the delivery of firewood," I replied.

"A blizzard," he repeated. "That's good."

I was astounded. "Why is a blizzard good?"

"Old people in my town claim that if a blizzard swirls with huge snowflakes, the harvest will be excellent next summer, that's why. And today is Epiphany, the day the three wise men saw Jesus," he said dejectedly and fell into silence.

It was evening before he spoke again. "When are we going to be released, Bolotov?"

"I'm not a fortune-teller," I said. "How would I know?"

"I think you know. Tell me the truth and stop squirming."

I was growing angry and yet empathized with him and all the prisoners. A few days later, 10 prisoners delivered our firewood, and I said to the one-legged man hidden beneath his blanket, "It'll soon warm up."

He poked his head out, thanked me several times for this good news, and asked again, "When will our Kolyma sentence end and I can leave this hell?"

"Soon, my friend!" I replied.

The one-leg man squinted his eyes at me in disbelief and turtled into

Twenty-Six. My Broken Leg

his blanket. The next morning when I spoke to him he didn't answer. He had died.

That same day, my TB neighbor started making strange, straining sounds. He twisted at the wires confining him. He looked at the one-legged man and grumbled, "That man lost his leg, was racked with pain, and soon died. Unlike him, I've been bolted down by metal straps, and even the Devil doesn't want me."

For several days, the one-legged man's plight stayed with me. *All he wanted to hear were gentle words, but I was as rude.*

After three months, the doctor ordered me to leave the dispensary where I had slept well and grown healthier. Now I had to walk, leaning on a cane. Leaving, the bright sun and glossy snow in the 12-hour daylight, dazzled me after being cooped up so long. The March sun didn't look like winter's too-lazy sun that circled just below the horizon as if had stumbled behind the knolls. I could only walk slowly through the snow drifts the mile from the dispensary to my tent, and it took two hours before I arrived. It was empty.

Sidorkevich ordered me to work on the night shift. "You'll chisel stone, Bolotov."

"But I can't stand without my cane," I replied. "How can I chisel?"

"Chisel sitting!"

I had no choice. My first step was to go to the tailor's shop for mittens. And what a surprise awaited me! There stood Alekseev, the former director of the Leningrad clothes factory. An excellent tailor, he made uniforms and light silk dresses for the Kolyma administrators and their wives. It was odd seeing him cutting light silk fabrics with snow blowing in temperatures far below freezing! I begged Alekseev to speak to Sidorkevich and ask if he couldn't assign me to his workshop.[1]

"I can make mittens from old peacoats, pants, and discarded heavy coats," I offered.

The authorities respected Alekseev, and Sidorkevich soon assigned me to his warm shop with a large kitchen and sprawling dining room. Heaven!

---

1. In 1938, 93,978 prisoners worked in Kolyma camps. Shirokov, A.I. *Dal'stroi v sotsialno-ekonomicheskom razvitii Severo-Vostoka SSSR (1930–1950)* (Moskva: ROSSPEN, 2014), 178.

Twenty-Seven

My New Friends

Dining Hall at the Mine
Thursday, March 16–Wednesday, May 31, 1939

Leaning on my cane, I walked slowly and carefully to the dining hall and slumped against the wall to await lunch. Suddenly, an agile waiter approached carrying a tray of food. He looked like a gypsy. "Father," he said to me, "why are you standing here? Go take a table over there!" He pointed at a table by the window where criminals always sat.

I doubted him. *Why was he carrying food for me*? But I followed. As we wound through the tables, he said, "Father, always take this table, and I'll take care of you."

"Thank you," I said, and looked at the bowl he put down and saw a *miracle*.

The bowl looked like an administrator's lunch, a meal of the highest quality. Usually, my lunch was *balanda* and a small chunk of low-quality bread. For some odd reason, after this day, I began to eat better, and my belly was always full. And yet, I could not stop puzzling over the waiter's kindness. *What does he need from me? Does he need a pair of mittens*?

Strangely, the waiter never asked for a thing, and we became friends.

Time fled. May arrived. Ice melted. Streams flowed. Spring smells filled the breezes as days grew 23 hours long. *Stlanik* shot up through the lingering snow, intensifying my conflicting feeling.

On the one hand, I enjoyed the warmth of the constant sun, but I was distressed seeing the daily parade of noseless, armless, and legless men dragging themselves about camp. The cheeks of some young men had rotted away, and still they fought to live! My nagging doubts lingered. *How could the katorga mutilate them? These men needed warmth and care. Was our revolution for this?*

Soon these mutilated men disappeared. I suspected the camp admin-

Twenty-Seven. My New Friends

istration took them to an unknown place and shot them. The truth will never be known.

On May 16, 1939, the guards ordered me to leave the tailor shop and work in the mine. I discussed it with Mark, the man who slept next to me on the planks. He explained that he had heard that vast arrests had ended and there would be no more deliveries of fresh prisoners. Political prisoners became team leaders and watch-guards. The new guards forced criminals to work as hard as we did. All men were assigned a quota to deliver 100 wheelbarrows of rock to the dump per shift. Due to my slowly healing leg, I couldn't push a wheelbarrow and was permitted to be a loader. I worked with Mark, who ran with our wheelbarrow. We labored seven days a week, compensating for our "guilt" with blood and sacrifices before the eyes of the government. Meanwhile, with our increased productivity and spring work hours, our food improved, and sometimes we even received extra bread.[1]

Sidorkevich was replaced as my team leader by Pozyvnoi who entrusted me with counting the number wheelbarrow loads arriving at the dump. "Remember, Bolotov," he said, "my rule: Don't trust anyone. We must fulfill our norm every day!"

"I understand," I assured him.

Criminals heard our talk and snickered. Soon our group of 72 entered the mine. The first morning went well. We worked in coordinated teams and ran with wheelbarrows. By lunch, we were exhausted, and after eating, we rested 40 minutes. Many prisoners approached me and offered me *makhorka*, white bread, or canned meat from home if I would increase their wheelbarrow count. I refused, even though some men threatened me and my waiter, Kostia, who still got my tray.

My previous gypsy waiter, Aleksandr, stepped up to me and said, "Hello, father, how're you doing? I see Kostia is helping you as I told him to do yesterday."

"Yes, thanks, Aleksandr. Kostia's a great help bringing me extra rations."

"Remember, don't take gifts and don't fear anyone or alter their records. If you do, they'll sit on your necks and do nothing."

"I know that. I'll never alter my wheelbarrow count."

Just then we heard noise rise from the dump and hurried to the window. Pozyvnoi was shouting, "Time to get back to work, men!" And I started pushing through the crowd to get to the dump for my counting.

---

1. After July 28, 1940, all Soviet employees were restricted to working only eight hours a day, seven days a week. Batsaev and Kozlov, *Dalstroy Trust Sevvostlag OGPU-NKVD of the USSR as Presented by Documents and in Numbers (2 parts). Part 1 (1931–1941)*, p. 1, 187.

One man started to dump his wheelbarrow on the conveyor before I hobbled up to the top.

Someone shouted, "Who left this wheelbarrow here? We can't dump our rubble!"

"I'm coming; I'm coming," I said, gasping, and hurriedly grabbing my plywood board to write down his wheelbarrow number.

The gypsy stepped close to me. "Aleksandr," I said, "why do you worry so about me?"

"Because, father, you're different from the others. You're always patient, and that moved my heart. I'm so tired of criminals and weary of the disabled begging for food. Several times I tried to approach you but didn't, thinking you would refuse my help."

I thanked him as the conveyor belt started moving. Later that day, camp authorities arrived and looked at my tally board. "Is your count accurate?" one snapped.

"Yes, Citizen Chief," I replied. "It always is. I swear by it."

"And are the wheelbarrows fully loaded when dumped?"

"Of course. We'd punish men if they tried to dump half-full wheelbarrows."

Then Pozyvnoi shouted, "If you men don't deliver 100 wheelbarrows, you'll complete today's norm tomorrow and work the next 24 hours straight!"

After their visit, the authorities trusted me and asked me to fulfill other jobs.

Twenty-Eight

The Competition

The Mine
Thursday, June 1–Thursday, November 30, 1939

In June, the administration announced a new method of mine work: Socialist Competition. Pozyvnoi stood beside me at the top of dump hill where all the wheelbarrow tracks converged, shouting the method, and 150 men stopped to listen.[1]

"Come closer!" he shouted. "For you who work hard, I'll give you a cigarette."[2]

Prisoners started scampering like ants, pushing their heavy loads up dump hill. The clerk waved a box of cigarettes. "Who'll be first? Who'll bring the hundredth wheelbarrow of slag today and get a full box of cigarettes?"

I can't tell you how the prisoners rushed up the hill for real cigarettes! For the rest of that day, the clerk divided one box of 20 cigarettes among 150 men! Socialist Competition died a quick death.

Contrary to rumors, at the end of June, fresh prisoners arrived from western Russia. They said the government was still arresting people but fewer than in 1937. With their arrivals, the character of men convicted of Article 58 changed.

If you, dear reader, think that life in the camps was boring and monotonous, you're wrong. There was not a similar day in camp, though one day in Kolyma felt like one year at home. Eighteen-year-olds began to look like old men. Their faces reflected the price of prison, drudgery, and toil. Despite administration cruelty, political prisoners organized their

---

1. The size of a wheelbarrow was determined by Dalstroy decree of July 8, 1939, to be: 5.5 cubic feet. Batsaev and Kozlov, *Dalstroy Trust Sevvostlag OGPU-NKVD of the USSR as Presented by Documents and in Numbers (2 parts). Part 1 (1931–1941)*, p. 1, 180.

2. Socialist Competition is one of the principles of encouraging workers to meet and overfill production targets and receive various forms of reward. Wieszynski, *The Modern Encyclopedia of Russian and Soviet History*, vol. 36 (1984), 84–90.

lives and worked by removing criminals from leading positions, replacing them with their team leaders. We knew the government did not want to deal with criminals who tried to eliminate honest and hardworking men. Meanwhile, the guards turned cleverer.

Administrators allowed us to walk to the mine without guards. But, beyond the woods, we were only permitted to walk with guards, worried we'd escape. Guards inflicted their "justice" in the woods. One day, Tolia Bortsov, shouldered an unusually large log and started for camp. A guard yelled, "Get rid of that big log, Bortsov! And stick to the path!"

But Tolia dashed into the woods and hid.

The guards yelled at us, "Don't look back!"

The men, staggering under the weight of wet, heavy wood, turned at the fork in the path for our tents. The guards shouldered their rifles like soldiers, and soon we heard the echo of a rifle shot. The men dropped their firewood.

"Why are you stopping?" a guard yelled. "March!"

We hoisted our heavy loads and proceeded to camp. The next day, a guard read, "*We shot Bortsov while escaping from camp.*"

It was nonsense! No one could or would escape from camp; we were too exhausted from slogging in the mine. There's no fleeing the Arctic. These shootings often happened as authorities promoted murdering guards. If a political prisoner saw a guard stalking him repeatedly, the man would worm into a clutch of men and never leave. That was our safety net. Guards wouldn't shoot into the middle of a group to kill one man.

The second half of August saw long, wet days. Rain was rare in Kolyma, but it drizzled from August 15 to 18 and poured the next two weeks. Mud oozed down the mountainsides, ruining our work at the gold-mine and making work impossible. But the guards beat us to continue working. After two days, guards delivered bags of flour to the site. We quickly emptied them, gobbling the raw flour in hollowed hands like animals. Then, we used the empty bags to cover our heads. After a time, we dried out a little and warmed a little in the driving rain. The monsoon beat down harder and harder, and we looked for a shelter. Some men slid into the mud and hid under wheelbarrows. Of course, the guards remained in their nifty huts, warm and dry. Occasionally, they donned weatherproof tarpaulins and stepped out to yell at us.

Later, we learned that the flour bags were given us to build dikes, and guards ordered us to yank them off our heads, stuff them with gravel. Their order was useless. The storm had destroyed everything in its path. Floods inundated towns along the river under 15 feet of water.

We thought as the weather cleared our nasty treatment would end. We were wrong. August was ending, but our gold norms were unfilled,

Twenty-Eight. The Competition

causing a breach between us and the authorities. They demanded increased gold extractions. Some men had been too sick to work and were relieved of duty. Now they were commanded to work despite looking like death shades. Who would derive any value from their bumbling work?

Our dictators drooled over their expectations, but nothing changed. We produced less and less gold and often hid treasurers. For example, one day a man found a huge gold nugget and started to run with it to the guards.

His workmate grabbed his arm and asked, "What're you doing?"

"I'm going to the administration to give them this nugget," the lucky man replied.

"You're nuts! A watch guard, will increase your term for hiding a gold nugget."[3]

"Do you think so?" He looked shocked.

"Of course! Toss it or bury it in slag."

We all had seen guards shoot prisoners who found gold nuggets. After that, we always stomped gold nuggets into the ground, dreaming of lost bread but remaining alive.

The setting sun had dropped below the horizon briefly for the first time since May in early August, and then the days quickly shortened. By September, nights were nine hours long. October lengthened them to 16 hours, and by early November there were just brief hours of sun before it set for good the end of the month. But our schedule never changed. As nights grew longer and colder, nothing was done to prepare for Kolyma's winter. Every evening we still tramped to the mine to dig gold, and after those long night, we cut and carried logs to the camp and gathered grass for our mattresses. Usually, the guards, cooks, and criminals stole our grass, and we slept on bare planks all that winter.

---

3. On May 21, 1938, the administration of Dalstroy ordered prisoners to be paid 50 kopeks for 3.6 ounces of gold. Batsaev and Kozlov, *Dalstroy Trust Sevvostlag OGPU-NKVD of the USSR as Presented by Documents and in Numbers (2 parts). Part 1 (1931–1941)*, p. 1, 164.

Twenty-Nine

World War II in the Gold Mine

Maksim Gorkii Village
Monday, January 1, 1940–
Sunday, November 30, 1941

As 1940 arrived, we heard rumors of a war, and we were building a Maksim Gorkii village.[1] It grew fast as the number of gold mines swelled with the arrival of modern technical equipment that required trained, skilled workers for the compressors, pneumatic drills, hoists, sluicing equipment, and trucks.[2]

The administrators did not allow political prisoners to work these machines; however, we were the only men sufficiently educated to operate them. With me, my team-leader, Borodnia, began to fulfill his production objectives. Compared to other prisoners, his miners had cabins, beds, stoves, better food, and never had to carry firewood. Also, it was warm deep in the mine where the earth's temperature stayed a constant fifty degrees. Borodnia's miners worked 10-hour day or night shifts. He allowed me three days off the last of December.

"Bolotov, you will work with Anton. He's a good man from Kuzbas, and he'll introduce you to others.[3] Do you wonder why I hired you?"

"Yes," I admitted, puzzled.

"The other day, while at the smithy sharpening drills, I spoke with Suvorov. He said he'd worked with you at The Red Triangle." Borodnia added,

---

1. Gorkii, Maksim (1868–1936), writer and political activist. Wieszynski, *The Modern Encyclopedia of Russian and Soviet History*, vol. 13 (1979), 58–61.

2. In 1941, 45 gold mines and 12 tin mines were in production in Kolyma. Batsaev and Kozlov, *Dalstroy Trust Sevvostlag OGPU-NKVD of the USSR as Presented by Documents and in Numbers (2 parts). Part 1 (1931–1941)*, p. 1, 15.

3. Kuzbas is one of the largest coal deposit in southern Siberia. Wieszynski, *The Modern Encyclopedia of Russian and Soviet History*, vol. 2 (1976), 174–177.

Twenty-Nine. World War II in the Gold Mine

Mine trolley (Dal'stroi Territories Photo Album of 1942–1943, Ministry of Inner Affairs, State Archive, Russian Federation, Moscow).

"It was tough to arrange your transfer from the tents to my mine because the guards said you were dangerous, but I didn't believe them."

This turn of events made me forever grateful to Suvorov and Borodnia, for I soon became stronger and able to survive another winter. Together with other miners, we mechanized the mining process, increased output, and fulfilled the 1940 Work Plan.

In 1941, I became team-leader-assistant in charge of the night shift. Our mine fulfilled its gold production norm. By July, we were sluicing gold in the open air, and I received a letter from my mother. She told me that Nina was delighted to learn I was still alive as many husbands had died. Mother sent along a list of the arrested husbands of friends, hoping I could tell her what had happened to them.

In the summer of 1941, Borodnia completed his 10-year term and was sent to the western front. Golenischev, sentenced to Kolyma for 25 years, took his position.

That fall, the arrival of new men—and women—crowded the Gulag! Muscovites told us of the Nazi's unprovoked attacks. Young women and well-fed men (who had dodged military service), became our team leaders despite not knowing a thing about gold mining. The girls sat on rocks 12 hours, watching us work. Sometimes they gossiped about news from the

Information Bureau to which we hungrily listened. Moved by the invasion, we asked camp authorities to send us to the war. However, "enemies of the people were prohibited from fighting." Although this saddened us, the camp's tyrants began valuing our gold production as it promoted Soviet glory.

Every day my team-leader fulfilled his gold extraction goal by bringing one-tenth of an ounce of gold to the camp administration for our country's defense. We never rested. Underground, in Mine 21, when we needed light, we used our torn clothes as wicks for cans filled with grease. The administration stopped yelling at us and started calling us tenderly, *kontriki*. The work was so coordinated and productive we nicknamed it "Two Hundred Percent" as we always exceeded our quota by 200 percent and received new benefits. Sadly, we never received cash for groceries as the criminal did, so we were unable to purchase from local vendors. Surprisingly, soon we began eating American oatmeal, white flour, sugar, and butter: a joy. Years later I learned this was a benefit of America's Lend-Lease Program.[4] With these gifts, life went on underground. Enemies of the people, most feared by the government, had long sentences, and for most, these became death sentences. Men whose terms ended were automatically given new, longer terms without trial or notification.

I remember the authorities appointed a 20-year-old girl, Claudia, as my team leader. She was modest and faint-hearted and didn't have a clue about mining. Dressed in a thin coat, she came to the mine early each day and sat under a light until lunch. From the first, she feared us and never spoke. Once, I suggested she stand and jump up and down to get warm. She refused. Later, miners gave her three padded jackets, one jacket to sit on, another to wear around her shoulders, and a third to cover her knees. That is how our young female team-leader led us.

One day, deep in the mine, our air compressor stopped pumping. Lights went out. Claudia, sitting like a doll wrapped in coats, screamed, "What's happening to me?"

"Hold on," a miner said and lit the rag-wicks in the grease pots. We proceeded to break rocks in the semi-darkness, moving the grease lights from cut to cut until the electricity was restored. Within two weeks, Claudia befriended us, and we taught her how to fix small hoist defects.

---

4. Under Lend-Lease, America supplied the Soviet Union with 400,000 vehicles (mostly trucks), 15,000 planes, 1,900 locomotives, 11,000 carriages, tanks, wire, grain, butter, sugar: $150 billion of supplies. Weeks, Albert L. *Russia's Life-Saver: Lend-Lease Aid to the U.S.S.R. in World War II* (Lanham, MD: Lexington Books, 2004).

Thirty

The Cave-In

The Mine
Tuesday, April 14, 1942

    I will always remember the first mild days of 1942 when a massive catastrophe struck the mine. Despite the Arctic's ferocious cold, the first spring days brought with them vast troubles. Warm air percolated deep into mine melting overhead arches and leaving us in the mud. Ceilings leaked. Stones fell. Lights failed. And the prevailing blackness turned fatal.

    I was plodding through thick, gooey mud when I heard the screech of an arch giving way. I plastered myself against the shaft's wall and dodged chunks of stone tearing loose. Huge pieces plopped into the mud around my feet. Nearby, on the narrow-gauge railway, a cart of rocks had flipped over at a break in the track. Criminals had claimed to have fixed it, but they hadn't. Men put their backs to the cart, got it upright, and began to push it forward. I decided to fix the track and ran to the shop as fast as I could, stumbling over rocks. I soon saw men on their knees, drilling holes in stone. They set the charge. We hid. The blast moved the rocks. When the dust settled, they loaded railcars and pushed them to the top of the mine and onto to a trailer. But then another arch fell, blocking the railcars. Again, the miners went to work breaking hunks of rock with their hammers and shoved the railcars forward, loading four railcars.

    Leaning on their elbows, one wide-shouldered miner joked with the trailer-hand, Mark, dressed to look like a sumo wrestler in layers of coats, said, "You've made yourself look frightful in all those clothes."

    "For sure," another miner added. "He looks like he eats with bears."

    Mark snarled, "Screw you! I work as hard as five miners."

    Mark did, indeed, work hard, and he was as strong as an ox. Only an exceptionally strong man could load railcars onto the trailer. The miners often asked the administrators to assign a second miner to work the trailer, but they were unable to find another strong man. Mark, known by the nickname Bulba, handled the job alone.[1]

Warmed by the mine, the miners continued to mock Bulba when suddenly, WHOOSH!

A CAVE-IN![2]

Dust, grit, and earth bellowed out of the mine entrance. When the air cleared, I screamed, "Let's go in!" And I dashed through the entrance.

Massive rocks blocked my path. I stumbled into the darkness. I switched on my miner's light. Rocks had smashed railcars. Aftershocks, deep within the mine, sent snaps and cracks up the shafts. I heard heart-wrenching screams, timber snapping, rocks crashing, and the screech of stressed-metal giving way. Air hissed out of broken compressors.

A deep voice pleaded, "Help me!"

It sounded like Bulba. I felt for him in the gritty dimness. I found him.

"Petrovich! I prayed someone would hear me. It's hard to breathe. Rocks crushed my left arm and leg, but my right arm is free." Sticky blood oozed down his cheek.

"We got to get you out of here," I said.

"I can't move," Bulba muttered, with a weak moan.

I looked around. There was hissing from the broken air pipe. Prisoners didn't have watches, but I counted the railcars and realized half a shift had ended. My light flickered, blinked, and died. In the darkness, I fiddled with the wires. It turned on. Bulba and I rejoiced. In the dim beam, we saw mutilated men and wrecked railcars. The young men who made jokes yesterday were silent. The wide-shouldered Siberian who spoke to Bulba a few hours ago threw back his arm and looked at us with sickening glass-like eyes.

I trembled but turned my light on Bulba. "Stop complaining!" I said, "You're only dirty!"

"But Petrovich, I can't move!" he wept.

"You can too. Pull one arm out, then pull out your leg." I ran my light over Bulba and saw huge blocks of the permafrost laying 60 feet from him.

"Brush yourself off and get up on your knees."

---

1. "Taras Bulba," a romantic novel by Nikolai Gogol (1809–1852), whose protagonist, Taras, symbolizes Cossacks' strong traits. Wieszynski, *The Modern Encyclopedia of Russian and Soviet History*, vol. 12 (1979), 216.

2. In 1943, 63 equipment-accidents occurred in Northern Mountain Industrial Administration's mines. Batsaev and Kozlov, *Dalstroy Trust Sevvostlag OGPU-NKVD of the USSR as Presented by Documents and in Numbers (2 parts). Part 1 (1931–1941)*, p. 1, 159.

Thirty. The Cave-In

The roof of the mine settled more. Bulba twisted his head and slid his shoulders to release his arms.

"Petrovich, there is a lump on my head." While I checked Bulba's head, I heard the miners' moans and groans. I turned; the lamp played over the cave-in. He brushed the dust off and asked me to shine the light on his legs. Although my left arm hurt, I clutched it and went to the moaners. Suddenly, miners' lights flooded the disaster. Others dashed in.

After we'd helped the injured, a doctor said, "Petrovich, your arm is broken." He torn the sleeve of his peacoat, wrapped my broken arm in it, and hung it around my neck.

Five miners died in the cave-in; two were disabled. The next day, we worked, as usual.

Thirty-One

The Unexpected Meetings

The Gold Mine's Isolator
Thursday, October 15–Friday, November 20, 1942

During the full cycle of the wash-season, an ideological inspector met with us after meeting with our administration. He grew furious over the lax and liberal relationships between the guards and political prisoners. I overheard his conversation with my team leader. "Enemies of people must work with chisels and shovels," he railed.

"But they're knowable professionals," our team-leader countered.

"Are you covering for them? Professors, engineers, and doctors must only work with wheelbarrows," the inspector snarled.

"Then who'll work in the workshops?"

"Criminals!"

"They know nothing about technical equipment."

"Teach them. Otherwise, *you'll* be the new wheelbarrow driver!"

About this time, a new mine manager arrived in camp, a colonel Rybak. Upon hearing his name my heart sunk. *Was he the same Nathaniel Rybak who wrote denunciations about us as a technician at The Red Triangle? Rybak was like Snopikov and Stepanov. These three scoundrels slandered many men at my factory.*

At the end of October, miners started blasting surface permafrost. Overwork caused the compressor to shudder and stop. The drillers couldn't work. The night shift couldn't get enough gold-dirt. Several times, team-leaders descended into the mine and got the compressor working and discovered a criminal sleeping by the compressor, doing nothing. We replaced him with a political prisoner, an old man. The team-leader ordered me to work with him as his assistant to keep all the compressors working. We worked all night and soon started fulfilling our norm again. Men found their strength and dragged themselves to and from the camp. I often stayed long hours in the mine to help the drillers checking the depth

Thirty-One. The Unexpected Meetings

of the bores. One morning, when finished, I went to the surface carrying my drill and found myself among a group of officers. Quickly turning away, one well-dressed man stopped me.

"Hey, Bolotov!" he shouted. "Come here!"

I stopped. In front of me stood colonel Nathaniel Rybak, the former technician from the Red Triangle Factory. *What is he doing here*? I heard NKVD officials had hidden him from Kochergin. Rybak approached and carelessly slapped my shoulder.

"Well, Bolotov! You look surprised. I'll be managing this mine and hear your team leader always fulfills his norm, so if you work even harder, I'll give you more bread and fifty grams of vodka every day."[1]

I said nothing. *Well, you betrayed us. I won't work harder for vodka.*

The next day, my team and I met Karpetin at the gold mine entrance. About 35 and well-fed, he was of average height and wore clean clothes. He ignored our eyes as he spoke, seeming overly-complaisant and obliging, probably playing up to the administration for favors. A few days later, I heard rumors that he was a *stukach*[2]: *Who was there to spy on here in the Arctic?*

I was sure he was not spying on me, like most miners, and never discussed politics. Plus, I had no time for idle gossip and felt isolated; men arrested between 1939 and 1941 comprised my team. I, alone, was arrested in 1937.

I worried too about my earlier meeting with Rybak. Three of my fellow engineers had disappeared under mysterious circumstances, Fedor Suvorov, Lazar Alymenko, and Vasilii Serebrennikov.

I never dreamed the lead investigator wanted to examine me again, for Karpetin often spoke to me, sharing his schooling about graduating from Moscow's Institute of Red Professorship.[3] Simultaneously, he also sold himself to the *kum, or kommissar*, for an extra scoop of *balanda*.

"Bolotov," he said to me repeatedly, "I want to pour out my heart to you."

"I don't have time," I objected, waving him off. "I've got to fill my quota."

I was wary; his desire to talk would slow me down. All the other miners avoided meetings with Karpetin, too, and he soon realized it. Mean-

---

1. On November 22, 1940, the authorities ordered prisoners given 1.8 ounces of spirits per day, which had to be consumed immediately outside the mine. Batsaev and Kozlov, *Dalstroy Trust Sevvostlag OGPU-NKVD of the USSR as Presented by Documents and in Numbers (2 parts). Part 1 (1931–1941)*, p. 1, 273.

2. The word *stukach* means a secret police informer. Rossi, *The Gulag Handbook*, 435.

3. Institute of Red Professorship was founded in 1921 and abolished in 1938. Wieszynski, *The Modern Encyclopedia of Russian and Soviet History*, vol. 14 (1979), 199–203.

while, the *kum* began investigating all miners. Usually, the men never mentioned their questionings, but once Anton Gutnik told me, "Bolotov, the *kum* has been asking us about you; putting you in danger."

That made me furious—at both the *kum* and Rybak. "I mine gold for my country!" I exclaimed, frustrated.

One day, Rybak and Karpetin called on us deep inside the mine. Rybak carried a big teapot in his spotless hand that smelled of alcohol. He looked at us and pattered, stressing the loud *r* sound, "Your team took first place among all the others. I want to treat you." Rybak poured vodka from the teapot into the can our 10-man crew shared. When he looked at Karpetin, they both smiled. My heart skipped a bit. When Rybak offered a shot of vodka to me, he smiled. His eyes opened wide and sparkled with wolf-like gratitude.

Yagodnoye Mountain Notch (Dal'stroi Territories Photo Album of 1942–1943, Ministry of Inner Affairs, State Archive, Russian Federation, Moscow).

Thirty-One. The Unexpected Meetings

He filled my cup shouting, "Bolotov, to your health!"

His toast shocked and puzzled me. Camp administrators never descended deep into the mine. They never rewarded us with anything! His treat made the men giddy: "Rybak, you're an excellent mine manager! You're the first man ever to see our work."

Later, when investigator Kulakov called me, I realized that Rybak had made this banquet because he planned to bury me. As I suspected, on November 10, 1942, at midnight, guards scurried me away from the barrack and drove me to the courthouse in Yagodnoye. The night was quiet and clear. The guards took me to Camp 6 and locked me in a three-by-five-foot cell of welded steel sheets. I couldn't sit. I couldn't stretch. I couldn't stand.

There was a small stove in a narrow hall that guards stoked once a day. Along the back wall were 10 other similar isolation boxes—all occupied. Guards gave me a can of murky warm slush and a half pound of bread once a day. Sometimes I heard mumbles. I spoke to my neighbors. They never replied. I folded my body over and tried to sit cross-legged, pressing my knees against my stomach, head to my chest, like a baby in his mother's womb.

Ten days passed.

Thirty-Two

Investigator Kulakov

Yagodnoye Court House
Saturday, November 21, 1942

On the 11th day, guards unlocked my cell door and marched me to a new investigator. My legs felt like wooden pegs, and I struggled to walk without stumbling. My head spun dizzily. *Why had they left me caged so long? Probably trying to break my will?*

We stopped at the investigator's office, and guards ordered me to sit on a bench while we waited for him. I assumed his apartment was in the same large building: *Why had we built such a huge house for him and then constructed metal boxes for us?*

The investigator's door was open, and I overheard his side of a phone conversation: "Yes, this is Camp Six—Listen to me, Karpetin will be visiting you soon. Support him. He'll be speaking to political prisoners—Do you understand?—*But Karpetin is your informer, and he's treading on us. He asked me to help them with cases and promised me a new mattress and better food, so I agreed.*"

"Bolotov, in here!" Kulakov yelled, and I stepped into his office.

"Sit on that stool," he directed. Kulakov was a dark-skinned man of 35. Like Rybak, he was well-dressed and closely shaven. Unlike my Leningrad investigator Baryshnikov, he didn't scream at me but began quietly. His wooden chair creaked when he leaned back and folded his palms behind his head. "Well, Bolotov, tell me about your counter-revolutionary activities. I see the Party has controlled your life."

"This sounds like 1937 all over again," I said.

He smiled patiently. "No, this is 1942. Answer my questions."

"What do you want to hear?"

"Tell me about your political and social activities."

"What's there to tell?"

"Everything! I see you didn't spend enough time in the metal box.

Thirty-Two. Investigator Kulakov

Listen...." Kulakov started reading Karpetin's denunciations of me. When he finished, he asked me to sign them.

"I will *not* sign lies!" I protested, knowing it meant more time in the metal box.

"You denied Karpetin's evidence ... you didn't tell the miners Stalin would let Germans occupy Moscow, or he would abandon Moscow and flee?"

"Citizen Chief," I pleaded, "I'd never make those outrageous lies!"

Kulakov shook his head, amazed. "So, you don't want to confess?! Maybe you need more time to think!" He turned to the guards. "Take him away!"

I spent another 10 days in the box.

Then Kulakov called me to his office, repeated the interrogation, and I again refused to sign, which earned me my third 10-day confinement in the box.

After that third confinement, Kulakov gave up on me. My grilling ended. On December 12, 1942, Kulakov sent me to the infamous locale for Soviet executions, *Serpatinka*.[1]

At 10 in the morning, a new guard opened my box. "Bolotov, follow me!" He wore two sheepskin coats; I wore rags. Outside the jail, the day was pitch-black and bitter cold. The wind was soundless, as if resting for the next blizzard, and the guard prodded me with his rifle butt, pointing with his flashlight into the dark. "It's 12 miles to your new jail from Yagodnoye, over the northern pass of the Chersky Mountain."

We walked about two miles in the blackness when headlights and the groans of a truck signaled an approaching vehicle. *A ride*! It came up behind us, slowed, and stopped. The driver rolled down his window. He did a double take, looking right at me, standing in his cab's light. "Hey, is that you, Bolotov? Where are you guys headed?"

I recognized the driver from the mine. I didn't know his name. "*Serpatinka*," I replied.

"Well, get in. I'm going there too."

My guard growled, "No! Our orders are to walk!" and waved him off.

Neither the driver nor I could believe his refusal. The driver hunched his shoulders and tromped on the gas. We plotted on through deep snow another mile, and the slog turned the guard face beet-red and sweaty. "Let's rest," he said, yanking off one coat and setting it on a large rock beside the road. I was freezing and didn't want to sit as I could barely walk.

Once rested, we started walking, and soon, the guard asked repeatedly, "Slow down."

---

1. Serpantinka is derived from *serpantin*, or a serpentine road. Translator's note.

Finally, we approached a sentry box on the side of the road. He immediately entered. I stood outside and watched him peeled off his coats, sit, and smoke while I hopped, foot-to-foot.

At this latitude, the sun had only hinted at rising above the horizon two hours late, and the frost grew severe. I was terrified. An hour dragged until he pulled on both, coats, and came out, rested and fed. We started down the road again, me dragging my feet.

He muttered, "Why didn't I take that ride?"

Soon, the road forked. We saw a string of weak lights in the distance.

"Houses," the guard said, relieved.

"Maybe they're the eyes of wild animals, wolves or bears," I offered.

"Do they live here?" he asked in wide-eyed astonishment.

"Certainly!"

The road snaked between steep canyons beneath towering mountains. Eventually, we arrived at *Serpatinka* jail, from which prisoners never returned. When we entered, guards were playing dominoes beside a small, red-hot stove. No one searched me. More guards accompanied me to a warm and uncrowded cell. I collapsed on a cot and slept. The guards didn't feed me as it was a transit stop on my way to yet another jail. In the morning, prisoners gave me a chunk of bread and a bowl of *balanda*. I ate half the chunk and stuffed the rest in my pocket for later.

And then we left. The guard broke a rule and stopped a passing truck for a ride to the next jail. Arriving, to my great surprise, prisoners overfilled the jail squeezed together like sardines. A few hours later, guards dragged me outside to a court building surrounded by majestic larches as tall as flagpoles for more Soviet justice.

In 1942, prisoners worked in snow 10 feet deep (Dal'stroi Territories Photo Album of 1942–1943, Ministry of Inner Affairs, State Archive, Russian Federation, Moscow).

Thirty-Three

The New Accusation

Serpatinka Jail
Friday, December 18–Thursday, December 31, 1942

Guards left me at a large office with a well-groomed man who sniffed at me, peered down his long, aristocratic at a scruffy prisoner who hadn't showered in months.

He scoffed, "I say, Bolotov, do you know who I am?"

I shook my head. "No idea."

"I'm the prosecutor who'll be sending your case to Moscow. I've read your file and have been directed to affirm your case as an enemy of the people and mail it to the tribunal since investigator Kulakov signed it. You'll be having another trial."

That same day, a middle-aged judge and young *VOKhR* guards sat at a wide table covered with green cloth. Karpetin, a witness against me, sat in silence against the wall.

The judge began, "Bolotov, admit all the accusations in the investigator's report!"

Humbly, I said, "Your honor, they are all lies. I will not sign them."

The secretaries yawned indifferently. The judge summarized, "For the record, Bolotov objects to the accusations in his case. He denied them in pre-trial investigation and in 1937, which I don't understand. Why, Bolotov, are the judges so wrong about you?" He rubbed his puffy hands and glared at me. "To you wish to make a final statement to this court?"

"Yes, comrade," I said. "I'm an honest Communist and weary of all these endless lies."

The judge read his verdict. "In the name of the Soviet Union, we order you, Bolotov, shot for organizing a rebellion."

I shouted, "Tell me, who did I organize? *Who proposed this bizarre verdict? Kulakov never accused me of such organizing any rebellion*."

The judge swiped his brow and concluded. "You may appeal this verdict."

"That would be useless. You're ignoring Lenin's laws."

The judge stood and left. With miserable resignation, I accepted my death sentence and was escorted to a small cell barely secured with a thin wooden door with finger-wide cracks. Inside the crowded space there was an opened, screened window overlooking Serpatinka's yard. The jail, built in the mid–1930s, was not far from the Khatynnakh River, and I'd heard rumors of how guards executed prisoners with machine-guns on the banks of Sniper Stream.[1] Eighteen condemned men were stuffed in the cell; one said we had been ordered to strip, hand over our clothes, kneel by the stream for shooting.

There were neither benches nor tables. There was one metal bed, a small *burzhuika*, which was incapable of throwing off enough heat to melt snow on the floor. I flopped into the snow to sleep. Soon, men let me lay in the middle, near the stove, and I dozed, thinking I'd never awaken.

But the next morning, I awoke to a bang, bang, bang. Someone said, "Water-carrier breaking ice off the water barrel for us." A crunch of snow followed by the bang of the bolt hitting its stop, the stamp of feet, the squeak of the door opening. Two criminals, accompanied by guards, carried out the *parasha* and brought in a handful of *stlanik*. The short, stumpy guard, nicknamed Ferocious, held a rifle.

One prisoner stoked the stove's ashes and added branches. With their backs against the icy wall, most men sat in the snow, ignoring the feeble attempt at the heat. Ferocious gave each of us a slice of bread and cup of warm water. With us fed, Ferocious wheeled around and beelined for his office, slamming the flimsy door behind him. The *stlanik* caught fire and crackled. Through cracks in the stove rose the odor of hot iron and sight of burning flames. Oddly, it seemed peaceful, life went on, and the *stlanik* burned and the cold seeped in.

I'd lived honestly and brought society some benefits from my existence. If I could start life over, I'd not change a thing. I dwelled on this and refused to accept my awaiting death. Criminals spoke of no man ever returning from *Serpatinka*. I knew no one could survive more than a few days. If men didn't eat their bread while guards watched, it was snatched from them when they left.

Political prisoners never resorted to criminals' swearing at our restraint. Knowing that prisoners enjoyed hearing historic and romantic

---

1. In 1980, miners found skeletons and bullets of the dead and refused to mine gold. In 1991, Ivan Panikarov and Stanislav Vladimirov erected a stone in honor of those executed in *Serpatinka* jail. Translator's note.

stories, I took a chance and told one, "The Gadfly."[2] Captivated, criminals listened eagerly, edging closer and closer, asking me to speak louder until I finished. The next morning, the top criminal ordered others to make room for me beside the stove. I thanked him and began Dumas' "The Count of Monte Cristo." Interestingly, criminals loved whimsical stories and asked for more, but, given my frailness, I said, "I must rest; maybe tomorrow."

After I'd spoken, a 24-year-old told us "his" story, describing killing a greedy old lady with an ax, hiding her money, and going to the police. It sounded like Dostoevskii's "Crime and Punishment," but I said nothing even when he described himself as Rodion Raskolnikov. Criminals never knew and often retold tales of Vol'ka Kain[3] and Golden Sonka.[4]

An 18-year-old prisoner relayed how he killed a teller carrying money for the miners. He claimed he'd dug a hole in a snowdrift, buried the corpse, and hid the money. But, foolishly, he began to spend his bounty, and the administration caught on and sentenced him to death. We could only guess about the truth of his story as men all exaggerated their adventures and police difficulties, but the criminals loved the kid's story, which began by his claim to have brought drills from the mine to the smithy for sharpening. One day, he said, I arrived and discovered he hadn't finished. He asked me to wait for a half hour. Not thinking about anything, I stood close to the fire, leaning on the brick wall. I was depressed because the administration had delayed our salaries, and I'd lived on bread and water for a week.

Suddenly, the smithy's phone rang. I heard his half of a conversation with the bookkeeper and realized that soon he'd be at the smithy with our salaries. I was overjoyed! I'd return the drills to the mine and return for my salary. On my way to the mine, I planned how I'd kill the teller and snatch the payroll. With the snow falling to cover our tracks, no one would ever guess what happened to him, and all the money would be mine. So, I returned to the mine, gave the drills to the miners, kept one, and snuck back to meet the teller. When he approached, I saw his briefcase with money. I asked him for a cigarette. He stopped, pulled a pack from his pocket with one hand, and, at that instance, I clunked him on the head with the drill.

---

2. Voynich, Ethel Lilian (1864–1960), British author of "The Gadfly," which was made into a movie in 1928, sold 2.5 million copies in the USSR. Taratuta, E. A. *Istoriia dvukh knig: "Podpolnaia Rossiia" S.M. Stepniaka-Kravchinskogo i "Ovod" Ethel' Lilian Voynich* (Moskva: Khudozhestvennaia literatura, 1987), 139–141.

3. Bolotov speaks about Van'ka Kain whose real name was Ivan Osipov (1718–1756), a well-known criminal character in Russian folklore. Emin, F., et al. *Van'ka Kain* (Moskva: EKSMO, 2008).

4. Sonka, the Small Golden Hand, born Sofia Ivanovna Blyuvshtein (1846–1902), was a legendary female thief exiled to the Sakhalin Island. Chekhov, A., Reeve, B. *Sakhalin Island* (London: Alma Books, 2013).

He fell. I checked his pulse, none, and tugged his body into a drift, emptied his briefcase into my pocket, and hid the briefcase. Then I went to the smithy, took my three sharpened drills, and returned to the mine to work. Workers waited in vain for the teller who never arrived. I heard that the head of the mine called the bookkeeper and asked him about the teller. Someone claimed they had no idea what happened to him and proposed they check the road to the smithy. Miners ran to investigate, but the teller had disappeared, the money was gone.

The blizzard continued, and soon another teller arrived with our meager salaries. I was lucky. I received my small salary, but with the stolen loot, I paid off all my debts. Men always went to the store when paid because they'd been hungry for a month. After I'd paid my creditors, I purchased some expensive food in the dining halls and store. When my salary was gone, I found my buried treasury and bought a new hat and sturdy *valenki*. For weeks, no one suspected me. Talk faded about the teller's death, and that calmed me, but one night, in the barracks, a man noticed blood on my old *valenki*. He wrote a letter to an investigator; it launched a flurry of activities, and they discovered I'd paid off all my debts and bought new clothes and food. They compared my purchases to those of others and arrested me. I soon admitted my crime and received a death sentence.

When he ended his story, criminals asked me to tell longer stories. I retold Hugo's *Les Misérables* and Pushkin's "Dubrovskii."

On the day before New Year, we overheard the tromping-steps of Ferocious: *Whose turn it would be today? As terrible as life was in Kolyma, no one wanted to die.* Ferocious opened the door with the usual jingle of keys and stepped in.

"Bolotov, outside!" he commanded. "Hurry!"

Fear paralyzed me! *My death will be today!*

I turned and said, "Farewell, Valjean, Cosette, Fantina, and Javert.[5] Sorry I can't tell you more stories."

Outside, pointing at the watchtower, Ferocious ordered, "Run, Bolotov!"

I ran and stumbled, as my underwear fell. Ferocious followed and shoved me inside the watchtower. He and the chief warden chit-chatted, looking at me and mocking my helplessness. One of them poked my underwear; the other poked my bare feet.

"Dress, you imbecile!" roared the chief warden and laughed.

"You look like a brand new state criminal," giggled another man.

Then, the door opened, and a new guard barged in. "What's going on?" He pulled off his fur mittens and held his hands to the stove.

---

5. The characters are from *Les Misérables* (1862).

Thirty-Three. The New Accusation

After a while, the blizzard subsided, and the moon and stars appeared. As I warmed, I slowly slipped my feet into *valenki* and pulled on my shabby peacoat and hat.

"Go out that door over there!" a guard ordered, pointing.

I opened the door and stepped into the taiga.

Behind me, someone said, "Turn right!" I saw a path leading to the mountains.

Sorry, my life. No one will ever know when I died or why. No one will know of my innocence. I looked at the sky. The night was crystal clear; the stars radiant. The Great Bear ruled the northern sky.

The path wound up and down and down and up. Sometimes it aimed straight as an arrow through deep canyons; the encircling mountains felt like they were squashing in on me. It was hard to breathe and deathly quiet except for the crunching of snow underfoot and our gasping for air. The guards, a few steps behind me, hit me when I looked at the stars. How many songs of praises I'd read about them? Now I had to ignore the stars although I felt one with the universe. I was overwhelmed with the desire to prove my innocence and live. *If this is your end, you've slept on cement floors five years for nothing. Fight!*

The guards ordered me to go around a large, snow-covered snag jutting out. I turned, and a snow-covered log cabin appeared; smoke rose from its iron chimney. "Go in the cabin!"

I glanced at the guards. They folded their arms behind them and swore at one another as we entered the warm cabin.

The guards looked at me. "Well, state criminal, take a bath!"

I couldn't move. Then, as if waking, I rushed to the blazing stove to warm myself.

"Hold it! Don't fall to the floor! Go ahead, get warm and bathe," a guard said.

Soon, I warmed enough to undress and wash. The guards gave me a new uniform of patched cotton pants, a greasy soldier's blouse, and a warm hat. What a transformation! After my bath and dressing, the guards shoved me into a Black Raven, and we drove away; I had no idea where, but with warmth and clean linen, my heart stilled.

Thirty-Four

Jail

Vaskov's House[1]
Friday, January 1, 1943

On New Year's Day, a Black Raven truck with a cloth-covered-top hauled us, stuffed like *Zakhar Kuzmich*,[2] to another jail. When others learned I'd spent two weeks in *Serpatinka*, they allowed me more space. Our truck tilted, plowing over curvy roads and snowy passes, and, hours later, stopped at a new jail. Guards ordered us out, striking us as we disembarked. Most men entered one door, but a guard ordered me to another. Emaciated, I could barely walk across the yard's knee-deep snow. On passing another guard, I smelled alcohol and his face looked red. He grumbled, groaned, and shook the snow off his coat. "This blizzard is a disaster; I wish we're in Moscow."

A supervisor said, "Here's a new prisoner. Read this instruction and take him away!"

Guards surrounded me like a small animal to study. One, with thick, black eyebrows and a wooden nose that didn't move, said, "You're in Vaskov's House; toss all your rags and check in!"

With frozen fingers, I untied my small rope-belt around my peacoat, thinking: *You want me to take off all my linen.* But I slowly undressed.

"Engineer, do you need my help?!" he asked impudently.

"Slam him!" another guard, with a flat head, croaked.

I took off my pants, and guards stared at my skeleton. Then a guard with a flat head wheezed, "Arms forward! Spread your fingers! Open your mouth! Lift your right leg!"

---

1. Vaskov's House was the official name for Magadan's jail. It was established by the NKVD officer, Rodion Ivanovich Vaskov (1891–1961). Batsaev and Kozlov, *Dalstroy Trust Sevvostlag OGPU-NKVD of the USSR as Presented by Documents and in Numbers (2 parts). Part 1 (1931–1941)*, p. 1, 349.

2. *Zakhar Kuzmich* is the collective name for a group of men, equivalent to Tom, Dick, and Harry. Translator's note.

They're like neuropathologists; perhaps, they'll order me to close my eyes.

Then, I asked the supervisor, "Citizen Chief, may I have my peacoat?"

"Maybe you want your wife too. I don't have her," he laughed, proud of his wit.

Once redressed, we walked down a low hall, and I slumped my head into my shoulders and put my arms behind my back. The two guards hissed, "Faster!"

After turning a corner, we went to the end of the hall where guards ordered me to stop before a heavy, iron door, and I entered the cell of condemned prisoners. Unlike the cell in *Serpatinka*, there were two-layers of plank beds, lights, and steam-heat. *How lucky I am! This place is warm. What's next?* And I fell asleep.

When I awoke, I saw a tall, bald, old man with a blanket covering his head. He poked his head out, glanced at me, and asked, in a low voice, "Where are you from, friend?"

"From *Serpatinka*," I replied.

The old man waved his hand at that. "I'm from another camp, but I was a professor of mathematics before my arrest and exile. Maybe the guards won't shoot us."

I was sleepy, but the professor kept talking in whispers. "Where did you live before?"

"Leningrad. I was born in Saratov."

"Since 1937 all roads lead to Kolyma. How parallel our paths!"

He started bustling about and climbed to the second tier of planks to rummage in a small bag. When he climbed down, he sat next to me and gave me a crust of bread and block of sugar. I ate the bread and sucked on the sugar, but I couldn't taste if it were sweet, sour, or salty. As it dissolved, I took it out several times and placed it under my tongue to distinguish its flavor.

Suddenly, the professor slapped his forehead, reached in his small clothing knot, and produced a red-colored pack of Saratov *makhorka*. "My dear fellow-townsman forgive me. I'm forgetful. Please take a cigarette!"

I looked at the old man with reverence and took the extended *makhorka*. After six years in Kolyma, tears clouded my eyes, unable to respond to his kindness.

He told me how he had induced the jail's administration to buy sugar and *makhorka* for our cell. "At first, they resisted, but then agreed to buy *makhorka* for each condemned prisoner. Unlike others, old men got two packs. That's yours, my last pack!"

My weak hands held this piece of my Volga River hometown, and beautiful Saratov stuck in my mind surrounded by mountains on three sides: the Sokolov Mountains, the Altynnaia Mountains, and the Bold Mountains with the Volga River flowing through them.

The red-colored pack of *makhorka* also brought back memories of student days, dates with Nina, and games on Bold Mountain. I shared with the old man how we, as kids, formed two groups, Whites and Reds. Whites attacked us Reds. We hid on the edge of the woods, in the front of Kumysnaia Glade. We loved games and relished attacking Cossacks, and yelled, "We will slay you Whites; we Reds are stronger than you, and there's no escaping our guns!"

The old man smiled with comprehension.

I continued. "Our hearts never wanted to submit to our enemies. But now," I began, "what's happened to us here? Who are our guards and investigators? Why did they arrest and exile us to Magadan? Is this what our fathers fought for in the Civil War?" With that, I pulled a cigarette from the pack and smoked. After a few inhales, I closed my eyes and slept.

When I opened them, I realized I'd had a tobacco hangover. My neighbors said I'd slept 24 hours. The strong tobacco had sickened me. The next week I slept nonstop while the professor still talked. One day, he exclaimed, "Maybe we'll return to Leningrad, and I'll see you. Wouldn't that be a miracle?"

"Yes," I agreed. "There all kinds of things could happen to us."

Thirty-Five

Brevda's Story

Vaskov's House
Saturday, January 2, 1943

A slight, near-sighted man climbed down from the second-tier bunk and said, "Bolotov, I recognized you when you entered the cell, but I was too weak to climb down."

Astonished, I exclaimed, "Doctor Brevda, you're still alive!"

Like me, the doctor, also arrested in June 1937 and then exiled to Kolyma's Valley of Death. It had seemed strange that Brevda had disappeared like so many Leningradians, banished to this eternal permafrost, "the homes of Communists." I hadn't seen him in five years, yet here he was: ALIVE!

I stood on my frost-bitten feet and gave him a bear hug. "Man meets the mountain here! I see you're sitting on the edge of death, my old friend."

"A company in distress makes me less trouble," he replied. "You, Petrovich, are 15 years younger than I am. You must survive to tell the world the truth!"

"Maybe we'll both survive," I countered. "There's so few of Leningradians left."

"Petrovich, I've survived, but so many young died. And for what? Nothing! Now, I'm creeping to the slaughterhouse."

"Tell me, how did this happen to you?" I'd never heard his story.

"My medical occupation saved me. Remember how we loved Leningrad's white nights and how we came to hate the same white nights in Kolyma?"

"Yes, I certainly do," I replied.

"During 1938 and 1939, we both labored in the gold mines, pushing wheelbarrows. I'm thankful to you because you always fixed my wheelbarrow when its handle broke. One day I was so weak and laid on my belly, criminals beat me mercilessly. I remember how you tried to help me, but I kept falling as my legs couldn't hold me. Finally, I decided to let criminals kill me since death would come to us all. I bid farewell to this earth and sky.

"But then, suddenly, guards came running to the goldmine. One took my hand and pulled me up, but I still couldn't walk. I took two steps and fell. *Will he shoot me?* Several times, a guard lifted me up when I closed my eyes, needing sleep. Petrovich, you know guards are gods in camp. They could do with you whatever they wanted. Finally, one grew tired of helping me, and yelled, "Aren't you a medical doctor?"

"Yes," I said, "I was a medical doctor before Kolyma."

"Well, we need your help, a woman is dying."

"I felt a burst of energy and started walking. It felt like I could run, but I was only dragging my feet. Soon, we met the manager's coachman; the guard and I climbed on his wagon, and I immediately fell asleep. The next thing I remember, we arrived at a small clinic. The coachman and guard pulled me off. One called me a fascist; the other yelled, 'real medical doctors die in goldmines like Soviet heroes. Only good-for-nothing people are in the barracks where no one works.' Slowly, they calmed and gave me tea. I warmed up and recovered."

"Then, suddenly, someone said, 'Please help me, doctor, my wife is dying.'

"Strength welled up inside me. I thought my wife could be dying as well, for how many innocents have died in the goldmines? Maybe my children are starving. Who will help them? I thought about my occupation and let the authorities know. Maybe this woman was arrested like a wife of an enemy of the people and now is dying in the mines.

"I slipped on a white surgical coat, and with my dirty face—I hadn't washed in two months—I entered a ward where a woman lay in bed. Her face was pale, her eyes wet, and she writhed from pain. She said, 'Doctor, help me.'

"I examined her and ordered her placed on a surgical table. I drank another glass of hot tea, and, for the first time since arriving in Kolyma, I washed my hands. See, Petrovich, we enemies of the people are like lepers. Criminals and guards don't want to have any dealings with us. They often bolt from us, but we're the majority here. Soon after this, I became a medical attendant in the clinic, for I'd saved the manager's wife.

"Also, another case helped me avoid mine labor when another manager and his family arrived in the area. A truck struck their five-year-old son. Young doctors brought him to surgery with his slashed stomach and entangled guts. The boy could have died. His mother dashed about us. His father said, 'If you kill my boy, you'll all work in the mines.'

"I'd heard his words and asked his permission to examine the boy.

Thirty-Five. Brevda's Story

The inexperienced doctors grew nervous because they did not know how to stop the internal bleeding. I knew they would kill the boy. The manager, 'Who are you? What was your article?' And I replied, 'I'm Brevda from Leningrad, a surgeon, and received Article Fifty-Eight.'

"'Fifty-Eight, fine; now save Vladimir's life!' Then he took me by my dirty uniform and hoisted me up in his strong arms and prayed.

"I pulled on a surgical coat, mask, and gloves and lifted my face to the sky; I imagined that I was in Leningrad with my graduate students in a surgical room covered with the bright lights. I forgot I was a Kolyma slave and said to the other doctors; you're my assistants. Follow my instructions. Don't breathe heavily through your noses. You will contaminate the boy.

"We worked in silence. The surgery went well. In a week, the Kolyma authorities called me to Magadan and allowed me to work in the clinic. That is my story.

"Petrovich, you're young, and I'm a professor. We'll both die, but you'll survive. Please tell our stories to Leningradians, let them know of our humiliations and how much Russia paid for its Communism."

Then Brevda asked me to tell him my story, and I did as other prisoners gathered around us. When I ended, guards brought us lunch: porridge in one bowl to share, warm water in one tin can, and one tiny piece of bread. After lunch, we smoked.

"Petrovich, how many survived from Leningrad?" Brevda asked.

"Ten in a hundred," I replied, closing my eyes to avoid seeing my decrepit friends.

Thirty-Six

My Last Judgment

Vaskov's House
Sunday, January 3–Friday, March 12, 1943

For two months in jail, my frostbitten feet ached terribly. The skin around my toenails had turned black. One day, when a guard entered the cell; I asked his permission to see a nurse.

My request angered him. "Condemned prisoners aren't permitted to see nurses."

I protested and, finally, another guard allowed me to ask for help. "So, what's happened to your feet?" a guy in a white surgeon-coat asked me rudely.

"My feet are frostbitten. I needed them looked at."

"But you're condemned. If the Moscow authorities cancel your execution and give you another sentence, then see me."

After this exchange, a nurse chitchatted with a guard. Both giggled. I hobbled back to the cell and laid on the plank. Since *Serpatinka*, I hadn't changed my uniform, and, with poor food, my face had turned whiskerless. Often, my thoughts turned to my mother, *Dear Mom, I'm at my Last Judgement Day and often think of you. You suffered raising us during Nicholas II's reign. We grew up in a new Russia built on socialism. But look at your children. Their lives turned out otherwise. Your son is working in labor camps, and you're raising my orphans. How is your sick heart? Are your tender hands still stroking my children? Where is the happiness Lenin promised us? I'm awaiting death bravely; should I sleep on a plank until being killed.*

Soon the investigator from Khabarovsk came to my mind. In Vladivostok, he'd said investigators always arrest criminals because they had proofs of criminal acts; but they create fake dossiers for political prisoners.

Drowsiness scrambled my thoughts, but *cogito, ergo sum* prevailed. I knew I was thinking and would see the end of this prison as this was my sixth year. Sometimes I worried my time was running out, but I found comfort knowing I'd completed my duties honestly.

One March morning, I received a small portion of breakfast. Lunch was far off, but a guard opened the door, looked around slowly and ordered, "Bolotov, follow me!"

At first, I remained on my plank unmoving and stared at the big man.

He yelled, "Bolotov, are you dead or alive?"

With care, I stepped down on my sore feet. We left the cell. I hobbled down a long corridor for six or seven minutes before entering the warden's large office. He sat at a wide writing table with layers of belly-fat heaped on the table. His eyes, like buttons on a big, round globe, stared at me. His white, well-cared-for hands held a paper. He studied it. He put on airs, ignoring me. Then he stood and stepped to an armchair, turned, and looked at me. He flapped a paper. "The case of Bolotov Leonid Petrovich, arrested on June 17, 1937, and convicted of Article Fifty-Eight, paragraphs seven, eight, and 11, was brought before the Military Board of the Supreme Court of the USSR and decreed to abolish his execution to be replaced by 10 years of imprisonment in the labor-corrective camps. This decision has come forthwith."

I barely heard him, still debating about this repulsive man. His bottom lip hung loosely from his disgusting face. "Bolotov, do you understand; the government has set aside your execution and given you the right to live? Bolotov, you'll live!" he yelled.

Neither my execution nor the new sentence told me anything. The head of the prison stroked his belly and kept on talking. In front of him, I stood barefoot with black toes and filthy long johns in rags, my long-sleeved undershirt rotten. I don't know why, but I was embarrassed about my boney knees bulging out of the rags. The warden's bulk swung in the armchair. He asked me about arrests in 1937 and 1942, and I could only stand there in silence like a soldier. From somewhere strength arose within me, and I replied, "I've always supported Soviet power and honestly completed all my duties."

The warden hated my responses. His round face wrinkled; his lower lip drooped down. "I need your signature," he said with irritation and handed me a paper. I took the offered pen and signed the strange paper, astonished by my handwriting that looked like hen scratches. I'd forgotten how to write my own name! Thoughts flew through me. *Maybe I'd not worked for the six years you harassed me in Kolyma for nothing. Maybe I'll get to see the nurse about my feet.*

In a few minutes, two guards took me by the elbows, led me out of the office, and gave me new clothes. When I put them on, I looked like I had in 1938. They issued galoshes, ripped and too large, and walked me into the snowy yard. The bright March sun dazzled. I was drunk on fresh air. Nature returned hope, and I uttered a deep sigh and tromped around. I slipped and fell and stretched out in the snow.

"What're you doing?" one yelled, and I chimed, "Let's raze this jail for a church."[1]

The next morning, guards allowed me to see the nurse. After two weeks in the clinic, I was ordered to work at the transit camp, near Vaskov's House, two-hours walk from the jail.

---

1. The quote is from *March of the Red Army*. U. M. Sokolov, ed. *Krasnoarmeiskii fol'klor* (Moskva: Izdatel'stvo Sovetskii pisatel', 1938), 121–122.

Thirty-Seven

The Finnish Shingles

The Transit Camp
Monday, March 15–Friday, March 31, 1944

When we arrived at the transit camp, a guard completed my paperwork and handed me over to the administration. The new head of that camp showed me a barracks for 200 men. Since work had long started, I took an unoccupied plank, stretched out, and closed my eyes. The next day, I was unable to rise as my body ached so badly.

Despite my ailment, guards ordered me to shovel the local road with other prisoners. I was breathless and in pain most of the 12 hours and often leaned on my shovel. Ten days later, I was sent to work at The Finnish Shingles, a tool used to cut roof shingles. Here, the administration fed prisoners well in preparation for our work in the mines.

One man, Osipov, about 40, was our manager. He was thickset, wide-shouldered, and cruel with a weather-beaten, Mongolian-looking face. His assistant was a former prisoner.

The next morning was frosty as we left for tree-falling in the tai`ga. We split into pairs: one man issued a saw, the other an ax. The blacksmith gave us a thick, short saw with widely-spaced teeth—I called it my toothless saw. When the sun appeared, my partner and I picked a tree, and soon, axes whacked, saws screeched, and high larches crashed. Falling trees snagged standing trees, breaking their branches with muffled cracks and crashed into the snow in the virgin taiga, sounds of civilization in Kolyma, a symphony to my soul.

The team-leader interrupted my reverie. "You and your helper must produce four cubic meters of wood a day.... EACH! Now, trample snow around that larch, cut off its branches, cut the tree into six-foot lengths, and stack it! Then burn the branches and stumps."

Unfortunately, my helper was an angry man. Before the tree-falling, he'd spent two weeks in isolation. After a talk with him, I realized that he'd been a thief. I started thinking: *Thieves ignore all the jail policies. Should I tell him about my Kolyma jails because all those survivors became heroes in the criminal world?*

I started talking, "Well, dear bones, it's time to stretch you out and relax; you've spent too much time in *Serpatinka* and Vaskov's House." I hadn't finished my lament when my helper stopped and stared at me.

He asked, "Were you really in Vaskov's House?"

"Yes. I was ordered shot." I said and looked up at a lofty larch tree. We must fall it, and then I'll be able to start my new life again. "Let's work or we'll die in this wasteland."

"Do you want to chop or saw?" he asked.

"Both. Chop a notch to direct the fall and then we'll saw on the other side; it works."

I didn't expect much from him. We stamped waist-deep snow around the tree. Then we notched one side, knelt behind the notch, and sawed. We dragged the dull blade back and forth for two, long hours, but we didn't topple the tree.

Others bawled at us. "Come on!"

We tried our best. Around us, men fell trees and chopped their branches. Our larch was full of a yellow, sticky resin that gummed up the saw. Then the wind blew, and the larch tilted, binding the saw. We needed to tilt it back, yank out the saw, and clean pitch from its blade.

The team-leader and workers gathered around us, laughing and making crude jokes. "Get your saw out or I won't feed you!"

My helper said, "I'm a criminal, and we don't work!"

"I'll break your neck if you don't," the team-leader threatened.

Their squabbling bothered me. I asked, "Comrade, how can we get the saw to work better?"

"Grab that thick branch; we'll push from the opposite side and get the tree off your saw."

We did. "Watch out! It's falling!" The larch swayed, cracked, and fell.

My helper became kinder. The team-leader started explaining the steps needed to chop, notch, and fell trees to control them. After a break, I crawled up the larch and cut off its branches. My helper sat in the snow. I soon saw that our cutting had turned forest into a glade stacked with wood. The other workers sat by small fires and burned branches. Only our larch was uncut. In the shining last rays, the sun slid behind the knoll, the day grew cold, and I dragged branches into a pile.

The team-leader yelled at us, "I won't give you bread unless your quota is filled!"

Other fires burned down. It got dark and sinister. Soon the team-leader and guards took the men to camp, but my workmate and I were left with

Thirty-Seven. The Finnish Shingles

larch to cut up. Besides us, two other workers chopped trees. My helper and I sat on the larch and started to fall asleep in the dark and quiet taiga as the cold turned ruthless.

One of the guards offered us to join him at the fire. We added to a small fire and soon went to sleep. In an hour, the guard woke us, kicked snow on the fire, and ordered us to camp.

Next morning, guards brought us to the same glade. My helper grew weaker as we walked; he couldn't hold the saw, and I dragged it. He was supposed to push as I pulled. And we still hadn't cut the branches off our larch.

The team-leader grumbled, "Who sent you here? I'll freeze you to death."

At the end of the day, prisoners again left us in the taiga. The guards had grown tired of us and asked, "Why don't you two work harder?"

I told them that prisoners need more food and rest. Then I asked about the German invasion and why the Red Army failed to protect the country. Guards explained the government did not have enough guns, tanks, and planes, and that German planes covered Ukraine, Moscow, and Leningrad like clouds of mosquitos. After being wounded near Moscow, the *osobists* sent them here.[1]

Within five or six hours, they told me many war stories. While they talked, my helper dropped into the snow and died. Someone dragged off his corpse. When I got to my barracks, I flopped onto my plank, and fell asleep thinking of war and my helper's death.

On the third day, reveille was sounded, as usual, and a man on duty started shouting as they had in 1938, "Get up!"

The men rose quickly; they wanted to pick the best tools: crowbars, axes, and saws. Some of us were pushed aside with fists and elbows. I was the last man in line.

"Give me saw number 32," I said to my team-leader, Anton.

"No, Bolotov. You've been ordered to use saw number 10. You're like it a lot." Anton gave it to me. It had thin, sharp, steel teeth that rang when I flapped it. Smiling, Anton said, "This is the best bread-winner and will help you complete your quota today."

Men surrounding me grumble. "Look, a *dohodiaga* got the best saw."

I pressed my breadwinner to my body. The taiga rang with cutting saw as we approached the glade. One healthy looking guy, carrying a Ca-

---

1. *Osobist* means a member of the NKVD branch of political trustworthiness. Artemiev, V.P. "OKR: State Security in the Soviet Armed Forces." *Military Review*, vol. 43 (1963): 21–31.

nadian ax, and said, "Bolotov, I'll work with you. My name's Demon; I'm from Siberia."

Demon, 10 years older than me, commanded a division under Muralov and had a picture taken with Trotskii before his exile and arrest.[2]

Together we got to the glade where he selected a tree and adroitly notched it. When we started to saw. Demon said, "You push; I'll pull. You'll become strong and healthy again."

Demon and I completed all our work over the next days, and we carried heavy logs to the stack. He always took the heavy ends. I was ashamed. Demon said, "Your time will come to carry the heavy ends." In a month, we doubled our quotas.

Spring came. Snow drifts melted, and we discarded our heavy, winter clothes. Larches and willows budded. Frequently, a special committee visited us and selected the healthiest men for mine work. After tests, doctors sent Demon to gold mine 40 miles from Magadan. They reassigned me to a glass factory. I knew nothing about making glass, other than it came from quartz, or silica sand, lime, and sodium carbonate heated to a high temperature.

A taiga truck (Dal'stroi Territories Photo Album of 1942–1943, of Inner Affairs, State Archive, Russian Federation, Moscow).

---

2. Muralov, Nikolai Ivanovich (1877–1937), a Red Army Commander and prominent Trotskyist. Wieszynski, *The Modern Encyclopedia of Russian and Soviet History*, vol. 23 (1981), 189–191.

Thirty-Eight

Glass Factory

Seventy-Two Kilometer
Monday, April 3, 1944–Friday, November 29, 1946

The glass factory was one of the main industrial plants in Magadan Province. Since its manufacture of glass required a long, flat area to cool, planners located its lengthy building alongside the Magadan-Tayga Highway[1] in a lush, sprawling, mountain-hollow protected from harsh winds and numbing temperatures that plummeted to -13°. The *Krasavitsa River* flowed through the valley, and the glass factory's opportune location gave birth, in 1941, to the bustling town of Stekol'nii on the banks of its two intersecting rivers.

We arrived in the back of a *ZIS-5* truck,[2] which reminded me of an American truck. The tarpaulin of two huge tents flapped in the summer breeze; prisoners' homes, and, further off, three log cabins rose in a grassy meadow, managers' homes. Tractors pulled vehicles through the mud. The head of camp, Seventy-Two Kilometer—its distance from Magadan—Petr Ivanovich Zheerov,[3] ordered us to the second tent to await lunch.

I went into the tent and flopped onto a middle plank. At 1:45, without yelling, banging rims, or striking men with rifle butts, guards awoke us. I hustled down to the river to wash my face, surprised to hear the flutter of bathing birds. But I was astonished to see not birds but a huge school of black-spotted, blue and turquoise hunchback salmon feeding. There were so many I could have scooped them up in bucketsful and drooled at the thought of eating one.

---

1. The distance between Magadan and Tayga is 2,312 miles. Translator's note.
2. Built under license to *Zavod Imeni Stalina*, or *ZIS*, the truck was produced from 1933 to 1941. Kochnev, E.D. *Avtomibili Velikoi Otechestvennoi* (Moskva: EKSMO, 2010).
3. His name is listed in documentation of glass factory employees between 1944 and 1946. The Khasyn Archive.

Back at the tent, guards ordered us to form a column and marched us to the dining room. I'd never seen such an orderly, clean area in my seven years of Gulag meals! We each relished a pound of bread, a piece of salmon, and hot tea! *With salmon meals, I'll get fit fast.*

After lunch, we marched to the factory where a glass blower, Iakov Iakovlevich Babeikin, gave us an overview of the glassmaking process: silica-sand mixed with soda ash (sodium carbonate) and limestone (calcium carbonate), melted to 3,092° and then the substance poured into sheets.[4]

Babeikin took us into the workshop, a large, wide, wooden building with ventilators in its metal roof near a pair of tall chimneys. A boiler house stood to the left side; a mechanical shop rose on the right. Outside, I noticed a horse barn. After our tour, an administrator explained that we would be allowed inside the factory to work once the administration had issued our identification papers. Excited about an inside a warm job, we returned to our tent. That evening, we introduced ourselves and listened to men who had worked in the factory for a month tell us of their experiences. We were astonished to hear that trucks brought disabled prisoners

---

4. Babeikin, Iakov Iakovlevich, was born in the town of Elensk, Khvastovich District, Kaluga Province, into a glass worker's family. His name is listed in employees of the glass factory during 1944–1948. The Khasyn Archive.

Glass factory (Dal'stroi Territories Photo Album of 1942–1943, Ministry of Inner Affairs, State Archive, Russian Federation, Moscow).

from mines here; they were fed better, regained their strength, and started jobs in the factory.

I knew that the glass factory work would be difficult, but I'd survived the mine, and, with my engineering qualifications, I knew I'd earn respect for my professional abilities.

That evening, the glass veteran Nikolai Nosov told me that prisoners had constructed a bridge over the *Krasavitsa River*, which flowed through the center of the town, linking the growing town's two sides. He, sentenced to 20 years, told us the legend of the river's name.[5]

"When geologists arrived here," he said, "a hardy woman named *Krasavitsa* befriended them. In her honor, geologists named the river after her, immortalized it on Soviet maps."[6]

In spring, the *Krasavitsa* always overflowed its banks, and after its waters receded, there was a profusion of salmon in the small lakes, easily hooked. The factory had a job called Fisherman for Sea Animals. The man assigned this position was Grigorii Cherepanov.[7]

On the shore of the Khasyn River sat the charming house of Ivan Fedorovich Nikishov, the Administrative Chief of Far North Development.[8] I often admired his home and still remember its honeysuckle and large berries that turned navy blue in August, setting among the wild, red roses coloring the hollow and glades peppered with cowberries and pine trees with cones loaded with pine nuts. His house inspired me to plan a cottage of my own.

Late in August 1944, I was assigned the position of glass factory worker. One day, Babeikin called me to his office. "Leonid, we must fulfill our annual objective. I've many engineers, three chemical industry workers, two mechanics, and two electricians, but I've no one to be our heating engineer, a critical and difficult job. Will you accept it?"

Honored, I assured him, "I will, Iakov Iakovlevich, gladly."

Babeikin then relayed how he considered my new position vital and how one NKVD officer had doubted my honesty as they still regarded me as an enemy of the people, but he'd said he had objected to his doubt and felt that I was honest and smart. Babeikin added if the administration didn't

---

5. Nosov, Nikolai Mikhailovich, began working at the glass factory in 1942. Shalimov, Yu. B. *Legendy i byl' kolymskogo stekla* (Magadan: Oblastnoe gazetnoe izdatel'stvo, 1992), 15–17.

6. The literary translation of *Krasavitsa River*, Beautiful River; its length is 12 miles. Translator's note.

7. Cherepanov, Grigorii Petrovich, is listed in documentation of glass factory employees between 1947 and 1948. The Khasyn Archive.

8. Nikishov, Ivan Fedorovich (1894–1958), concentrated his enormous power in Kolyma; he died in Moscow, having achieved the rank of Lieutenant general. Batsaev and Kozlov, *Dalstroy Trust Sevvostlag OGPU-NKVD of the USSR as Presented by Documents and in Numbers (2 parts). Part 1 (1931–1941)*, p. 1, 360.

approve my work I'd be sent back to cut trees. He explained my duties, concluding with, "I know I've made the right decision. But Leonid, I also hired you because you've been working from 8 a.m. to midnight, is that right?"

"Yes, but when I train new pyrometer technicians, things will be easier for all of us."

"I'm sure they will be. I want to combine you into two positions: as our engineer of heating and shift-head, working four p.m. until midnight."

His words were a vote of confidence and I agreed.

Iakov Iakovlevich looked at me and cautioned, "Now, Leonid, these are temporary positions. I'll try to replace you in one of the jobs as soon as I am able. I'm always at the factory until 8 p.m. Now, you'll replace me from 8 until midnight."

"Iakov Iakovlevich but I don't know glass production well, despite spending hours in the laboratory trying to master the process."

"I know your concerns, but there's no other way out. As for glass production, it's not hard to master the concept. All our workers are Kolyma locals. I heard you've been reading Kitaygorodskii's works on glass technology."[9]

Babeikin introduced me to Vasilii Nikolaevich Sokoulin, master of factory production, and Ivan Petrovich Logunov, main engineer; he had received a 15-year sentence. I befriended Sergei Petrovich Vasil'ev, head of the chemical laboratory, Iosif Ignatievich Polevoi,[10] and Frido Seydewitz, who cut cold glass with a glazier's diamond.[11]

General Nikishov visited the glass factory to check our work and suggest new ideas. During World War II, no one supplied high-voltage insulators to the mainland. Our engineers welcomed the challenge and were the first to produce them from locally mined minerals. Several times they tried to cast insulators from basalt, but they came to nothing

---

9. Kitaygorodskii, Isaak Il'ich (1888–1965), invented types of citall glass and published the book *Teoriia stekloobrazovaniia i metody varki stekla* (Moskva–Leningrad: Geezlegprom, 1935).

10. Sokoulin, Vasilii Nikolaevich, is listed in documentation of glass factory employees between 1944 and 1945. The Khasyn Archive. Logunov, Ivan Petrovich, and Vasil'ev, Sergei Petrovich. Shalimov, *Legendy i byl' kolymskogo stekla*, 16–17. Polevoi, Iosif Ignatievich (1886–1959), was condemned to death June 14, 1938, but the Supreme Court of RSFSR modified his sentence with twenty years confinement September 14, 1938. Orlov, V.P., et al. *Repressirovannye geologi* (Moskva–Sankt-Peterburg: VSEGEI, 1999), 248.

11. Seydewitz, Fridolin (1919–2016), visited Lake Seliger in Tver Province, was arrested in Moscow on March 8–9, 1938, and taken to Lubyanka. In Kolyma, Fridolin labored in the gold mines, was sickened, and deported to the invalid camp "Kilometer 23." After the beginning of World War II, Fridolin worked blowing glass until the end of 1947. In 1948, he was permitted to travel to Germany after much effort by his father, Max, prime minister in the Land of Saxony. Dehl, O. *Verratene Ideale. Zur Geschichte deutscher Emigranten in der Sowjetunion in den 30er Jahren* (Berlin: Trafo-Verlag Dr. Wolfgang Weist, 2000), 25, 208–217.

as high-voltage glass insulators must be able to withstand 35,000 volts, a goal not achieved before the war. Our chemists developed a process for making them from volcanic ash. Soon, our engineers attempted to produce them. It was hard to calculate the correct ceramic composition for firing as the weight of one insulator was 10 pounds and the thickness of its walls varied from one to five inches. These size variations complicated ceramic firing, but soon solved the blending problem by instructing the pyrometer technicians in new ways. The fusing of each set of 200 insulators required 64-hours in the kiln, including adequate slow-cooling time. They provided reliable transmission of power over the long distances between mines and towns.[12] Fulfilling this goal was a great victory, and it demonstrated that enemies of the people had achieved great success.

Sadly, this ended all too soon, when, one day, General Nikishov arrived at the factory to check our work. It had only been 40 hours since we'd loaded the kilns; the insulators required firing for 24-hours longer. But the general barked out orders, "Open the kilns!"

Glass factory ovens (Dal'stroi Territories Photo Album of 1942–1943, Ministry of Inner Affairs, State Archive, Russian Federation, Moscow).

---

12. At the end of 1945, it produced 4,000 insulators used for transmission lines from Elgen to the Lazo mines, a distance of 33 miles. Shalimov, *Legendy i byl' kolymskogo stekla*, 28–40.

We could do nothing else and called our stove man, Fedor Alekseevich Sidorov.[13]

Following Nikishov's orders, Fedor opened the kiln and removed the first row of bricks. The insulators, lacking sufficient time for cooling, started cracking in the cold air.

"Let me see an insulator!" Nikishov demanded.

Fedor removed an insulator with a hook, and he held it out. It exploded!

"I see you've been working," Nikishov said carelessly as he knew we had produced the first insulators.

---

13. Sidorov, Fedor Alekseevich, is listed in the glass factory employees for 1948. The Khasyn Archive.

Thirty-Nine

Young Thieves

Glass Factory
Monday, December 2, 1946 –
Monday, December 30, 1946

During the winter of 1946, fresh convicts told us that World War II was rapidly concluding. The Red Army had won decisive battles on the Eastern Front and recaptured Poland and the Baltic countries. The Nazi fled. We waited impatiently, basking in victor's glory and anticipating release from the Gulag. What a dream!

Fathers of our country had decreed the 1932 law, *plundering Socialist State Property*, which kept the Gulags full. According to this decree, all Soviet citizens, regardless of age or sex, were punished and given sentences of five to 10 years for stealing anything.[1]

I was astonished to meet an attractive young woman convicted of stealing two thin French rolls at the bakery where she worked to feed her starving children, sentenced to eight years. *What kind of socialism had we built? Why did we hate capitalism so when a young mother, like Fantina in Les Misérables, could not feed her babies? Had Soviet society not advanced in the eight decades since Hugo? The truth was: the country could not feed itself.*

As the weeks passed, I came to know more arrivals; many were 17- and 18-year-olds sentenced for stealing as little as an oil cake or raw sunflower seeds. At the end of September, more teenagers, mostly orphans,

---

1. The state law, "Plundering Socialist State Property," was dated August 7, 1932. Soviets called it the law of three spikelets, or seven-eights for the month and date, as people were arrested for stealing grain from collective farm fields. On June 4, 1947, it was replaced with a new law, "About Criminal Liability for Theft of State and Public Property." Davies, R.V. et al. *The Stalin-Kaganovich Correspondence 1931–36*. Russian documents trans. Steven Shabad (New Haven: Yale University Press, 2003), 168–170.

arrived at the factory.² Losing both parents during the war had left their lives shattered and them hungry. None had experienced personal warmth and kindness, and the least expressions of thoughtfulness, care, and compassion resulted in their surprised loving thanks. Girls were more responsible than boys, though they often acted as wild as caged animals. I soon started writing petitions to the administration on their behalf, pleading for them not to be sent to the taiga.

Sadly, there was a top thief among the youth who the boys and girls greatly respected. On the first day of their arrival, some kids, under his direction, stole the crimped, silk, Chinese, crêpe curtain from four windows in the director's office. I asked around and found the leader of the gang, spoke with him, and told him about the feared taiga. I asked him to return the curtains, and he vowed he would. The next day, some boys returned the curtains. When I examined them, I discovered 30-feet of fabric had been sliced off. The thieves had cut off the ends of the curtains to make blouses for the girls.

Another winter day, the boys were at it again. This time, when General Nikishov drove to the factory for a directors' meeting, he and his driver left the car unlocked near the office. The daredevils watched the general get out of the car, take off his coat, and toss it in the car before entering. The young crooks snatched the general's coat.

Two hours later, General Nikishov returned to the car, opened the door, and reached for his coat. I was in a group of engineers, and we watched his face turned as dark as a summer rain cloud. He screamed, "Who stole my coat? Someone tell me, where is it?"

The factory director and all of us engineers wheeled around and ran on a search mission. I peeked around a corner and watched the driver look under the car. Then he beelined into the director's office and returned empty-handed.

"There's no trace of your coat," he said sheepishly.

The factory director took me aside and asked me to speak to the young thieves. I found the top thief and warned him, "Return the general's coat, or he'll send you all to the taiga."

The pack leader's eyes widened. "I don't want to be sent there to die."

I nodded at his followers. They hadn't heard about the taiga, and he explained it was a death trap. "I'll return the general's coat if the boys haven't already made mittens from it. Vasia!" he yelled. A skinny little 12-year-old appeared. "Get the general's coat, right *now*!"

---

2. In 1949, 365 teenagers, in one Magadan camp, worked six hours a day and fulfilled 75 percent of an adult's norm. Batsaev, I.D. "Kolymskaia griada arhipelaga Gulaga (zakluchennye)." *Istoricheskiie aspekty Severo-Vostoka Rossii: ekonomika, obrazovaniie, kolymskii Gulag* (Magadan: SVKNII DVO RAN, 1996), 57.

Thirty-Nine. Young Thieves

Vasia, the thin, frail kid, scampered off.

"Leonid, he's the same kid who stole the curtains," the pack leader said. "Now, if we return the general's coat, we won't be sent to the taiga, right?"

"Of course not. No chance," I replied, praying that wasn't a lie.

"Leonid, is it the truth? A thief's honest word?"

"I'm not lying to you, but I can't give you an honest thief's word."

He looked at me seriously. "You can't because you're not one of us, a wise guy. Mezgleek helped steal the coat. I told him he couldn't steal from the bosses, but he didn't listen."

"Tell them never to steal stuff from the administration. It's okay to steal from other prisoners while in training: *But no stealing from the bosses*! Where's the coat?"

The pack leader asked me to follow him. I placed an arm around his shoulder. He shook off my arm. One doesn't hug a gang hero's shoulder. The hero continued toward the director's office and stopped at the accountant's office beside it. We entered and continued through the outer office, lined with clerks bent over ledgers. In the inner office, there was a closet on one side. He opened its door, knelt, and dug behind a pile of files and pulled out the general's coat.

The accounting clerks gasped. They couldn't believe a thief had stolen the general's coat and hidden it in their inner office.

I asked the gang leader, "But when did Vasia have time to steal it and hide it here?"

"The accountant left the office for a minute, and I snuck it in," little Vasia confessed.

"I left for a minute," the accountant admitted. "But you couldn't have come through the outer office; someone would have seen you. And there is only one tiny window here."

The skinny young thief remained silent. We asked the boy, "What's your name boy?"

"My first name is Small Child," the boy replied. "My second name is Old Man. Will you send me to the taiga?"

I never heard about him again. As weeks passed, the glass master taught young thieves at the factory to become glass production workers, which made me proud.

Forty

Katia Maksakov's Story

Generator Station
Monday, January 6, 1947–Friday, February 28, 1947

Life at the glass factory was always interesting as challenges with the supplies of minerals, heating gas, people, and wood arose daily. I feel the destinies of some people deserve detailed description, and I'll relate a few stories still lingering in my memory.

One story happened two years after the war ended. Prisoner Lev Rybas worked with me three years of his 10-year term. A tall, wide-shouldered, impressively large man, Lev came from Belorussia. With his beak-like nose, which looked like a sweaty half-moon all the time, he wore short pants and a short-sleeved military shirt. He was a painstakingly watchful and disciplined worker, but he was slow and lacked initiative.

After two years, one day, a pretty girl named Katia caught Lev's eye. Twenty years old, Katia had an interesting gait, walking like a peahen strutting; her face was oval, her eyes green, and I got along well with her. Katia had told me her parents died in the war, and she received her sentence for hiding her brother, an army deserter.

Both Lev and Katia mastered pyrometry, the vital measuring of temperatures during glass production. They became friends, thick as thieves, and often stayed after work. If either of them started work before noon, the other appeared at the factory early too and vice versa. Though they usually worked from 8 p.m. until midnight, they often could be found in the shower, which worked 24 hours, washing their clothes. Gulag-prepared lunches arrived at the factory daily, and Lev and Katia often ate from the same dish.

Everything was fine until misfortune struck. The glass factory received orders to join the Magadan effort of producing more gold at the Golden Key Mine. Mining prisoners had not panned enough gold. Thus, the administration ordered a dozen glass factory workers to join the gold

Forty. Katia Maksakov's Story

effort for several months. Lev Rybas was among those men selected. He received training for panning and measuring of gold. His jobs were simple, but the gold mine was bitter cold and a wet, dirty place to work. Lev missed the warmth of the glass factory and Katia. His troubles started when he wrote a letter to her and sent it with a driver. Unfortunately, his mournful plea bemoaned his grueling. The head of the ideological affairs censored his letter and ordered Lev to remain on the wheelbarrow. He performed poorly. Lev wrote again how he could not understand how criminals, in these post-war days, had free reign over political prisoners. He wrote one day miners decided to take revenge on their night-shift team-leaders. A dozen political prisoners beat two team leaders almost to death and decided to burn them in a furnace. They dragged the team leaders to the furnace, but guards stumbled across them and sent the injured leaders to the hospital. The rebels were convicted and shot, and our glass factory workers returned to the factory. Sadly, for Lev, the head of the ideological affairs ordered him to continue working at the mine during that long winter. When Lev received his extended term, Katia grieved. Previously, she had snuck out of the women's tent to be with Lev. Now these meetings had ended. Katia, who cried easily, was moved to tears over his new sentence and dwelled on seeing him.

As winter set in, Aleksandra Romanovna[1] complained to Magadan authorities that they needed Lev Rybas and requested his return to his position at the glass factory. Aleksandra Romanovna sent petitions and finally convinced them Lev Rybas was a highly trained glass professional. Lev soon returned to the glass factory.

Elated, he told me he felt doubly blessed. He'd be with his beloved Katia again. But life had gone on. When Lev entered the factory, Katia did not meet him. Distraught, Lev ran to the bench, near the kiln, where Katia made jars. Seeing her, Lev smiled broadly, his eyes shining, his heart trembling at the thought of holding Katia again. But she didn't acknowledge him. He watched the girls working with Katia begin to whisper to her while looking strangely at him. One approached him and said, "Lev, Katia will soon marry Nikolai Kolychev, a guard."

Unlike Lev, Katia had been counting her dwindling days until being released, staying cheerful and happy. But her new boyfriend, Nikolai, often dropped by my office evenings, wanting to ask me questions about

---

1. Gridasova, Aleksandra Romanovna (1915–1982), arrived in Magadan aboard "Feliks Dzerzhinskii" and led several camps for prisoners that often played in her own theater. Later, she became Nikishov's wife who promoted her to glass factory supervisor. In 1948, she moved to Moscow where she died at 67. Batsaev and Kozlov, *Dalstroy Trust Sevvostlag OGPU-NKVD of the USSR as Presented by Documents and in Numbers (2 parts). Part 1 (1931–1941)*, p. 1, 351.

Katia. "Katia is a careful and modest girl," I said. "You shouldn't worry about marrying her. Lev is nothing to her."

That didn't seem to impress the guard, so I sat at my desk and he stood in front of it, and we talked on about Katia. The office had an unobstructed view of the workers in the workshop and Katia working at her bench. She undoubtedly realized that Nikolai and I were talking about her. When he left, satisfied, he offered me help in buying groceries in Magadan. At break time, Katia ran to my office, wanting to talk, but other workers surrounded me.

When the howl of the big exhaust fans began, indicating the end of the break, Katia stepped closer. I rose. "Katia, what do you want to talk about?"

"Leonid Petrovich, did Nikolai speak to you about me? Please tell me everything."

"Nikolai told me he loves you above all others and is waiting for your release."

"What did you tell him for so long?"

I smiled. "Katia, I told him to hurry and marry you as many men will be released soon."

Cheerful, Katia ran to the bench where her five co-workers waited to hear the news. Instead of gossiping, Katia picked up a pipe and started blowing the red-hot glass globs into water bottle shapes. Beyond her, I saw Lev had been spying on her, even from the roof, looking down from an open transom at her and Nikolai.

On the day before her release, Lev hid among the wood piles, waiting for Katia and Nikolai. Lev plotted his revenge. Close by, the first glass oven was roaring with blazing firewood and brewing its sand. The second, more powerful oven, was thundering and bellowing, fired by gas, not wood, piped in from a generator station located in another building. Fifteen feet above it, a bank of nozzles released gas from the melting sand, which quickly rose to 3,092°, capable of burning everything. From time to time, four glass masters, directing bottle-making where Katia worked, allowed people to come in and stand beside the oven to warm up.

Lev Rybas and Dmitrii Kuznetsov operated the second, powerful oven. Before I left the glass factory that evening, I asked Nikolai Vladimirovich Ivanychev, the chemist on duty, to advise the glass masters to monitor hourly the quality of the gas.[2] Also, I directed gas master Kuhorenko to careful watch the gas generator station's work. When the four

---

2. Ivanychev, Nikolai Vladimirovich, is listed in documentation of glass factory employees between 1947 and 1948. The Khasyn Archive.

Forty. Katia Maksakov's Story

glass masters went to the chemical laboratory to inquire about the gas pressure, Lev quietly snuck up on Katia.

He said, "I heard you'll be released tomorrow."

"That's right," Katia sang out joyfully.

"Going home?"

"Oh, no. Leonid Petrovich promised to increase my salary to 1,000 rubles a month."

"Guess you'll be a wealthy bride," Lev said sarcastically.

"Wealthy? I have nothing," Katia said quietly.

That pained Lev. "Perhaps, Katia," he said, "I'll show you where I work throwing two-meter-long wood into the oven."

Suspecting nothing, Katia agreed. They descended to the fire chambers beneath the melting sand.

"Watch this wood; it'll burn in seconds," Lev said insidiously.

They stared at the fire devouring the wood. Lev set an arm around Katia's shoulders and pulled her to him. He put his hand under her chin and lifted her face to his.

"Lev, what's happening to you?" she pleaded as he pulled her closer to the flames.

"What do you think?" Lev snapped. "How long will you last in those flames?"

"What do you need from me?!" Katia bawled. Lev shook his head and kept talking. "I'll not throw you into the flame right away. I'll fry you gradually. I'll let your boyfriend suffer with you."

"Lev, you're frightening me!"

He wrapped his arms around her and tightened his grip. His big hands grasped her throat. Just then, I returned to the factory. "Petrovich, help!" Katia pleaded.

I pulled Lev's arms off her and he fell onto the firewood and rolled into the hole. Katia dashed to the other side. Trying to get out of the hole, Lev caught Katia's right leg.

"You're a hateful creature!" Lev yelled and dragged Katia to the edge of the pit.

Katia fought him and screamed, "He's trying to kill me!"

With the glass masters in the laboratory, other workers charged Lev. I was responsible for the ovens, which must have a constant flow of gas. And the regulation of gas flow depended on the gas generator's station coordinating with the firewood in the furnace.

Katia made mournful pleas. Now, in the firelight, I saw Katia's struggling with Lev next to the mouth of the furnace. If I waited one second longer, the raging fire would consume her. Sometimes a second decides our fate. I leaped down. Shoved between Katia and Lev, rammed him

Glasses and bottled produced at the glass factory (Dal'stroi Territories Photo Album of 1942–1943, Ministry of Inner Affairs, State Archive, Russian Federation, Moscow).

aside, and felt flames on my leg as my trousers caught fire. "What're you doing, Lev?" I screamed.

Lev trembled. He seemed to want to say something but couldn't. Then Lev took a log and pushed it into the oven instead of Katia who had slumped against the log pile, moaning.

"Katia, don't cry," I said to her, and to Rybas, "Fill the oven to overflowing! Kuznetsov will help you."

Katia sobbed. We went to the chemical laboratory, found needles

Forty. Katia Maksakov's Story

and threads, and she mended her blouse. Abrasions covered her face. Ivanychev opened a drawer and gave her powder and lotion. I explained to him that Katia jumped into the wood hole and scratched her face. On the way to the workshop, we met Nikolai, guarding the glass factory. He looked at her, and I said she'd bruised herself while warming up. He quieted.

I went to see Lev. He told me he hadn't expected Katia to leave him and it made him angry. "Leonid Petrovich," he begged, "forgive me. I'll work as hard as an ox for you."

"Lev, I never thought that a wild beast lives inside you. Katia needs our help."

"Nothing will happen to her."

Next morning dawned sunny and frosty. I had a cold shower, boiled water for my tea and ate a piece of salty salmon before running to the factory.

Katia never spoke of the incident before marrying Nikolai.

Forty-One

Ivan Zelenin's Story

A Ukrainian Village
Reflections on the Summer of 1945

At the glass factory, I met Ivan Zelenin, 18, when he entered the workshop appearing sad and dejected. "Ivan," I began, "what's the matter?"[1]

"Yesterday, I received a letter from a sister in my hometown. There are no men there. My mom's alive, but she lives with my two sisters. She wrote about our neighbor, Oksana."

"Tell me about it," I said.

Ivan poured out his heart. "My relationship with Oksana began last year and soon became intimate. You've been here so long you don't know, but in the war years, boys grew up fast and matured young, far beyond their years. Women often kidded us, calling us *muzhiks* as we worked and ate with them. They told us to sing, and we imitated the voices of adult men.

"When I was 13, I had grown slowly, and girls were indifferent to me. But over the next two years, compared to others, I grew tall and filled out. My voice changed. Boys called me rake, a reference to my thin height. It was about then I caught the eye of 20-year-old Oksana.

"One day, returning from the rye field, I dropped behind the others, and as I passed a field of sunflowers, I heard a woman's voice. 'Ivan,' she called. 'Come here, let's pick sunflowers, and I'll show you something!'

"I turned off the path, shoved towering sunflowers aside, and there was Oksana, sitting in a grassy spot surrounded by sunflowers. When I stepped closer, she grabbed my hand and pulled me down. I was startled. Then she started stroking my chest to calm me."

Oksana chimed, "Ivan, if you'd like, I can make you a real man."

"I was stunned. Oksana, I don't know anything about that."

---

1. Zelenin, Ivan Grigorievich, is listed in glass factory employees between 1947 and 1948. The Khasyn Archive.

Forty-One. Ivan Zelenin's Story

"Oh, so you're still a boy," she teased.

"I must have looked puzzled for Oksana laughed at me, then she threw her arms around my neck and licked me. She even reached between my legs and started stroking. I got home very late that night. And the next evening, Oksana again called me from the sunflower field. This time, she wore a blouse, unbuttoned, to show off her breasts. She pulled up her skirt. She was naked. I sat down. Things happened. Later, we walked to her house and sat on the porch.

"Oksana stroked my head resting on her breasts and said, 'Ivan, you're such a handsome boy! Your neck is young and thin but you're strong. How old are you?'"

"I said, 15, and next year, I'll join the Army because I want to fight Germans."

"Oh, God, save you!" Oksana exclaimed. "Come into my house. She pointed to a bench beside the wall. Then she sat next to me and began to stroke my skinny body with her strong hands. After that Oksana pressed her lips against mine, and I lost my head from her caresses and couldn't move as she laid her naked breast and hot body against mine.

Oksana said, 'Ivan, don't you like me?'"

"Aunt Oksana," I said, "I like you very much, but you're heavy."

"If you like me, kiss me, hold me tight, and you'll see I'm all woman."

"Aunt Oksana, I don't know how to do that stuff."

"What kind of an aunt do you think I am? I'm 20, and you'll soon turn 16," she said with a laugh. She rested her naked breast against me, and I felt her pressing and moving with all her strength. "Ivan, stroke me gently and quietly."

I stroked her wiry pubic curls, and she smiled with pleasure. I lost control and flew into a wild passion, spending the rest of the night with her. Oksana tormented me those first nights; I fell in love with her, but my arrest and sentence separated us.

And that was Ivan's story. Years later, when he turned 22, he was released, married, and had a pretty daughter. But he never forgot Oksana.

Forty-Two

Our Raskolnikov

Barracks 7
Monday, June 2–Sunday, August 31, 1947

During the summer of 1947, work went on smoothly at the glass factory. Director Babeikin and I regularly discussed the fulfillment of our goals and possible workers' raises as production increased. After work, I had time to care for personal needs: shoes and clothes repaired and finding new books at the library before returning to my Barracks 7.

One night, the shift glass masters woke me unexpectedly. Ivan Danilenko, a worker, slept in a bed across from me. Earlier that evening, instead of sleeping, Ivan had changed clothes and taken his dish and cup to the kitchen to cook dinner. Minutes later, he brought his dinner to the table near our bed, ate, changed his clothes again, and left. Ivan never wore the camp's uniform, always wearing white dress shirts. For five years, he lived with a caring female thief.

Ivan was about 28 years old. A tall, large-boned man with blond hair and rounded-faced, he had a grouchy character, but he worked well with me. One night, a guard came to Ivan's bed and woke him as a woman's leg stuck out from his blanket. The guard took Ivan's girlfriend to the isolation ward for the night. She was an actress in a local theater.

After work, Ivan visited her rehearsals, sitting quietly in the hall. But one evening, Petrov, the head of the theater, rashly ordered Ivan to leave the rehearsal in front of a large group. That embarrassed Ivan as Petrov let the others remain.

"Why are you ejecting me?" Ivan asked Petrov, glancing at his love on stage.

"Don't ask me silly questions!" With that, Petrov pointed at the door.

Mortified, Ivan left. The ejection sent his anger boiling, and he zeroed in on Petrov.

Somewhere, deep in his mind, Ivan decided that Petrov could not

Forty-Two. Our Raskolnikov

live. As his plan matured, Ivan said nothing. Even his girlfriend never guessed his deadly plan.

When the last day of Petrov's term arrived, he opted to spend it in the barracks. The authorities had allowed him to visit Magadan to receive his passport and release documents. That same day, I ran into Ivan. He was quiet and cool and said hello to me on his way to the second barracks where the carpenters lived. By its entrance, he met a guard and asked him where Petrov slept. The guard told Ivan where Petrov's bed was, and Ivan went to bed, pulled back the blankets, and made sure that the sleeping man was Petrov. He covered him and left. He returned at one in the morning to a silent barracks as 100 men were sleeping with an ax under his coat.

He turned down the blanket, assured it was Petrov, and axed him. The guard, for some reason, had left for a few hours. After the stabbing, Ivan couldn't calm himself and walked back and forth at the scene with his bloody ax.

When the night shift returned from the factory, the glass master, worried about me, and thought Ivan might have killed me, too.

"Leonid, leave the barracks now," he insisted.

Ivan, waving an ax, rushed in chased by five guards. He yelled, "I won't touch you," at me, washed his hands and sat at the table as the guards warily stood back. "Let me finish my dinner, and I'll leave with you guys. Try to take me by force and I *will* kill you."

Ten minutes later, Ivan said to them, "I'm ready."

All eyes watched Ivan. He said, "Petrov should have left me alone, but he ordered me out."

After this murder, Babeikin allowed me to move into a small house for my safety.

Forty-Three

The Blue-Eyed Blonde

The Glass Factory Sawmill
Monday, November 3–Wednesday, December 17, 1947

October ended in numbing cold with temperatures plunging to -13°. Despite it, young women felled taiga trees for the factory. Downed trees were sawn into six-foot lengths and pulled to the factory where other women, from the West,[1] using circular-saws, cut them into 20-inch furnace-sized lengths. The women always fulfilled the daily quota of 150 cubic meters. The administration resisted replacing the women with men; men never worked as hard.

Women split the firewood into narrow chunks that more women stacked on cradles. Winches hoisted those cradles to a 20-foot overpass over the production line, and then lowered them into the gas-and-wood-fueled furnace pit that maintained the kilns at 3,092°F to dry.

In my position, overseeing and regulating the factory's heat source, I always examined the cradles, overpass, and temperatures and discussed problems with my assistant, Kuhorenko. Once resolving problems, I descended 30-feet to the pit to monitor temperature control. This required special clothing and thick glasses to check on the melting sand and key minerals. Once satisfied, I returned upstairs, crossed the overpass, and watched the women cutting firewood. One day, several women noticed me and beaconed me to join them.

"Leonid Petrovich," one sang out, "come on down! Why only look at us?"

Surprised, I replied, "Give me a minute, and I will!"

They laughed. Another said, "Oh, girls, the big engineer is finally coming to see us!"

As I approached the area, one, a blue-eyed, curly-haired blonde with

---

1. The West infers the Baltic States, Poland, Western Ukraine, and Romania. Rossi, *The Gulag Handbook*, 129–130.

Forty-Three. The Blue-Eyed Blonde

rosy cheeks, looked at me seductively and said, "Oh, Leonid Petrovich, why don't you cut firewood with me so that Valentina can have a break?"

One thought came to mind: *She's an actress*, but I said, "Sure, beautiful, I'll cut wood with you anytime."

My promise delighted the girls. One yelled, "Sawing logs with an engineer! Careful Natasha; you'll have to teach him how to work hard!"

I stepped closer to the blue-eyed girl's workbench. Her eyes flashed excitedly. "Leonid Petrovich, do you like me?" She smiled coyly. "You do, don't you?"

"Yes," I admitted, glancing at her again. She *was* pretty.

Her head turned left and right. "I bet while we're talking, people will gossip that engineer Bolotov will brag about a certain girl. Let them. Hey, my name's Natasha."

"Nice to meet you, Natasha. You and your friends do one of our hardest jobs. Now turn on the circular saw," I said.

Natasha made a couple of cuts in a six-foot log but quickly slowed, as if weakening, passing me the saw.

I increased the speed and sawed. Natasha's face turned beet-red as she threw cut-chunks aside, and her curls drooped with sweat, but she did not give up. *How she looks like my Nina. Same curls but Nina's were thinner and softer. In winter, Nina hid them under heavy hats or shawls; she always wore light knitted hats, and her light brown hair curled over the top of her hats, a charming contrast with her radiant blue eyes.*

"Leonid Petrovich, where did you learn to work so craftily?" Natasha asked, bashfully, untying her *ushanka*[2] and shaking sawdust from her hair.

"I learned to work in Saratov, Leningrad, and Kolyma."

"Leonid Petrovich, you make sawing look easy. I hope you'll help us again. But next time, please saw slowly; after all, I'm a woman," she said, shoulders slumped, exhausted.

"I'll return tomorrow," I promised, thinking, *I'll sleep better tonight after this workout.*

"Leonid Petrovich, criminal women don't work hard as we do," Natasha said.

"No, they don't. And we send slackers to collective farms or fishery."

"I've seen them come into our barracks, but they disappear quickly with new assignments," Natasha complained.

Criminals never submitted to Gulag instructions and regulations, but they received privileges. Youth, like Natasha, received unfair prison terms for their parents' sins.

---

2. *Ushanka* is a hat with ear-flaps that can be tied up or fastened at the chin. Translator's note.

Natasha interrupted my thoughts. "Well, Leonid Petrovich, let's go," she said loudly.

While I'd cut logs with Natasha, Kuhorenko had looked at me askance.

"Natasha, we're done for today!" I concluded, picked up an ax and sunk it into a block.

After that, Kuhorenko motioned to me for a serious conversation.

"Bolotov," he said, "we looked for you when the truck from the mine arrived. We looked at their order, but it was not as stated in our purchase order."

"Why are you cutting firewood?" Mazurkevich, another glass master, asked me.

"I wanted to help the girls," I said.

"Well, I need glass," the truck driver said.

"I'm coming," I said. "But let me warm up first."

They left, and I wiped my forehead and went slowly into the factory. On the way, Natasha stopped me. "Leonid Petrovich, may I have a word with you?"

"You can have 10 words," I replied, smiling. *And at that moment, my son, 17, and daughter, 11, came to my mind. Will investigators persecute them for being the children of an enemy of the people?*

"Leonid Petrovich, today we'll finish work one hour early. May I see you after work?"

"Of course." I wanted to get her transferred to another position. Several times I'd watched her work in severe weather 12 hours a day while I worked eight hours. I smiled and tried to keep my spirits up, but I was sick at heart.

"Natasha, do you want to work inside?" I asked.

"Leonid Petrovich, all the girls dream of it. But I know the administration won't permit it," she whispered. "I received the severe Law of Three Spikes. My parents were both teachers. In 1937, the NKVD arrested them. I was 12, then I was arrested a few years later, charged with plundering socialist property."

"All right, tomorrow, I'll meet with you."

"Leonid Petrovich, thank you. God sent you. I'll come without fail."

Entering the factory, I met Kuhorenko, and we started talking. "Kuhorenko, my legs are aching, and my arms are shaking from cutting logs. Every day, girls must cut 25 or 30 cubic meters of them. It's tough work."

"Leonid Petrovich, girls chop wood because the camps won't send men to do it."

"Have you ever talked to the administration about that?" I asked.

"No chance."

"Tomorrow, men will start cutting the logs. If there are not enough

Forty-Three. The Blue-Eyed Blonde

men, you'll join them. And tomorrow the wood-cutters will work eight hours daily."

I explained to Kuhorenko that he is a good master, but he must take care of his people and watch their welfare and food when they work outside. Kuhorenko smiled.

"Why are you smiling?"

"I know you stayed too long with Natasha Vorobieva. I'll feel sorry for her, but there's nothing I can do." There was grief in his voice.

"Kuhorenko, I want her to become a pyrometric technician."

Over the next 12 months, work continued, and glass production increased. Natasha and other girls, thankfully, were reassigned inside to vital positions and proved to be more capable than men. But working in the factory, where temperatures stayed over 120°, and then walking in bitter cold to my cabin caused a viral infection in my pleura. Shooting pain spread to my back and shoulders, and I was hospitalized. For two weeks, I could barely open my eyes. I lost weight. My temperature stayed at 100.4°.

Close friends visited me. Babeikin's housekeeper brought a bottle of wine. It didn't help. The wine sat on my bedside table a month until I returned it. Raisa Mikhailovna, the head of the hospital, permitted my coworkers to visit at the end of my third week. They often brought bad news: my absences caused a production fall, especially of high-voltage insulators.

Maksim Petrovich Girich, director of the chemical laboratory, replaced me, but he had no idea about controlling the temperatures. He made small mirrors, shoe polish, and tooth powder. Wages dropped. Babeikin asked Raisa to allow me to work a few hours daily. She refused, but she did allow my coworkers to spend 15 minutes with me. Girich said the glass masters violated the rules of fritting and one burner on the stove had seized up. I stayed upset and bored.

On Sunday, I stood by the window, looking at the snow-covered hospital yard. A nurse stopped to take my temperature. She covered me with three wool blankets and said that Natasha wanted to see me.

"Leonid Petrovich," Natasha exclaimed, "we miss you!"

I enjoyed this news. "What have you been doing evenings to fill your time?"

"Knitting! Your body needs warmth," Natasha said. "I made a waistcoat for you." She opened a small bag and took out a knitted waistcoat. Also, she put on the end table a jar of condensed milk, cookies, and melted butter. I looked at her and thought: *Natasha, your heart is kind and responsive.*

Somehow Natasha's clothes came to my mind. When she chopped firewood, she wore quilted pants and a padded jacket that made her look like a boy teenager. And here she is with no heavy winter clothes. She looked different, and I relished seeing her thin, sexy body, her eyes gleaming with joy and beaming with charm.

"Leonid Petrovich, we want you to get better fast! I'll visit you next Sunday."

"I'll wait for you but please don't bring any more gifts," I said.

"We'll all be offended if you refuse them," Natasha whispered.

"Natasha, I'll get better," I said haltingly, wanting to give her a hug and kiss.

Natasha visited me the next Sunday and again brought food and put a two-quart jar of delicious cranberry jam on the end table.

Two weeks later, I was released. When I returned to my small room, the floor shone, curtains hung in the windows, embroidered pillowcases covered the pillows, and a white cloth with the embroidered roses looked splendid on the table.

Natasha had sewn all these items from cloth-bags of American wheat and baking soda.

Forty-Four

Bears and Berries

The Taiga
September 1948

After touches of frost in late August, surprisingly, September arrived with unusually balmy days that warmed our sprawling valley. One day, after work, I set aside my factory cares, packed a bucket with fresh bread and a water-cup, and left for a berry-picking hike in the taiga wilderness. Leaving town, I soon climbed the slope of a mountain range out of the basin. An hour later, at its ragged summit decimated by storms, I descended into a promising deep canyon and soon discovered a cornucopia of wild lingo berries. I picked a pail full, felt famished, and plunked down under a shady spruce tree—pine, spruce, and larche characterized the taiga's coniferous forest—to munch yeast bread and juicy lingo berries until I was full, Then I slumped against a tree, drowsy in the autumn sun. I licked tasty tanginess off my fingers and shut my eyes.

After a nap, I walked up a bluff to get my bearings. Endless taiga, stretching 3,600 miles from the Ural Mountains to the Pacific Ocean, rolled out in front of me. For a moment, I was disoriented and couldn't make out where I had walked. I checked the sun; I spun around and looked at a clone of mountain peaks. *Was I lost?* One peak looked familiar with its tattered silhouette of evergreens. Once I was sure it was the ridge that had been on my left when I descended meant I'd keep it to my right on my way back. I relaxed and continued to pick wine-red lingos and tiny, wild strawberries. *Fantastic: big, bright, juicy berries and sweet strawberries! My bucket will soon be full again.*

Then I heard a noise. I sprung around. Not 10 yards from me was the largest omnivore in the taiga: a towering, shabby, brown bear! A second later, I dashed to the far side of the clearing and started yelling, "Ah, ah, ah!" I clung to my bucket of berries, my only weapon! I kept yelling. It startled the bear. It lumbered around, stumbled over some brush, and disappeared. I took one last look over my shoulder and ran for 10 minutes. Only after entering a glade, far from the ill-fated knoll, did I relax.

When I looked around again, my berry pail spilled. I listened: no bear sounds. I raked up the berries, headed for the barracks, and never went berry-picking alone again.

At the factory, I told my bear story to my friends. They were open-mouthed astonished. Two weeks later, the glass factory administration asked me and Iosif Polevoi to go to a quartz mine 125 miles from the factory. The mine area was bisected by a small river. The driver refused to cross it, as it was spiked with rocks and sand piles. We washed our faces with icy cold water, sat and talk about our challenge, listening to the babbling river.

Suddenly, I heard a familiar, "Omph! Plunk! Omph! Plunk!" followed by a splashing.

"What is it?" Polevoi asked as I smiled.

No one else was around. When we set our bread on a big rock, we heard the noise again. This time, we turned toward the sound and saw a frightening picture. On the opposite shore, a pigeon-toed brown bear was throwing rocks into the water. Sometimes, its rocks fell short of the water, but it was undeterred. Tiring of that sport, the bear reared on both legs and plunged into the river. It seemed to admire the waves and spray flying up in all directions.

"What a bundle of mischief he is!" I exclaimed.

"Just like a kid," Polevoi seconded.

We watched in delight for about 10 minutes, but then the brown bear spotted us and made for the bushes. Despite our fear, we slowly forded the river, and climbed the steep slope where the mine geologists waited for us and we retold the story to their joy.

Forty-Five

Special Camp 5

Beregovoy Camp
Tuesday, September 20, 1949

One September morning, a truck drove up to the factory's main entrance, and two young officers jumped down and dashed inside. They showed their identification to the watchman, and he took them to the personnel office. At the time, I was checking kiln temperature and had no idea that their truck would soon be taking me away. But, within an hour, a watchman ordered me to board the back of the truck with other prisoners.

As I climbed in, Captain Parnachev, a good-natured man, said to me, "There is no more work for you here. Don't look so worried; we gave you an excellent reference."

I was puzzled. "Tell me the truth, then, Captain; where am I going?"

Parnachev didn't reply. Babeikin approached with kind words. "Leonid Petrovich, where you're going, please remain the honest and confident man you've always been here." His words did little to comfort me. When the truck sped off on the Kolyma Road, different thoughts came to mind. *Why have I been arrested again? Why didn't my friends among the factory's guards let me know about this arrest? Did Moscow place me on a secret list? When the Kolyma administration desperately needed engineering help, they recruited me. I even evaluated the ground with geologists and builders for a huge new building in Stalin's empire style with a deep basement for shelter, inner and outside pillars, and stucco molding. Since I began working at the factory, Moscow's authorities must have wanted me sent to the taiga, but the local administration took the trouble for me to stay at the factory. That was my life! Will I be living in severe isolation with no contact with the outside world and my relatives? Once, when ordered to help build a barracks for dangerous prisoners in Magadan Berlag, I met some of those prisoners. Three rows of barbed wire surrounded Berlag, and when the carpenters and I completed the construction plans, the authorities ordered these men into the barracks with thick iron plates covering the windows. When the last man stepped over the doorsill, the guards bolted the door with a heavy lock and placed the men in irons. The prisoners secretly told me they used to work on secret constructions. For 10 years they worked like this, in irons, but with a truck ready for them all the time to take them to other places. The old men among them never spoke to each other; they developed eye contacts and facial expressions to express themselves. Am I like them? Will Kolyma authorities bury me alive?*

But then Babeikin's encouraging words came to mind. I realized he had tried to give me secret information. I slowly interpreted his words, and suddenly, a thunderstorm crossed my mind. *I'll be working in a new place. He had wished me success. It meant I wouldn't die. How wise he is!* My heart leaped. Babeikin had not disclosed secrets but found a way to give me support.

Now, the body of the truck was bone-chilling cold. I had feared of leaving the factory but looked up at smoke-colored clouds racing across the sky. Soon, puffy white clouds and blue skies replaced them and the darkness outside and within my soul. There were a few men in the truck with me, and they began to speak.

"If we're to be released, the guards should know," one man offered hopefully.

"Yes, they'll let us know if our future is secure," another man seconded.

"Ahh, don't say that, brother; we've no idea what'll happen to us," a third scoffed.

Yesterday I worked; today, my factory work ended. If I can work again, I'll survive. That seemed plausible to me, and slowly, jarringly, over the bumpy road, I fell asleep. A factory dream appeared. It had an 800-seat theater, library, art and music rooms. Prisoners, guards, and unrestricted men enjoyed the club. The wives of the unrestricted men hated when prisoners sat next to them, and they often asked guards to take the prisoners' seats. Movies were free. But women never watched them. They were spying on young girls and their admirers to see who was being hugged and kissed. Although my fantasy club was in the men camp, women were allowed in during specific times.

My dream ended when the truck struck a washout, tossing me, and my eyes popped open. Sitting near the tailgate, I looked out at a mountain ridge. A cold wind whistled in, penetrating my clothes. Sharp, prickly sleet thrashed my face. I yanked my hat down, turtled into my coat, and watched the endless taiga roll past. I wanted to press my body against the truck bed as we climbed the dizzying heights of a moun-

Forty-Five. Special Camp 5

tain peak. Descending, we passed the big town of Palatka. We stopped at a cafeteria in Atka, another large, well-developed town. Our driver and the guards ate. We didn't. And then we rumbled past the towns of Miakit, Strelka, and stopped in Orotukan. Just beyond it, the truck stopped. Guards had us get down, stretch before they had lunch. When they returned, the guards ordered us to climb into the back of the truck, hungry.

A Ukrainian boy said to a guard, "We'd like some bread too."

Another man shoved him aside. "Don't ask them for a thing."

A guard explained, "You'll eat in your new camp."

The driver filled the truck with gas, and we rattled on. When we passed a bridge over the Kolyma River, it reminded me of the rains that burst the Kolyma's banks and flooded the mines in 1939. Prisoners had hidden beneath wheelbarrows, and we ate bread and *balanda* in the flooded mines. Some trucks loaded with food and equipment from Magadan sank in the flood waters, and yet authorities blamed us—not the storm—for not fulfilling our norm.

We drove on in darkness. It reminded me of my truck ride into prison obscurity in 1937, but soon the flicker of far-off lights appeared, and guards interrupted my thoughts. "This is your new home, *Beregovoy*," he announced. The truck braked and stopped outside the raised-hackle-wires forming double-gates around the camp half-buried in snow drifts. *Beregovoy* was Special Camp 5 for political prisoners.[1]

"You prisoners wait in the back!" a guard yelled.

I looked at the sky, sprinkled with a firework of stars. We wanted to dash into the warm barracks, but the guards were indifferent as we listened to their chatting. We looked around. Watchtowers rose at four corners. Electric lights glowed over the entire camp. Far beyond the camp, to one side, rose high mountains; to the other side, sprawled Elgen Valley and its coal mines. An hour later, when guards finished talking, they approached in quiet, measured steps and took a head count. Once concluded, they allowed us to enter the low, long barracks; snow buried its locked doors and windows beneath towering drifts. Despite it being night, the guards marched us to the cafeteria for bread and *balanda*.

I undressed, slid under some real blankets and slept.

Next morning, I received a hat with my designated number: HII-425, and told I'd be working in mine BES-21, in the ventilation branch, measur-

---

1. The *Beregovoy* Camp was founded in 1948 by the Council of Ministers Decree No. 416–159. On January 1, 1949, it held 15,570 prisoners in a compound surrounded by three rows of fences and patrolled by guards with German shepherds. Like men, women worked in the mines ten hours a day. To maintain control, guards used straight-jackets and handcuffs. Batsaev, "Kolymskaia griada arhipelaga Gulaga (zakluchennye)," 62–63.

ing gas pressure and checking ventilation systems. Then two carpenters, an electrician, plumber, and I built the station.

Days later, before the October Revolution holiday, our routine was toughened with inspections and harassment every two hours. Once, during the night, while 200 of us slept, a guard appeared in our barracks.

"We're frisking everyone!" he yelled, wheezing as if something had caught in his throat.

Behind him, the door of the barracks banged open, and 20 guards burst through, intimating us. Men hurriedly hid small treasures. The guards acted like hungry wolfs and rushed from side to side, shoving sleepy, barefoot men into the cold hall, frisking us roughly. As always, they took everything they wanted. Their bags grew by the minute with our military uniform, mittens, scarfs, small knives, etc. When the guards' frisking ended, they carried their booty to the office; prisoners spent the rest of the night rearranging the barracks.

Seating on his bed, an old man complained, "The guards stole my needles and thread."

A former mayor, boiling with anger, moaned, "They stole my long winter mittens."

Sitting near the mayor, an Uzbek wailed, "Guards sliced my pillow and took my vest."

"Well, I'm lucky," a former combat engineer said thankfully. "The guards didn't find the shaving blades I'd stashed in a crust of bread."

"Cut out the complaining, lay down, and sleep!" a watch guard warned.

"The night is ending but you, guys, are still howling," another guard echoed. *How could prisoners sleep after this barracks frisking?*

But the sleepless night did end, for soon the banging of the rail started, and the watch guards bawled, "Get up!"

Guards never spoke softly as they feared the Kolyma Administration would banish them to the mines. When the guards opened the door of my barracks, they carried out our two *parashas* on heavy poles. Tired and angry prisoners jumped off their beds and fired desperate questions, "Have you got an extra pillow or blanket?" But the guards ordered us to form a column and marched to the cafeteria to hurriedly eat a scoop of *balanda* and chunk of bread before work. A few minutes later, a guard yelled, "Follow each other out!"

On the snow, our black-clad stretched out like a line of obedient dolls. We formed lines of five-across behind team leaders, and then guards checked our pockets before an officer opened the outside gates. When 35 of us were inspected, an officer opened the outside second gate and we proceeded to the mine.

Forty-Five. Special Camp 5

As we walked, guards called out Soviet "prayers": "March together tightly, don't lower your arms, don't talk! Don't step to left or right, that's an attempted escape; we'll shoot you!"

A minute later, the guard ordered us, "Run!"

In another minute he yelled, "Stop!" We stopped. "Now march!"

At the mine, guards re-counted us, from the front of the column and the rear. "Is the number of prisoners correct?" the head of the guards asked our guards.

"Yes, they agree with the count!" the guards replied.

Guards counted us every two hours all day. We wanted to work in the mines, but it was not easy to do. The guards never descended deep into the mines, but, instead, they called us to take a lift to the surface for a recount again and again. Whenever the guards' count came up short, they'd order us all to the surface for a recount, impeding out productivity.

In *Beregovoy*, the guards never considered prisoners people. They referred to us by initials and numbers "Hey, Ш II-763!" "Oh, УII-960!" "Come to me, Ф II-565."[2]

If a guard called a prisoner from across the camp, he had to stop 10 steps from the guard. If he did not calculate the distance correctly, the prisoner spent the night in the punishment cell. If a prisoner attempted to speak to a guard, he spent two nights in that cell. Prisoners were also put in that cell if they sneezed, coughed, or yawned. We were lucky when the guards ordered us to wash the floor or cut firewood instead of spending the night in the cell. The guard's revolting behavior never considered mine production, but they admired their power over us.

After four decades, these *Beregovoy* Laws and Ethics stay embedded in my mind.

---

2. The Cyrillic characters are the equivalent of calling the men CHP, UP, and FP.

Forty-Six

A New Order

The Commandant's House
Saturday, November 10, 1951

A year passed since arriving in *Beregovoy* Camp, and it was here I celebrated the 1951 October Revolution with other convicts. During the renowned holiday, guards shut down the camp, locked up everything, and ordered us not to work as they feared an uprising. Our day off was in near-total darkness a blinding snowstorm. We spent the day in the barracks under dull lights. Some men ate bread crusts they'd saved; some slept; some re-mended shabby clothes, and all relived the past with retold stories.

Among the prisoners, I was always the *new* guy, and, after all these years, I never stopped asking myself: *Why was I there?* Unlike the others, I lived mostly in my mind and rarely spoke.

The next morning brought a typical day, roll call, breakfast, waiting in the snow to work in the mine, and then being locked in for yet another night. When November 10 arrived, another "typical" day started, but when our workday ended, we returned to the main gate. Something was happening. Guards failed to open it. We waited impatiently. An hour later, they let us in, and a guard yelled my last name. "Bolotov, go to the head of *Beregovoy*!"

I was bewildered and froze. *Now what?*

Following order, I plodded through the snow to the commandant's small house.

When I opened the door, two captains sat at a table, one headed the fire department; the other was the ideological affairs chief. He was ferocious to prisoners, always deeming us outlaws. But now he said, softly, "The Dalstroy major is waiting for you in the next room," puzzling me and my ears pricked up. He'd addressed me using my name, not my numbers, always used.

Forty-Six. A New Order

I opened the door and stepped into the room. Thoughts of hunger flashed through my mind. *Will I be sent to isolation? Was there something hidden in his kind words?* But another voice whispered: *Don't be afraid, whatever the news you'll survive.*

The room was hot. The Dalstroy major sat in the center of the office at a big table. Four young lieutenants sat in the four corners, staring at me. They did not know me personally, but they seemed to crave the meeting—*their chance to see a Soviet prisoner jailed 14 years.*

"Bolotov, I'm glad to meet you finally! How was your day?" he added admirably.

The young officers remained silent, but they appeared discouraged.

"My day went well, comrade."

"I understand there was a big problem in the ventilator plant."

"Yes, there was." *Where was this warm greeting headed?*

"What did *you* do about it?"

"I repaired it with the help of others. Accidents occur daily in the mine because of low-quality equipment."

"I agree, Bolotov, but you fix our equipment with baling wire and duct tape."

"That's all we have. In this instance, the miners need to clean blocked ventilator holes immediately. Improved ventilation fixes the breathing problem."

The major nodded, smiled, and moved on. "Are you receiving letters from home?"

"Rarely," I said dejectedly. "Postage from Saratov is expensive."

"And who is at your home?"

"My mother, wife, son, and daughter. My father died."

"That's good you still have them in your life."

Good? I couldn't understand why he was cheerful. My term ends in another year. The Kolyma administration could arrest me again and issue a new sentence if I leave early.

"Citizen Bolotov!" the major said. "As of today, Saturday, November 10, 1951, you are a free man! Here is the document, sign it, and go enjoy life." His voice was joyful as he slid my release across the desk. My hand shook as I picked up the paper and began reading.

I was free! I was stunned. *Were the major's words a malicious joke?*

But he leaned over the table and repeated kindly, "Citizen Bolotov, sign it."

Well, my life is unique. Arrested without reason, now I'm being released before my term ended and, for the first time in 14 years, an officer called me a citizen. I took a deep breath, picked up the pen, and signed the release document below the Soviet Hammer and Sickle.

The Major stood, he took off my hat, and tore off my number HII-425. He looked at me kindly and instructed, "Citizen Bolotov, stay in the barracks until tomorrow when you'll receive new documents." And then he told me about my future life.

I barely heard him. My mind was racing. I'd soon see Nina and the kids. I stood, thanked the Major, returned to the barracks, and flopped onto my bed. I missed supper.

Since I had no friends in the barracks, I couldn't share the fantastic news. It took me hours before I could relax. I rested and slept for a few days until summoned to bring my bag. The last time they had searched me they had found one ruble. The head of the camp did not allow them to take it from me. He said that it is prohibited to confiscate money from released prisoners. That one ruble became the start of my capital accumulation. I cherished it as it meant contact with my family, the price of a stamp to the mainland.

When I did not leave for work the first morning, it told prisoners I was free. Surrounding me, they asked, "How long have you been in Kolyma?" "Who helped you get free?"

I answered their questions, but I could not be honest as they were strangers. It took me time to realize I was, indeed, free. A guard told me a letter from Moscow had released me, but I'd be in external exile, living in Seymchan, for an unknown time.

I ripped off all the I.D. numbers from my clothes, cleaned my peacoat, and dried a pair of *valenki*. I sewed a new pair of mittens that extended to my elbows. They were snug and warm, and I wore them under the sleeves of my peacoat. Of course, I was dying to pass on my good news to my family and asked the guard about transportation to the city.

He said, "Snow buried the highway."

"So, when can I leave camp?" I asked frantically.

"When it's plowed."

A few days passed as I waited in eager expectation. I lost my appetite; I couldn't sleep. The story of Ignatiev occurred to me. He'd worked at the Nizhnii At-Uriah mine and was a muscular, cheerful, and healthy man with an even temper. When the end of his 10-year term approached, he became limp and dull, lost his appetite, and grew thin. After a medical exam, there was no explanation for his poor health. The team-leader allowed him to spend a week in the barracks, but even that wasn't helpful. He melted like burning candle and died three days later.

Outside the commandant's house, I mumbled, "Don't fret over Ignatiev."

A guard asked me and others, "Where are the numbers on your hats?"

"Gone! I'm like you now. *Free!*"

Forty-Six. A New Order

"I see it," he said. "Climb in the back."

An hour later, when we stopped, the senior lieutenant jumped down from the cab and said, "Well, get out, or you'll turn into ice cycles. Come on, warm up!"

As ordered, we jumped out and ran around the Studebaker to warm up. The sun faded. Twilight brought a fresh snowstorm. It covered the road and truck and roared while we re-boarded. Fortunately, the American truck was sturdy. When it plowed into a snowbank, the driver shouted, "Guys, hang on; Ivan Kolyma's your driver!" The truck jerked sharply, and we flew through snowdrifts as if they were cotton balls.

After a while, Ivan shouted, "Look ahead; those lights are Seymchan."

Soon, the truck stopped. The senior lieutenant jumped down and ordered us to and stand beside a house. Next to the door, I read the commandant's order: *All released prisoners must report to this office for valid documents.*

I waited 30 minutes. Once inside, the short, middle-aged commandant said gruffly, "Bolotov, I'm Ukhnalev, head of Srednekanskii District. How did you manage to slip away from two executions?"

"They were wrong," I replied.

Ukhnalev explained the rules for living in Seymchan. According to the instruction that he'd received from Moscow, I must live under the supervision of the Department of the Inner Affairs of Magadan Province. Twice a month, on the 1st and the 15th, I had to register at his office. Also, walking outside town and changing jobs required his permission. Then Ukhnalev's secretary passed me my new identification card No. СП 5209 with the year and place of my birth, nationality, signed by him, which must be carried at all times.

Ukhnalev told me to leave, and all barracks were opened to newly released prisoners. I picked up my suitcase and left, pausing to get my head around all this. Then I returned.

"What now?" an officer fired.

"May I sleep here?" I asked.

"Not allowed!" he growled.

"Can you loan me 10 rubles? My savings account is at *Beregovoy* Camp, and I'll repay you when it gets to Seymchan."

"I don't make loans!"

"You should. We are all people; newly released prisoners need your help."

Shortly, Ukhnalev finished his work and left the building, leaving a soldier on duty. There was nothing I could do. I stepped outside and stood on the porch watching the snow drift around the yard and thought: *this is my free life*. I sat on the suitcase and dwelled on Ukhnalev's character. *He's afraid of any relationship with a released prisoner. How could he push me outdoors with no money and no place to sleep?*

Shivering and blanketed with snow, I finally abandoned those thoughts and walked. I passed one street. Another. I spotted a bright light in a little house. I wanted to knock on its door: *Maybe they won't let me inside.*

I kept on walking, stomping my ice-covered *valenki*. I slid and fell several times. House lights turned off. I craved sleep. *I'll freeze to death laying here.* I remembered a story of a released prisoner who received his freedom, took off his clothes, and stripped naked on Seymchan's streets, clutching his new ID. He had walked and walked and finally froze to death.

I don't know what came over me, but I decided to fight for my life again. I picked up my suitcase, and plodded on, heading for whatever.

Forty-Seven

Freedom—With Restrictions

Seymchan
Saturday, November 10—Tuesday, November 20, 1951

After a long slog, I turned down a nameless street and squinted into the blizzard lashing my face at what looked like a doll house, tilted by permafrost and half-buried in drifts. Wisps of black smoke curled out of its chimney. Tugging my *ushank*a-hat down, I aimed for a dim light flickering in a window, probably obscured by ice two-feet thick. I passed a picket fence, leaning drunkenly, slipped, and fell into waist-deep snow as soft as a feather pillow.

I shoved an outer door into a drift and stepped inside. It was a degree or two above freezing. I almost tripped over a wooden box used as a refrigerator. A man sat in the kitchen.

"May I come in?" I asked softly.

He beaconed me closer to study my face. Except for the crackling fire, the room was silent; the one thing it needed was fresh air. He said, "Yes," and pulled out a dirty handkerchief from his hip pocket and honked. "Come in and warm up."

He pointed to a second stool, a twin of the first; it looked like one farmers use to milk cows. I pulled it over and sat across from him, back to the stove. I took off my mittens and held my hands out behind me. Dried branches clustered with the yellowed needles of lurch trees filled the wood-box; the stove cast soothing heat and a pleasant aroma that couldn't annul the stale smells of cigarettes and old grease, burned black, splattering the stove top. The old man fingered aside strands of gray hair, narrowed his eyes, and studied me some more. Deep wrinkles etched his wizened face. He pursed his lips enough to reveal yellow teeth and pointed a dirty fingernail at me with hands knotted and scarred by a lifetime of hard work.

"You a prisoner?" he asked with a voice as taut as a *balalaika's* E string.

"I was," I replied mildly. "Fourteen years. Now I'm free, but I can't return to Saratov." I changed the subject. "Lived here long?"

"Been a prison watchman for decades. So, you plan to live here?"

"Yes. I must remain in Kolyma. Tonight, I'm looking for a place to sleep."

The old man nodded, understandingly. "Sleep on that bench by the fire. Now, that'll solve your sleep problem, tell me your story. I'll make tea."

A clock on a wall shelf struck 12. "Sunday," the old man said.

"For years, I've had no idea what day of the week it was."

"That's sad. You hungry? I've bread and butter."

I smiled at the old geezer. When the teapot boiled, he poured black tea, set a loaf of bread the size of a shoebox on the table and went to the entry-refrigerator for butter. His kindness reminded me of my family, and that made me think of all the things I must do before I could see them. I relished the bread and salted butter and finished my tale and meal at the same time, brushing up a few crumbs. Exhausted, I thanked the old man again, pulled off my *valenki*, and flopped onto the bench, instantly falling asleep.

Next morning, my host repeated his kindness that I hungrily devoured. When finished, I took my suitcase, and left for the unknown. Outside, swirling snow veiled my view, but I aimed for what I calculated would be the main street and found people walking in one direction. I joined them, asking a man where everyone was going.

"To the market," he replied without stopping.

When we arrived at the market, a freezing-cold shed and horseshoe of tables staffed by three dozen, shivering, irritable clerks waited impatiently for buyers.

While I gawked about, two men approached. "Got anything to sell?" one asked.

"I doubt it," I said. "But have a look." I opened the suitcase. "Will any of it sell?"

"You bet." One man picked through my clothes, selected a few, and gave me enough rubles to buy a loaf of bread.

Sunday was a short market day; it ended at noon. Outside the blizzard raged. I decided to leave the area for a larger section of town and asked for directions to the highway, but most people, shielding their faces, hurried past, ignoring me. *I'm free, but where should I go? I must find a place to live and work, maybe for the rest of my life.*

"Excuse me," I said to a tall, attractive woman, wearing a hooded, mink-trimmed, leather coat that rested on the top of her boots.

She smiled and paused to look me over. "You lost?" she asked.

"I need a place to stay," I said gratefully.

Forty-Seven. Freedom—With Restrictions

"The next section is that way." She smiled and pointed. "You'll find two warm barracks for released prisoners there with beds and food. I'm on my way; join me."

She was a privileged local. I relaxed, and we talked as we walked until the blizzard grew so strong it left us panting and gasping and unable to converse. On the way, she touched my arm. "When we get there, you'll find criminals live in one barracks and political prisoners the other. The criminals' barracks faces a field; the political prisoners' barracks faces the market."

In a while, the shape of twin barracks appeared. The tidy yard of the building facing the market was cleared of snow; the other, facing the field, was drifted.

"Go ahead, enter," the woman encouraged. "Don't be afraid. No one will hurt you."

This woman and last night's old man strengthen my beliefs in life's fairness and the goodness of ordinary people. I entered the barracks. Three-dozen former prisoners were resting in the warm space. Some drank tea at a big table in the middle of the barracks; some chatted sprawled out on *real* beds; some shaved; some slept.

"My name's Bolotov," I said, approaching the table. "I'm newly-released and need a bed—if you've an extra."

"Yes," one man said, standing. "Take that bed by the stove and warm up!"

I pulled off my mittens, hung up my peacoat and hat, sat down on the bed, and held my hands up to the stove. Questions followed: "What camp were you in?" "When were you released?" "Where're you from?" "Where'd you sleep last night?"

I responded in detail, closing with "I just finished 14 years in Kolyma."

"Now you're free but exiled here to fulfill your term?" a man with a wavy hair asked.

I nodded. "Hopefully for only six more years."

The men shifted to open a spot at the table. Someone gave me strong black tea with sugar and asked, "What did you do today?"

"I visited a market and met a woman who helped me find you. She was surprised to hear I was from Saratov."

At the word, Saratov, a skinny guy jumped off his bed. "Hey, Bolotov!" he exclaimed, "I'm from Pokrovsk, 10 miles southeast of Saratov!"

"My father mentioned Pokrovsk when we drove our horse across the Volga years ago."

"Then we're almost neighbors once. Here, I work at the local bakery. Tomorrow I'll bring you a loaf of *real* bread. Now, sleep right here in my bed; I work nights and sleep days."

All the men were friendly. I never expected such a warm welcome. As I ate, they told me how difficult it was to find a well-paying job, the best positions are taken, but hard-labor jobs abounded. They said not to accept the first hard job offered but look around and wait, I could stay with them for as long as needed. After all these years, I still remember their care, help, and inspiration as a snowstorm wailed and we shared stories of arrests and confinements. I learned about the tough life of released prisoners—nothing compared with my past ordeal—and my spirits soared. *Life goes on. I had a warm place to sleep and eat and could write Nina.*

Next morning, Monday, November 19, 1951, I walked to the post office.

> *Dear Nina!*
>
> *My Gulag release came on November 10, 1951, and I'm writing you from the post office. The Dalstroy administration gave me an officially-sealed document of freedom; however, it restricts me to living in Seymchan. The town is not far from the prison camp on the Seymchan River where we worked in gold and coal mines. There's an 8-hour time difference, but I will try to call you. The days are short and cold with 21-hour nights this time of year I'll look for a job that pays well. Maybe this freedom ends our nightmare. I can't leave, and I am eagerly awaiting you joining me. All my love!*

With one ruble I bought an envelope and stamp and sent the happy news, airmail, to Nina from the Seymchan airport, constructed during World War II for delivery of American airplanes.

After sending the letter, I left and started looking for work. At the time, the town flourished with administrative, cultural, and economic organizations. Central heating existed in most buildings. There was a stadium, daycare, hospital and clinic, three groceries, a bakery, vodka factory, Russian baths, a brick factory, garages, auto repair shops, wood factory, and horse and pig farms. The two government administrations in Dalstroy included a Development Industry and a Geological office, headquartered in Moscow. Every year it sent 150 prospecting parties out to evaluate geological sites in Kolyma for mineral extractions.

I spent my first day knocking on tin-covered windows at Seymchan employment offices. I saw only beet-red faces of people sliding open peepholes that disappeared when I asked for a job. As the day ended, I went to the Development Industry, located on the second floor of a new building. The first room was warm and exceptionally clean with carefully painted floors, shiny doors, and walls covered with deeply embossed lincrusta. In it were four large tables filled with women with abacuses and a man, about 36, watching them. His cheeks were as pink as ladies' cheeks. I said hello, but he didn't look up or speak to me.

Forty-Seven. Freedom—With Restrictions

Despite this, I said, "My name is Bolotov," and handed him my papers. "I'm an engineer-economist able to develop action plans, write reports, and estimate the cost of mine work."

The man looked at my papers scornfully and snarled, "You're still alive after being arrested in 1937!?" He wanted to boot me out.

A woman tried to say something but only managed to stretch out the vowel a-a-a as the man yelled, "We've got no jobs for people like you!"

"I understand," I acknowledged. Leaving, the women gaped at me as if I were a leper.

I fled their boorishness and returned to the friendly barracks to share my dinner and day before sleeping. "Tomorrow," I vowed, "I'll try comrade Ukhnalev."

Tuesday morning, I went to the commandant's house. Ukhnalev quickly assigned me to work at the uranium mines in Lazo, 36 miles from Seymchan and gave me a bus schedule, saying the next bus departed in 20 minutes.[1]

I hurried to the station filled with well-dressed men in fur coats that

A Kolyma bus (Dal'stroi Territories Photo Album of 1942–1943, Ministry of Inner Affairs, State Archive, Russian Federation, Moscow).

---

1. Lazo, Sergei Georgievich (1894–1920), was considered a "local Lenin" in the Far East during the Civil War. Wieszynski, *The Modern Encyclopedia of Russian and Soviet History*, vol. 19 (1981), 85–88.

made me feel ashamed in my shabby peacoat. One man approached and inquired as to my plans. I was telling him my goals for a high-paying job when the bus arrived. He paid my five rubles fare, and on the hour-long ride said he was the commandant of Lazo and could help me find work.

When we arrived, I gazed left and right and grew upset. High mountains, masking the low Arctic sun, surrounded a deep canyon so narrow two trucks couldn't pass simultaneously. The convicts' camp and small log cabins were across from the bus stop. The uranium mines were a 10-minute walk away. *How will I ever live here with Nina?* I wanted to run to Seymchan. But I had nowhere to go with Ukhnalev's employment documents, so I went to the office of the head of the mine. People crowded it. I waited several hours.

A miner asked bitterly, "Couldn't you find a better place to work?"

That did it! He was right. I wouldn't stay. *What would I say to the head of the mine?* Finally, I was called. "Do you want to work today?" the head of the office asked.

"No," I said resolutely. "Not in the mine."

"There's no other work."

"Then write that on my paper: you have no positions for me."

"There's hard work here; I need people," he yelled.

"I know, but my lungs ravaged from years in the mines."

"Why in hell does the administration send me sick men?" he growled and grabbed the phone, repeatedly calling Seymchan. No one answered. He cursed the cold and rotten equipment. He yelled, "Ukhnalev, who did you send to me today? Bolotov! He's sick."

He motioned for me to leave his room. I left, but the walls were so thin I could hear his conversation as if I were still there. "Ukhnalev, you're sending me cripples!" There was a pause. "How can I do my job? I don't have healthy men!" Pause. "Bolotov's clever. I'm sending him back; I'll write he's disabled." Pause. "He's yours again."

He slammed the phone down and called me.

I was delighted. The head of the mine scribbled on my voucher: *Disabled.*

Outside, small lights sparkled like fireflies from tiny log dwellings. A man told me a bus would arrive in the morning. Distressed: *Will I spend the night outside?* But far from it! A woman appeared out of nowhere and asked me to be a servant for her family. I was surprised but refused her offer. There was no stopping her.

"Oh, come with me. You're cold, and my house is cozy, with lots of food."

"Thanks," I said. "Your sympathy is warming, but I want to stay here and find work as an engineer." It is disheartening to see former engineers,

Forty-Seven. Freedom—With Restrictions

doctors, and teachers opt to work as butlers and maids. I left the woman.[2] Another stranger appeared out of the darkness.

Laughing, he asked, "Would you like to become the new head of Lazo mine?" The malice in his voice was revolting. I turned away and returned to the commandant's home; he lived on the only street in the town, and he invited me in. I saw one bed and two chairs. He gave me food and five rubles for my trip back. The clock on the wall read midnight, and he opened another door to a Russian bathhouse. It was clean, quiet, and warm, and I slept on its wide, wooden bench. Tossing and turning, I worried about missing my bus. But the commandant, too, worried about me, and early the next morning, November 20, 1951, he accompanied me to the bus stop like a best friend. The morning was cold, and a thick fog hung over the canyon, but my heart sang: *I was leaving the Lazo mine and the area's gloomy canyon.*

Sadly, I don't recall the commandant's name, but I still remember his kindness.

---

2. On June 9, 1941, General Nikishov decreed that a narrow circle of family authorities would be allowed to hire disabled and released prisoners to work at their homes. Housekeepers and their assistants made 190 rubles a month. *Dalstroy Trust Sevvostlag OGPU-NKVD of the USSR as Presented by Documents and in Numbers (2 parts). Part 1 (1931–1941)*, p. 1, 275.

Forty-Eight

Dishwashing

Hospital
Wednesday, November 21, 1951–
Monday, March 31, 1952

Standing in the narrow, wooded canyon, I looked at the towering mountains while awaiting the bus to Seymchan. On my hour-long return, I decided to go back to Ukhnalev's office and asked to be sent back to the factory as it needed a well-trained staff to function. Ukhnalev listened to my appeal and explained, "I can't send you there. All my requests must be first mailed to and approved by Moscow. You'd best find work here." He leaned back in his chair and stared at me. "And Bolotov, I worry the Soviet authorities might change their minds and alter your status."

I left his office and relaunched my job search. Results: repeated job turn-downs. On November 21, 1951, I accepted a hospital's dishwasher job. I sawed firewood, kept the boiler room heated, and washed kettles and dishes. Evenings, I logged in groceries and supplies of dry potatoes, dry milk, jelly, powdered eggs, meat, butter, bread, and onions. I had no days off; just like the Gulag.

The winter dragged on dark and long, but I was free to come and go. I soon found a monk-sized room and hung white curtains over the bed and a white cloth on the table. I started saving money, and every month I sent a money order to Nina.

Evdokiia Semenovna Simakova, the hospital director, visited me with doctors and ordered them to make their rooms similar to mine. "Comrades," she bragged, "Leonid Petrovich is a man, but his room is a model of cleanliness and neatness." She called me an honest worker who she could trust.[1]

---

1. In 2006, Yuri Shapiro in his memoir, "Kolyma i Kolymchane," satirized her character. *Zdravyi smysl*, No. 1 (38): 45–50.

Forty-Eight. Dishwashing

In the kitchen, besides me, there were three cooks, all former criminals. The eldest, Arkadii, was about 30, lived with his wife, a nurse. Another man, Ivan Kian, 28, was a thief. The third, a baker, Petr Karpov, 26, had served in the artillery and received awards. After suffering shellshock, he was ordered to guard a military warehouse in Kuibyshev where he exchanged a wagon of soldiers' boots for a barrel of spirits. For this, he received a three-year sentence, authorities rescinded his awards, and sent him to Seymchan where he married and had two children. At his request, I wrote a petition for him, and months later, his awards re-appeared.

The cooks lived in peace and friendship in a dormitory. They drank after dinners and ate deer meat with sour, salty cabbage and cranberries. They often invited me, but I refused, telling them I didn't drink. During these months, people often addressed me as a father. As the weeks dragged by, I met new colleagues, including doctors, who often checked the quality of food in the kitchen. Several times, Vladimir Onuphrievich Mokhnach, the former director of Chemistry Institution in Vladivostok, visited me.[2] He was a tall, thin man of 60. Like me, Mokhnach was from Leningrad. I remember how he sat on a chair beside the zinc-coated tub where I washed dishes, and we'd chat. One night he told me about the benefit of using iodine to treat dysentery. Unfortunately, the young doctors called Mokhnach an enemy of the people. They believed he made attempts on the lives of Shcherbakov, Vasilevskii, and Govorov.[3]

Besides Mokhnach, Lopatinskii, from Saratov, often came to the kitchen. He was arrested in 1937 while studying veterinary science. When released from the Gulag, Lopatinskii sent me a letter saying he'd graduated from Saratov Veterinary Institution at age 40. He mentioned he'd married, received a free apartment, and was raising two sons.

Long, black, December days past slowly and finally ended, and I greeted New Year 1952 alone and watched Petr Karpov fire his rifle while others lit fireworks and sang songs.

---

2. Mokhnach, Vladimir Onuphrievich (1899–1974), arrested July 20, 1937, received 15 years confinement. During a dysentery breakout in Kolyma, he successfully used "black porridge," a mixture of alcohol, iodine, and potatoes peels, as a cure. He was released in 1956. His methodology in using iodine was also used during the Chernobyl nuclear catastrophe. Mokhnach, I.V. "Sinii iod." *Repressirovannaia nauka*, ed. M. G. Yaroshevskii (Sankt-Peterburg: Nauka, vyp. II [1994]: 145–158).

3. Shcherbakov, Aleksandr Sergeevich (1901–1945), directed the Soviet Information Bureau during World War II. Wieszynski, *The Modern Encyclopedia of Russian and Soviet History*, vol. 34 (1983), 187. Vasilevskii, Aleksandr Mikhailovich (1895–1977), Soviet Marshal and Minister of War from 1950 to 1953. Wieszynski, *The Modern Encyclopedia of Russian and Soviet History*, vol. 41 (1986), 208. Govorov, Leonid Aleksandrovich (1897–1955), another Soviet Marshal, directed the efforts to break through the 900-day German siege of Leningrad. After the war, he held a succession of the posts as commander of the Leningrad Military District and Deputy Minister of Defense. Wieszynski, *The Modern Encyclopedia of Russian and Soviet History*, vol. 13 (1979), 13, 86.

February arrived and ended with me still washing dishes and checking in supplies. Late that month, I began hearing rumors that I'd become an engineer. I went to a local factory that wanted to hire me, and they promised to pay an excellent salary. After my interview, I had to refuse their offer as there was no place to live.

Three months after my freedom, with better food and money, I looked healthy and bought a new suit, *valenki*, and *ushanka*. Voting day, I saw Aleksandra, a 36-year-old, attractive nurse.

She ran up to me and exclaimed, "Good gracious, how handsome you look, Leonid Petrovich! Let's go vote together!"

"Sure," I agreed and took her arm. When I looked back, I saw the cooks in their white aprons and hoods standing on the porch watching us.

Arkadii shouted, "Father, we're all for you!"

Soon, we entered a large light hall where buffet tables sagged under delicious appetizers of black and red caviar, cheese, bologna, smoked fish, and a variety of desserts.

Beautiful waitresses offered us tea. "You look hungry," Aleksandra said. "Want to eat?"

"No. I need to get back to work."

"Not me. Sit here a sec and save my seat. Stay with me!" she exclaimed.

"I've no money with me."

"That's no problem. Buy a small gift for me on March 8.[4] Today I'll treat you."

We had a few cups of tea and ate some sandwiches, then we went to another hall to watch movies. I felt ashamed as all the doctors and nurses stared at us. When the movie ended, we voted and went home together. While walking, a story came to mind: Communists at a meeting sharply criticized a non–Party woman who had fallen in love with a released prisoner. The Communists threatened to fire her, but she was firm and said that they could fire her, but she was in love. *Was I a threat to Aleksandra?* On the way, we had a nice chit-chat, but when we approached the hospital's kitchen, I closed my mouth. Aleksandra turned to the left, and I turned to the right.

---

4. March 8, International Women's Day, was established to recognize the world's women political rights and their equality with men. Wieszynski, *The Modern Encyclopedia of Russian and Soviet History*, vol. 46 (1987), 24.

Forty-Nine

The Family Cares

Seymchan
Thursday, May 1, 1952–Friday, June 13, 1952

After six long months, I decided to speak to Ukhnalev about Nina coming. There was an eight-hour time difference between the Far East and Saratov, and I needed his permission to call her, find property, and secure a suitable job. At the time, Kolyma was a closed region; one needed special permission to enter.

Comrade Ukhnalev explained, according to the law in 1951, I must have at least 172 square feet of living space for the two of us and a salary of 1,200 rubles or more per month. I made that wage but lacked adequate living space. Knowing that I planned to leave the dishwashing job, Evdokiia Semenovna tried to entice me to stay by offering me a warm, barn space and an increase in salary. I thanked her, but said I wanted to *own* a home. Also, hospital authorities could rescind their offer at any time.

As April ended, I readied to celebrate the May Day Holiday as a *free* citizen for the first time in 14 years.[1] Unexpectedly, Aleksandra dropped by my kitchen with an invitation to attend inauguration speeches and a concert. While giving it to me, she stressed the limited number of cards issued and that all hospital Communists opted to give me one.

On April 30, 1952, I went to the town hall and took a seat in the last row. Aleksandra spotted me and motioned me down to a seat near her in the third row. At the function, we listened to speeches and watched awards to outstanding workers. I was one.

That afternoon, a cold wind brought fresh snow falling hard. The

---

1. May Day was established in Warsaw in 1890 to celebrate International Working Day. The holiday showed solidarity with workers in capitalist countries. Wieszynski, *The Modern Encyclopedia of Russian and Soviet History*, vol. 21 (1981), 148–150.

next day, snow canceled our May Day celebration, and the blizzard didn't die out until noon on the second. Fortunately, it was May and not November. The snow soon melted in spring's warm breezes and carried cheerful news of my permission to build a home. Criminals, political prisoners, and unrestricted men, too, stayed busy building the town. In my tiny room, I sketched a cottage.

On June 1, 1952, news of my long-awaited job doing cost estimates, project evaluations, and maintaining accounting records for the area arrived. I was delighted to finally work in my field despite having to sleep on tables in my office. My superintendent, Kazimir Sokolowski, often drank and didn't oversee work; soon, I took his position supervising 200 workers.

They labored hard, especially former political prisoners. Their self-discipline and honest attitude set an example for released criminals who slowly changed their views. My staff included women, typically tailors, bookkeepers, and office help who greeted me cheerfully.

One day, a well-dressed woman appeared. She was attractive, sexy, and swung her hips when she walked, cooing, "Leonid Petrovich, we're all interested in you. Don't you want one of us as a wife?"

"Girls," I joked, "my fiancée has not been born yet."

"Oh, please have tea with us," another said, raising her dress and showing me her shapely legs. "Are you on duty tonight?" a third girl asked, vying with each other.

I shook my head.

The attractive woman stared at me. "Do you have a wife? Is she coming?"

When I replied in the affirmative, she said, "But why? Isn't she old? We're young and beautiful. Just look at us; aren't we better?"

"You're all good-looking," I replied. "But...."

"So, what would you lose?" she persisted, curling fingers through her curly hair.

"You'll see we're all fantastic," a third woman said, leaning back to expose her splendid breasts and hairstyle.

"Oh, come on, ladies. Your tongues are growing long," I said sarcastically.

"Don't get angry with us, we love you," several howled.

The banter continued for a few minutes, but I could not continue. So, I concluded. "Girls, I'm happily married. I can't go to the movies with you. I'll go with my wife when she arrives. I'm up to my eyes in work on a building. Thank you for your tea and chat, but I must leave."

While visiting the bookkeepers' office, I often saw these beautiful, well-dressed women. I liked their lush breasts. *Why, they were so big!* Be-

Forty-Nine. The Family Cares 215

fore my arrest, I didn't remember women with such huge breasts. Fortunately, no one checked my employees' downtime, and I allowed one of my assistants to go to the cinema with the girls. As for me, as soon as I finished work, I left to continue my work on our new home at 6 Suvorov Street.

Fifty

Nina's Arrival

Hotel, Seymchan
Saturday, June 14, 1952–Saturday, August 30, 1952

On the night of June 14, I received a lovely letter from Nina. It began:

Dear Leonid!

While I was in the Gulag at Yaya Station, I embroidered a winter scene of a snowy night with the sky sprinkled with stars and a glowing moon. Our house is in the middle of the picture surrounded by fir and birch trees. It was my dream of our happiness, and I hope to find us in such a house now that we'll be together. After we reunited, our children can join us.

I received my official invitation from the Ministry of the Internal Affairs and will soon receive my passport. Valeria has passed her final exams. Gennadii is a student at Irkutsk pilot school. Oh, how difficult it was to live alone with the children. I took a rope to the barn and wanted to hang myself to escape this torment and slander, but life tugged me away. Reading your letters, I feel confident in our future.

Love, Nina

In a letter 12 days later, Nina wrote of leaving the Saratov Railroad Station:

Dear Leonid!

Finally, I'm leaving for Kolyma. I'm bringing linens and clothes. My sisters, Valentina and Olga, and our daughter, Valeria, went to the station with me. Gennadii couldn't come due to his classes. We took a neighbor's cart, and, unfortunately, a wheel flew off on our way. Somehow, we fixed the wheel and started driving faster as we were afraid of missing the train. I registered my large bag and carried a small suitcase aboard. My heart was light. I knew I'd soon be seeing you. I was also terrified, traveling alone to far off Kolyma. Nina.

Ever since freedom entered my life, Nina and I wrote constantly. The local postman found me and gave me her letters at my office, on the streets, and sometimes in my mailbox at home. When friends stopped me on the streets, they often brought the news that I'd received another letter.

Fifty. Nina's Arrival

In July, the postman rummaged in his bag and said, "Leonid, here's a telegram from Moscow."

"A telegram!" I exclaimed. "Let's see it!"

Nina wired: *I'm on the train to the Far-East.*

The postman looked at me curiously. "Is your wife coming here?"

"Yes, indeed!" I shouted. "She's coming! Now, I'm off to build our house."

"When will you finish?"

"By the end of August, if I'm lucky."

"Right," he said. "Your wife will arrive in Seymchan in a month since it takes 10 days to get to Vladivostok from Moscow. She'll probably spend 10 days in Vladivostok awaiting a ship. Then it'll take a week to get to Kolyma and more time to get to Seymchan. You know, Leonid, I'm envious. I was released four years ago, and yet you're building a house for your wife who'll soon join you. You're happy, and I'm a postman with a small salary. Before my arrest, I taught history. Now I'm living with a woman. We have two children, and we both have two children from previous marriages. There's no future for me here."

I ran to our house to work. I had all the materials from the wood factory, and I'd kept all those receipts as my workers joked I was buying materials from myself. Three weeks later, I received another telegram from Nina; this one from Nakhodka Bay, 50 miles east of Vladivostok: *I received your money and bought a ticket. Will leave Nakhodka in a week.* Sadly, August was ending, and, as bad luck would it have, all the engineers and workers, including me, were sent to the field for haying. I'd never hayed before, and my scythe often stuck rocks and dirt. One woman, watching me, said, "Leonid Petrovich, I can hay. I grew up in a village and started cutting haying at 10. Why don't you boil water and make lunch?" I didn't argue and went to the kitchen to cook lunch of macaroni with beef.

The next day, I rushed to the shop and bought a double bed, iron springs, and a mattress as the walls of the house was up. I began on the roof. At the end of that week Nina sent another telegram: *I arrived in Magadan and will soon bus to Seymchan.* My mind's eye saw the road from Magadan to Seymchan. She'd travel 360 miles in crowded buses, stopping for food and gas.

In those last days of waiting, I received a letter from my mother. She could not believe Nina and I would soon be together again after 15 years.

> Leonid!
>
> *I am old. I know how hard your life has been since your arrest in 1937. You suffered in the mines. But know that Nina also suffered terribly. Despite this, she is happy because she'll soon see you. I hope your reunion will go well, and, after all*

your sufferings, you two will find happiness again. My dear children, I kiss you and hug you, Love, Mother.

Mother was wise; she knew Nina and I would rebuild our lives. As I clung to her memory, I recalled a story from a carpenter. Like me, he'd asked his wife to reunite here after 12 years working in Kolyma mines. His wife, from Ukraine, arrived, but she left two months later. When I asked him why, he said before his arrest, his wife was tall and thin. Now she had grown big and he couldn't get his arms around her. After she left, he said, he remarried, built a house, and had a daughter. *What will Nina look like?*

On the warm, sunny day of Sunday, August 17, 1952, a crowd of joyous people surrounded me on the banks of the Kolyma River. While well-dressed people walked slowly around Seymchan to shop, play soccer, and fish, I knew something great would happen to me. I'd stopped working on the house, put on my new brown pants, a white dress shirt, and left to inspect the town.

As I passed a hotel on Lenin Street, an unknown man waved at me. "Leonid, your wife's waiting for you at the hotel!"

"She's here, three days early?" I shouted ran. He followed me. "Do you know when she arrived?" I shouted over my shoulder.

"A few minutes ago," the stranger yelled. "I was at the bus stop and heard a beautiful woman say, 'Bolotov's my husband.' Someone said you'd been here, and I darted to find you."

Within minutes, I spotted Nina on the porch. She hadn't changed: tall and slender as she'd been 15 years ago.

"Nina!" I called. Her blue eyes sparkled. She wore a dark-blue suit, white blouse, and gray beret. I felt like a lovesick teenager.

Nina threw herself into my arms and kissed me. Then she leaned back, looked up, and said, "Leonid! Oh, my love, let's eat and then...."

The stranger helped us carry Nina's suitcases to our room. We ordered black beluga caviar and strong black tea. After lunch, Nina and I went to our room on the second floor. She opened her suitcase and showed me pictures of our children. She said my father had died due to war starvation. We both wept. I silently thanked my father for his help, then we talked about our future.

Meanwhile, news of Nina's arrival spread across Seymchan. People remarked: "Do you know Leonid's wife arrived from the mainland?" "I see he dresses well on Sundays." "Where do they live?" "They kept their family intact for years!"

As my log cabin was unfinished, I called Kazimir Sokolowski and asked him about renting a room in his house, vacant as his son was in the army. Kazimir agreed; he allowed us to stay a month. When we went to our

Fifty. Nina's Arrival

room, people crowded asked for a reception, and Sokolowski's wife fried potatoes and baked bread. There were no vodka or wine sold in Seymchan at that time; however, someone brought moonshine. The guests enjoyed our noisy party with many toasts and wishes we'd have a Kolymian baby. Nina relayed stories of her journey from Saratov to Seymchan. When she finished her tale, all our guests cheered and toasted her journey and our reunion. When alone, we walked to the edge of town to see our log cabin. On our walk, Nina admired the town.

"Leonid," she began, looking left and right, "I thought there'd be small houses thrown up here and there, but these are solid two-story homes linked together by clean wide sidewalks studded with trees."

"Nina," I replied, "political prisoners built these homes for Kolyma managers and their families. Many of the prisoners, after their release, became servants for the homeowners. Among them were teachers, medical doctors, and engineers, like me, who had no choice as their relatives had been arrested in 1937 or murdered in Kolyma or killed in World War Two."

Soon we entered the road connecting Seymchan and the airport where a local bazaar with vendors was operating. Small, miserable homes built close to one another stood behind the bazaar. I pointed, "Nina, this is where former and exiled prisoners live. We'll be turning left to cut onto Suvorov Street, and beyond it is our log cabin. You can't miss the roof."

"Oh, Leonid I see it! I see it!" Nina exclaimed, jumping up and down. "Let's run!"

Clutching hands, we ran to the log cabin, festooned with the greenery, set beside a cherry tree. Birds swooped down to pick blueberries; wild roses added a touch of red to the scene.

"Leonid, you planted a real garden!"

But when Nina approached the house, her enthusiasm vanished. She stopped and stared at the bare logs and flimsy roof. "I see there are things to do. Will we have time before winter sets in?"

"Nina, I'll have it all done. We'll finish the roof, make the walls tight, doll up the inside, and build a canopy, barn, and chicken coop as my work permits."

We walked around the house. Nina's spirits brightened. "This is the *first* home we've ever owned!"

We talked about house details, and I grew excited as she warmed to the undertaking. Finally, on Saturday, August 30, 1952, Nina and I moved into our unfinished cabin.

The next Monday I met Larchenko, the team leader for calcining limestone, the process for making cement. He asked, "Where are you living and how's Nina doing in Seymchan?"

I replied, "We're getting along fine, and she loves the town and our new house, but she worries we don't have lights."

"Look, my team can install electric power. If you want, we can also wire your house."

"Great! What do you need?"

And soon lights glowed in our cabin. Nina and I listed things that needed to do, and we tackled them as soon as I finished work every day. I made a fire pit in the yard, and Nina cooked. For years afterward, we talked of the pleasant smells of those wood-fired meals cooked in the fresh air set among the plethora of aromas of wild berries and evergreen trees. Later, three feet of snow covered the town. The only break from the white monochrome was black smoke rising from chimneys like spilled ink.

In November, I built a protective entry hall off the porch. Nina found a sewing machine and began making quilts and clothes to customers' orders. With her earnings, she sent money to our children. Later, at the end of December, Nina found work as a bookkeeper at the Seymchan airport restaurant.

Fifty-One

Nina's Arrest

Arsenalnaia Street Jail
Reflections on the Fall of 1937

One evening, Nina cleared the table and said, "Leonid, three months *to the very day later*, I was also arrested. But I'm getting ahead of myself. After your arrest, the kids and I barely had money for food. We lived hand-to-mouth, and that next month things grew worse. The only valuables we owned were my bicycle, a radio, and your books. I sold my bike and radio quickly. Then I lugged your books to the flea market. Voltaire, Rousseau, Turaev, and Kluchevskii quickly sold for a few rubles. Desperate, I took your treasured Tolstoi volumes to a book-buyer. The man offered me pocket change, far below their real value. I refused his offer and sat in a market all that day, praying for a buyer, but no one was interested. At dark, I returned home penniless.

"By September, once arrested, Soviet enforcers grabbed the few valuables people earned honestly. I was unable to find a teaching position: *I was the wife of an enemy of the people.* But finally, I found a job at the Krupskaia Sugar Factory. Your parents and the kids were overjoyed, but that joy didn't last long. In those cruel days, joy never did. On September 17, I hurried home to Gennadii and Valeria, but on the way two NKVD officers stepped in front of me, blocking the sidewalk. They flashed their ID's and told me to sit in the back seat of their black car. They joked, they wanted to show me Leningrad. I was scared, but I got in the car, white with fright. I don't remember the homes and streets we passed. Forty minutes later, we stopped near a five-story, red-brick building with tall iron gates.

"It was the jail for women at 9 Arsenalnaia Street. The officers ordered me out of the car and pointed to a soldier who opened the gate and shoved me into the yard. After that, I was told to go into an entry hall, a long, narrow, stuffy space crowded with women wearing summer dresses, bathrobes, thin shoes, and clinging to clutches. I waited an hour, and then was prodded into a cell, found a tiny spot, and squeezed onto the cement floor.

"Some women seemed puzzled and asked me why I was arrested and what would happen to my children, which left me unable to sleep. Rumors buzzed around the cell. Repeatedly, the overseer slid open a Judas hole and ordered silence. It didn't happen.

"Every day for six weeks, I prayed they'd made a mistake and you'd be released and rush to rescue me. I'd believed in the honesty of Soviet justice. I waited and waited for you to come. I knew you'd be at the door any minute. Later, I learned our kids expected us both to return. We didn't. Comrade Nikitin, a Party Secretary in the Lenin District, held you in high regard, Leonid, and said you were in Kresty Prison."

I nodded and sipped some tea. "I remembered Nikitin well."

Nina continued, "NKVD investigators ordered me to sign a document saying you gave me gold rings and brooches, a saboteurs' pay. I protested, insisting I'd never got such gifts. The investigator countered, saying you made good money."

"Yes," I injected, "I did make good wages that year, but never enough for gold gifts."

Nina grew angry. "Well, I told him that. I said, you'd been ordered by the State Department of Chemistry to move to Leningrad after college and we only had one suitcase between the two of us and no money for food or housing. But the investigator snarled that I was obstinate, insisting I tell him the truth about you and he'd let me go."

"You must have been scared out of your mind," I said, going to the stove, filling it with wood, and setting the teakettle on it to heat.

Nina let out a deep huff. "I told the investigator all that, but I didn't know what he wanted. Then he changed his approach and asked me if you ever talked about your factory, and I said, of course you had. We talked about your factory work every evening."

"I'm sure that was okay," I said. "All couples discussed their workdays. What else was there in life but work, family, and listening to the radio?"

"The investigator wanted details of our talks—*all of them*—and I said, it's boring. He insisted, so I said, my husband tells me about new machines he and his fellow workers are making and what they'll do. The NKVD agent yelled, 'Why do you keep talking about machines? Tell me about the people in the factory and their salaries.'"

"But wives knew nothing of that!" I said.

Nina continued, "The investigator's face was red. I said you'd mentioned Stakhanov,[1] but I had no idea how much, and he screamed at me again. 'Don't give me Stakhanov! Tell me what your husband said about the factory administration!' So, then I spoke of Ordzhonikidze and Kirov how they visited the factory and how you admired them. The agent yelled, 'Tell me more. Did anyone offend your husband?'"

"That's a strange question," I said. "How would you know?"

"He was guessing. It suggested that perhaps the factory director, like you, was an enemy of the people. But I insisted, you were not an enemy of anyone! He replied with a question, 'Why do you refuse to tell us anything substantial?' and I said, because I don't know anything substantial. He ranted, 'Tell, ask, tell, ask,' taunting me and said I was responsible for knowing your every action and thought because I was hiding an enemy of the people who hid saboteurs from authorities and had already confessed to his guilt. I could not convince him I knew nothing."

"So, what happened?" I stood, poured tea for Nina, and held her hand lovingly.

"After that, the investigator said, 'If you don't admit the truth about your husband, you'll follow him to prison. But if you tell us the truth we're seeking, you can remain at home with your children.' I remained silent. The agent asked me to sign a confession about you. I refused. A NKVD guard took me to a cell. On the way, in the corridor, I noticed a small kiosk where women, like Nina Lekarenko,[2] were permitted to buy groceries. The rumor was that her mother gave her money every week."

Nina's interrogation was the extent of her "trial" for the crime of being married to an enemy of the people. She had no witnesses. There was no application of the Soviet law.

On October 29, Nina, along with 2,000 other women with husbands labeled supporters of Trotskii, Bukharin, and Zinov'ev,[3] the court ordered them to up to eight years in the Gulag with no right to correspond. Investigators took their fingerprints and photographs, profile and full-face, and drove them to Sortirovochnaia Railroad Station.

"Lines of cars and buses pulled in close to the train. Guards with snarling German shepherds surrounded the area. Despite their secret ar-

---

1. Stakhanov, Aleksei Grigorievich (1905–1977), the most famous worker-innovator and labor hero in the USSR, whose feat of hewing 102 tons of coal in a six-hour shift on August 30–31, 1935 in the Donbas Region touched off the mass movement which bore his name. Wieszynski, *The Modern Encyclopedia of Russian and Soviet History*, vol. 37 (1984), 60–61.

2. Lekarenko, Nina Alekseevna (1911–1995), illustrated children's books, was arrested in the fall 1937, worked in Novosibirsk Province until the end of World War II, and was rehabilitated in 1957. Noskovich, N.A. "Vospominania "pridurka."" *Neva* No. 4 (2001): 165–183.

3. Zinov'ev, Grigorii Evseevich (1883–1936), Chairman of the Communist International, was a leader of the Party. Wieszynski, *The Modern Encyclopedia of Russian and Soviet History*, vol. 46 (1987), 91–104.

rests and sentences, relatives and friends learned about the terrible judgment and the train's location."

Nina said, "When I stepped down from the bus, I spotted Lelia Dobronravova, also a prisoner. She ran to me. Then Elena Pamfilovna appeared from the shadows in the headlights of the cars and buses where she'd hidden.

"Elena Pamfilovna glanced left and right and shoved her way through the crowd, yelling, 'Lelia! Nina! I've been waiting for you here for three days with this!' I couldn't believe the mass of men, women, and children, trying to find their relatives. A few times, I heard desperate appeals: 'Where's my dear mother!' 'Have you seen my daughter, Olga?' 'What prison term did you get?' 'Did you have a judge?' 'Where are you being sent?' 'Goodbye, my love!'

"Elena Pamfilovna and Petr Antonovich gave us our winter coats, apples, and money.

"Sadly, soon, the press of the crowd shoved aside Elena Pamfilovna and Petr Antonovich, and we lost sight of them. We saw desperate parents move from our wagon.

"Inside the dark wagon, ice coated the floor and the temperature was below freezing. Lelia and I rushed to claim a plank-bed by setting my apples and spreading my coat over its narrow boards. We laid down, huddled beneath her fur coat, and ate apples. When I felt in the bag for a second apple, my fingers touched a folded paper. I pulled it out and read: *Nina! I took Gennadii and Valeria to Saratov. Your mom.* Soon guards locked our wagon door. Only thin shafts of little light shone through cracks and a small window. For hours, when it was light enough, and I could see out the window, I saw snow and woods.

"On November 7, we arrived in Novosibirsk for two days. Outside, workers celebrated the 20th anniversary of the October Revolution. But this was a glum time for us with weak *balanda*, no toilets other than the space between the wagons to squat. We were all sick at heart. Maria Vasil'evna Skachkova[4] and Lubov Orekhova, on other planks, withered in pain and cried for their children.

"As we waited with nothing to do, some women made warm clothes for those who had none. Emilia Markovna Ryvkina-Vainer gave her knitted mittens to Vilma Schmidt,[5] and Berta Skoblo[6] cut enough lining from her winter coat to make Vilma a cap."

---

4. Skachkova, Maria Vasil'evna (1894–?), worked at the Institution of Municipal Economy until convicted in 1937 and sentenced to the coal mines of Anzhero-Sudzhensk. She was rehabilitated in 1956, http://arch.iofe.center.

5. Schmidt, Vilma, died in prison, http://arch.iofe.center.

6. Skoblo, Berta Aleksandrovna (1903–?), worked at the Leningrad Ophthalmological Institute until convicted in 1937, and sentenced to five years in Tomsk. She was released in 1942, http://arch.iofe.center.

Fifty-One. Nina's Arrest

"While I'm listening to you, Nina," I said, "men were arrested and deported first. Zhdanov[7] and Kuznetsov[8] knew if women were exile before men, the crowds would disappear by the jails and their paperwork would be reduced along with appeals to the courts. Mothers, sisters, daughters, and wives protested. Children quickly realized guards stole their parents. Old people knew they'd never enjoy their retirement."

"Leonid, you're right," Nina agreed. "After our 14th day, we arrived in Tomsk. Ignoring the cold and deep snow, guards ordered us from the wagons to make five columns. For the next two hours, they counted us before handing us over to Tomsk' jail guards. Of course, guards wore sheepskin coats, elbow-length mittens, and *valenki*. They had snarling dogs baring their teeth and barking. Some women gave up and dropped into the snow. Vilma, wearing summer shoes, jumped in the snow for warmth and rubbed her hands together.

"We snaked through Tomsk to a two-story barracks on the edge of the city, passing stone churches, administrative buildings, libraries, theaters, cinemas, markets, and fur shops. We finally arrived at the jail."

---

7. Zhdanov, Andrei Aleksandrovich (1896–1948), party leader in Leningrad, was notorious for his repressiveness against artists, intellectuals, and scientists. Wieszynski, *The Modern Encyclopedia of Russian and Soviet History*, vol. 46 (1987), 31–33.

8. Kuznetsov, Aleksei Aleksandrovich's (1905–1950), career benefited from the many vacancies occurring in the Party resulting from the Great Purges of the 1930s. During World War II, Kuznetsov served in the Military Council for the Baltic Fleet and on the War Council for the Leningrad Front. He was executed in 1950 for becoming too popular. Wieszynski, *The Modern Encyclopedia of Russian and Soviet History*, vol. 18 (1980), 220–222.

Fifty-Two

Tomsk's Jail

The NKVD Inner Jail
November 1937–December 1940

Next evening, Nina went on, "In jail, guards ordered us into cells teeming with bed-bugs. We spent the next hours picking bugs off our bodies and grinding them beneath our summer shoes. A few narrow plank-beds of 14 inches lined the cell, and women sat on the lip of the planks, awaiting turns to sleep, jammed so tightly together, we had to turn like dancers in a chorus line.

"This jail became our 'home' for the next three years. I met repressed wives: Anna Larina-Bukharina, Sarra Yakir, Maria Tukhachevskaia, and Sofia Averbakh.[1] Guards called us traitors to the Motherland. To add to their cruelty, they swore and yelled that we were political supporters of Nikolai Bukharin and Iona Yakir.

"Over the coming months, we only saw one boy, Yuri, a two-year-old boy arrested with his mother, and one bitter man, Uncle Poop, carried out our waste.

"As for exercise, we were rarely allowed outdoors. On those rare times when we were allowed in the yard, we were ordered only to look at our feet, and we watched our steps tramp snow into a muddy foot-trail, which we labeled 'The Leningradians' Wives Boulevard' as we sang this song:

---

1. Larina-Bukharina, Anna Mikhailovna (1914–1996), was one of three wives of Nikolai Bukharin and spent twenty years in camps. Larina, Anna. *This I Cannot Forget: The Memoirs of Nikolai Bukharin's Widow* (New York: W.W. Norton, 1993. Yakir, Sarra Lazarevna (1900–1971), wife of executed military commander Yakir Iona Emmanuilovich (1896–1937) was rehabilitated in 1956. Larina, *This I Cannot Forget*, 174–180. Tukhachevskaia-Vladimirova, Maria Nikolaevna (1907–1995), was one of Marshal Tukhachevskii's sisters and spent twenty years in camps until rehabilitated in 1956; Averbakh, Sophia Mikhailovna (1882–1951), a sister of Iakov Sverdlov (1885–1919), Chairman of the All-Russian Central Executive Committee, was a pediatrician, arrested in Moscow and exiled to Siberia, http://arch.iofe.center.

> Here we are your wives and girlfriends,
> Here to sing you an anthem
> From this Leningradians' Wives Boulevard.

"Once, while walking on the 'Boulevard,' a man shouted from the men's barracks across the way, 'Maria! Maria!'

"A woman stopped, whirled around, and waved. Maria Yermakova was the man in the window's wife. And then, a guard yank him away just as a jet of water from outside the prison blasted him.

"Prisoners supplied the jail with cooks and janitors. Liudmila Kuzminichna Shaposhnikova,[2] the attractive wife of Mikhail Chudov, oversaw food preparation. I had no idea how she managed to make us tasty meals from frozen potatoes, cabbage, and poor cuts of beef, but twice a week we ate meat soup. One day, guards ordered her to ball her clothes into a knot and led her away.

"There were women informers, like Kahnovich and Zemskova, who never hid their connections with the guards.[3] They claimed our bones and blood would be their ticket out of jail. After their denunciations, investigators often called us at night and beat us. Many women lost their vision and hearing. We renamed our investigators and watch-guards: Tsarists' policemen. Rosa Ozerskaia, a history teacher, went deaf after her night interrogation.[4] When we asked her what happened, she only nodded her head to one side, meaning the informers had deafened her. Raisa Gluzskaia, a former employer at the Hermitage, acted just like Rosa had, her body trembling and cringing fearfully after questioning."

I said, "That must have been horrible."

"It was," Nina said. "Then Yekaterina Fokina, our medical doctor, like Cerberus, passed on all our conversations to the administration.[5] After a year, they permitted us to write a letter a month and receive parcels. We were each issued a sheet of paper and shared pens. Women begged for more pens, but guards ignored their appeals, screaming, 'There won't be any more pens!'

"Slowly, we succeeded in informing our families where we were and how we were living. In response, our relatives began sending us needles,

---

2. Shaposhnikova, Liudmila Kuzminichna (1895–1942), the Manager of the Red October Factory, arrested in 1937, executed in 1942, and rehabilitated in 1956. Larina, *This I Cannot Forget*, 339, 341, 361.

3. Zemskova, Aleksandra Antonovna (1898–?), a prosecutor in Leningrad's October District, was convicted in 1937, and rehabilitated in 1957, http://arch.iofe.center.

4. Ozerskaia, Rosa Abramovna (1903–?), a Tomsk history teacher, was convicted in 1937, and rehabilitated in 1955. Uimanov, V.N. Iu. A. Petrukhin. *Bol' liudskaia: kniga pamiati tomichei, repressirovannykh v 30–40-e i nachale 50-kh godov* (Tomsk: Upravleniie AFB RF po Tomskoi oblasti, 1992), vyp. 2, 335.

5. Fokina, Yekaterina, was a watch guard for women, http://arch.iofe.center.

A preserved Tomsk jail cell in 2018 (Collection of Angelina Azieva).

thread, and lace. Every day, we embroidered curtains, sewed clothes, and adorned shawls for the administration. We even created work fit for exhibition. Often, groups of six women huddled on one plank-bed, sewing under dim light, talking about families and celebrating birthdays, holidays, or discussing world history.

"I also remember the medical observations of Vasil'eva, a Leningrad gynecologist, who noted our menstruation cycles ceased. Mother Nature supported us during this difficult time.

Fifty-Two. Tomsk's Jail

Nina Lekarenko's sketch of women in Tomsk jail, ca. 1980–1985 (Saratov Radishchev Art Museum).

"Countless girls were jailed for the 'crime' of having fathers and step-fathers who'd been arrested and exiled to Kazakhstan and Kolyma. That is so ironic, for, at the same time, government newspapers and posters proclaimed children were not responsible for their parents' crimes. Women sobbed over teenagers receiving 10-year Gulag sentences and decades of exile. Anna Larina-Bukharina with her one-year-old son, Yuri, was abandoned in Moscow.[6] Like her, Vilma grieved over her son Gelia loss. Unexpectedly, when a Moscow special commission visited our jail, Vilma asked their help in finding her son, and, within two months, authorities found him in an orphanage. He mailed his mom his first letter, written in a childish scrawl. Reading it, Vilma wept all night, 'Who arrested him?'

"Her father, Martius Schmidt, had been a member of the Bolsheviks' party since 1905 and was killed during the Civil War. The Whites killed her mother in 1920. Vilma and her sister fled Latvia for Moscow and joined the Party. On October 2, 1920, Vilma heard Lenin's speech at the Third All-Russian Congress of *Komsomol*. Her husband, Avgust Kaleis,

---

6. Larin, Yuri Nikolaevich (1936–2014), born in Moscow to Nikolai Bukharin and Anna Larina, was raised by a Gusman family and then in an orphanage in Stalingrad. Yuri met his mother in 1957 for the first time. Larina, *This I Cannot Forget*, 318–322.

professor of history and editor of the *Leningradskaia Pravda* newspaper, had been arrested as a *Trotskyist*. Vilma told us that Estina, a party instructor, ordered her to publish a newspaper article denying her marriage to Kaleis. Vilma refused.[7]

"Three years later, the administration began sending women to Gulags in Norilsk, the world's northernmost city, the Altai Mountains, Magadan, and Yaya Station in Kemerovo Province. We all went through Mariinsk.[8] The garment factory made long-johns, pants, and prisoners' quilted jackets. When World War Two began, we made military uniforms.

"On June 22, 1941, we heard Molotov's radio declaration that Germany had attacked the Baltic Countries, Ukraine, and Belorussia, including the cities of Zhitomir, Kiev, and Kaunas. He encouraged all Soviets to join in defense. This horror became doubly incomprehensible for us as all Yaya locals considered us guilty of crimes and having caused the invasion that started the war! Nonetheless, we worked in good faith and stitched with aching fingers on night shifts and always over-fulfilled our tasks by up to 180%.

"In the spring, factory's administrators ordered us to dig holes and plant trees around the home of Ostapchuk, our manager. Trying to stab the earth, we discovered it was frozen as hard as granite. The only way to proceed was to hack it into chunks with sledgehammers, and we did. When exhausted from 'rock' breaking, we plunked down on Ostapchuk's porch to rest, and his wife rushed outside yelling, 'This porch is only for good people, not wild animals like you! GET OFF!'"

---

7. Kaleis, Avgust Simonovich (1902–?), instructor of history at Leningrad Communist University, was arrested in 1937 and exiled to Norilsk Camp 2, http://db.ranar.spb.ru.

8. In the 1930s, Mariinsk was a large, prisoner distribution camp in Kemerovo Province, located at the intersection of the Kiya River and Trans-Siberian Railway. Rossi, *The Gulag Handbook*, 215.

Fifty-Three

Nina's Release and Meeting with Children

Anzhero-Sudzhensk—Yaya—Saratov
Thursday, September 17, 1942–
Sunday, March 8, 1944

The next evening, after dinner, Nina continued her saga.

"On September 17, 1942, guards ordered Lelia, Vera Kulikova, and I freed after five years. However, the guards refused us permission to go home. 'You women are free, today,' one said. 'Now go find a place to live because you can't leave the area.'

"In true Soviet custom, we received no food or money from the administration or factory and were desperate. Landlords demanded rent and deposits. Frantic, we walked into town to look for free lodging. Locals were afraid to talk; we were untrustworthy. In a panic, we met a frail, toothless, old lady. She agreed to let us stay in her old wooden house for garden and housekeeping work. Digging potatoes and cleaning a little house was simple, and we quickly agreed.

"Like most poor dwellings in the village, her home tilted drunkenly on permafrost, and its slab-sides and roof blackened with soot and grim. Paint-faded shutters bracketed her windows, and, up three steps, her porch led to a heavy wooden door on iron hinges and a rusty handle that opened to a long, narrow, entryway and kitchen. A shabby table stood beneath the kitchen window, and a sturdy bench before it was polished by years of sitting. Gray embroidered curtains hung over the window and blocked the little sunlight, leaving the kitchen in near darkness that a weak light over the wood stove couldn't overcome. The doorway between the tiny kitchen and larger living room was opened. In Saratov, we draped that dividing space with a full-length-curtain. Not here. In this living room, an oil lamp sat on a table above the bare plank floor; four beds filled the corners. The privy was outside. Water was pumped from a pipe in the next street and carried in buckets that hung from a yoke leaning against the wall.

"The old lady told me that she knew we were from a big city by our accent. She guessed we were fashionable ladies before our arrests, but she was a peasants' daughter sent to the coal mines at age 14. She lived here all her life and had two sons, arrested, and three sons in the army. She finished by saying she'd be thankful if we'd help her reply to her boys' letters, claiming her eyes didn't see well. She probably couldn't read or write.

"After finishing at the mine, we dug potatoes and carried them to the kitchen. The old woman told us potatoes were vital for the winter as the shops were empty; all food was sent to the army. She asked us if we knew when Stalin would defeat Hitler in this terrible war.

"Nineteen forty-two was a difficult year for all women; many lost their families. Aleksandra Petrova lost a son, parents, and three sisters in Leningrad.[1] Like most of the convicted wives of enemies of the people who had received release papers, we had no information from home as to where to go or help leaving Tomsk.

"In the city center, there was a modern theater, city-park, two stadiums, libraries, and a cinema. Tall, white birches and leafy poplars grew along its sidewalks, and in the square, there were monuments to Lenin and Stalin decorated with posters of coal mines production achievements glorifying World War II: *Our labor is the strength of the military defense of the USSR! Miners give our coal production to the motherland!*

"We wore issued white pants, jackets, and *valenki,* and we looked clumsy in our baggy 'uniforms.' We shoveled coal onto conveyors, under the supervision of a man who constantly yelled, 'You're not working at full strength! Work harder!' At the end of every shift, black with coal dust, we all gasped for breath climbing out of the mine.

"We learned there were other functioning plants in the city, a large-scale, mechanized bakery, timber mill, meat processing and packing factory, along with a quartz mine, and repair shops. Locals used horses for transportation.

"We enjoyed the indefatigable Elena Pamfilovna when she discovered Lelia's address and visited us. Elena had grown so weak from lack of food after evacuation to the Road of Life on the Ladoga Lake, but she told us about the German's siege of Leningrad and that horrific life.

"Once, long afterward, I was overcome with joy when Varvara Iva-

---

1. In 1942, 3,500–4,000 people died per day from starvation. Platonov, S.P. *Bitva za Leningrad, 1941–1944* (Moskva: Voennoie izdatelstvo ministerstva oborony of the USSR, 1964), 194–203.

Fifty-Three. Nina's Release and Meeting with Children

novna mailed me a picture of Valeria and Gennadii. All my friends gathered around me to look at the picture of my children and read the letter.

"In late 1943, a medical commission arrived in Anzhero-Sudzhensk. I trembled when my turn in line came. An old doctor said, 'You have high blood pressure and can't work.'

"On March 3, 1944, walking home, I met Vera Vedeneva.[2] She yelled joyously, 'Nina, here's your document! You may leave Anzhero-Sudzhensk today!'

"I thanked her, took my documentation, and went directly to the local police station. Officers told me I could leave Anzhero-Sudzhensk in two days. My sisters, Olga and Valentina, had already sent me money for my train ticket and food. In my clothing knot, I put six pounds of potato flour and slung an old blanket onto my back.

"On March 5, 1944, a truck picked me up at 5:30 a.m. in central square to take me to Yaya Station.

"The station master said all trains go through Saratov. In the minuscule station, there was a post office and telegraph station, and I sent a wire with my expected arrival date. That settled, I stepped out into the blizzard to await the next train. Forty-five minutes later, a train stopped. The coach doors were locked. Frost masked the windows. Snow plastered the railcars, making them look like a giant, knobby icy snake. I knocked on a railcar door, but no one opened it. I ran to the next car. No one opened that door either. Meanwhile, other passengers entered their railcars. Conductors shoved me aside, probably because my clothes looked shabby. For hours, I was not allowed to board and slept in the station. Passengers dressed in fur coats boarded, but the conductors were rude and callous to me.[3]

"I repeatedly begged conductors, 'I have a ticket to Saratov, please let me in.'

"But they refused me aboard unless I bribed them. Hours later, I jumped onto a footboard, clung to a handle, and pressed myself against the outside of the railcar door as the train left, closing my eyes and gritting my teeth as we chugged off. The train sped on, not stopping at stations. I felt frozen to the door, covered in snow from head to foot. The wheels clacked over the tracks. The wind whistled in my ears. I thought about the last seven years and kept repeating to myself, I'm going home to Saratov!

---

2. Vedeneva, Vera Aleksandrovna (1906–?), worked at The Red Banner Factory, was sent to the Tomsk jail in 1937. After her release in 1942, she still had to work in the coal mines in Anzhero-Sudzhensk. http://arch.iofe.center.

3. Aleksandr Vinnikov, a local Anzhero-Sudzhensk historian, told me that at that time trains often missed their schedules and were overfilled, forcing passengers to stand between or outside railcars. Translator's note.

"Two hours later, the train slowed, the railcars squeaked, and the engine huffed and puffed, slowing to a stop. When the conductor opened the door, it struck me, and she watched me fall into the snow. Despite her anger at me for stealing a ride, she helped me up and told me we had arrived at the Taiga Station, 58 miles from where I had started.

"'Fifty-eight miles?' I repeated, shocked. I thought I'd been clinging to the door an eternity.

"'Are you a political prisoner?' she asked. 'Do you plan to go on riding on the footboard?'

"'Yes! I bought a ticket to Saratov, but no one allowed me in.'

"'Well, come in and sit in the aisle.'

"I entered and sat on my small knot until we arrived in Novosibirsk when I took an empty bed in the middle of the warm car. I laid down and slept until we arrived in Saratov.

"When the train stopped, I stood in the doorway and smelled spring in the air. Water covered the platform. I stepped down and immediately saw our 12-year-old Gennadii with my sisters. I recognized his childish features, but Leonid, he had grown so tall and thin. Seeing me, Gennadii rushed and threw his arms around me in a bear hug.

"Then Olga and Valentina hugged me, and we all left for home where I finally saw my little Valeria and Varvara Ivanovna in the yard. When Valeria saw me, she screamed and jumped up and down. 'Grandma, mommy came home! Hurry out here.'

"Varvara Ivanovna rushed out to the yard and sat on a small bench. Valeria hid behind her and asked me, 'Why were you taken from us?'

"Soon my sisters' husbands and my sister-in-law, Zenaida with her husband, Konstantin, and your brother, Aleksandr, and his wife, Elena, came to visit. We celebrated, talking until midnight. I asked Valeria to go to bed early. She was hurt, but she went to bed behind a small partition. Next day, all our relatives and I walked down Saratov streets, enjoying the beautiful weather. I craved to have you near the children and me because only you could make us happy.

"Later, I went to the police station to register as a wife of an enemy of people. There I saw the real face of Saratov when a policeman woman snapped at me, 'If you returned from Tomsk jail, take your little puppies and get out of the city within 24 hours! I don't want to smell you in this city!'

"My sisters advised me to go to Aleksandrovka village in the Saratov German District. In 1941, authorities deported all Germans residents as friends of the German army. In the village, I worked as a storekeeper and a bookkeeper of a collective farm. Slowly, the children grew accustomed to me.

Fifty-Three. Nina's Release and Meeting with Children

"Gennadii told me that he went to school in 1938. His first and favorite teacher was Olga Zakharovna. Your parents lived on Poleznii Street as they left their previous house to your brother Aleksandr. Petr Antonovich worked as a stoker at School 27, he constantly had to keep two large boilers fired. Gennadii often slept over with Petr Antonovich in the boiler-house. Varvara Ivanovna made potato soup from peels he found in Saratov dumps. Anna, your sister, worked in the school cafeteria and brought the children a thin porridge.

"In 1943, the school turned into a hospital for wounded soldiers, all the desks removed for armless and legless soldiers. There was not enough space for them in the school and they laid on the floor. Boys witnessed them. So, Gennadii saw the blood of war.

"We had a cow, and we always had milk, sour cream, and butter, but we didn't have bread. In summer, we cut hay and caught fish. Gennadii learned to fix *valenki* because neither children nor I had adequate shoes and clothes. Once, I gave money to Gennadii to buy a pair of school pants at the local market, but he bought a hunting rifle and shot rabbits for us to eat. Varvara Ivanovna gave me old fabric, and I made a pair of pants for him.

"Leonid, I hoped that we would meet in 1947; it was the last year of your 10-year exile. I never dreamed you'd receive another term, and our long-awaited meeting postponed.

Left to right: Gennadii, Nina, and Leonid in 1956 (Collection of Lana Bourret).

"I had no one to share my grief and our eternal separation. The undeserved offenses and humiliations rose inside me. I took a rope and went to the barn to commit suicide. Fortunately, my beliefs in life gained the upper hand.

"I listened to Nina and thought about how strong she is!"

Fifty-Four

The First Thawed Patch

Magadan–Khabarovsk
Tuesday, March 5, 1953–Sunday, February 19, 1956

In Seymchan, medical doctors strongly advised Nina to leave Kolyma as its severe climate was destroying her health with hardening of the arteries. But Nina did not want to leave me as we'd waited too long for our reunion.

After Stalin's death, March 5, 1953, without telling Nina, I began sending appeals to review my case to Moscow and the Military Tribunal of the Far East.[1] Nina feared we might get new sentences, but, two years later, on May 19, 1955, I received official notice, No. 9/5209, from the Magadan Province Ministry of Internal Affairs:

> On April 23, 1955, the State Security and Ministry of Internal Affairs of Magadan Province refused to review the sentence dated December 18, 1942 for Bolotov, Leonid Petrovich; however, he is free of exile in Seymchan. This notice is for the issuance of a temporary passport. /s/ Chairman of Magadan Province Administration of Internal Affairs. Colonel Shevelev.

On one hand, Nina and I were pleased with this as it allowed me to obtain a valid passport, but, on the other hand, we were upset that it had not revoked my 1942 death sentence by shooting. However, we could now fly to Khabarovsk with my new passport, and, from there, to train to Leningrad and Saratov before returning to Seymchan for a full passport.

After seven more months of waiting for various approvals, Nina and I explained to our bosses that we would both be leaving Kolyma. Our colleagues listened to our happy news, gave us money, and, in February, we

---

1. In the summer 1951, listed in the archives of the Administration of the Northeastern Camp, were the files of 501,271 prisoners, including 125,316 dead. Batsaev and Kozlov, *Dalstroy Trust Sevvostlag OGPU-NKVD of the USSR as Presented by Documents and in Numbers (2 parts). Part 1 (1931–1941)*, p. 1, 6.

flew from Seymchan to Khabarovsk, over a thousand miles southwest with fuel-stops along the way in Magadan and Nikolaevsk-on-Amur. During the trip, I experienced severe pains in my heart, and I took the heart medication, *corvalol*. The flight attendant didn't have water on the plane, but a fellow passenger gave me his beer and I soon felt better. During our layovers, we dined at a cafeteria, enjoyed fish sandwiches and joked with other passengers about the warm spring on the mainland.

We landed in Khabarovsk early the next morning. It had been a long time since we'd breathed such pleasant air! We took our heavy bag—and took a taxi to the Dalstroy Hotel. On the way, we admired city life that we'd forgotten in Kolyma. At the hotel, the receptionist, a lady in her mid–30s, asked us for our passports and gave us a room on the first floor. We showered, slept, and then went to a restaurant. Over the meal, we discussed our meeting with Colonel Dubrovin, Vice Prosecutor of the Far Eastern Military District who I'd contacted in Seymchan.

The next day, at noon, I entered Dubrovin's office alone while Nina waited in the hall. Dubrovin shook my hand, smiled, and confirmed that my case has been on his desk for two weeks. Our talk was long and pleasant. I asked him to cancel my death sentence and explained that Karpetin had slandered my character. Dubrovin called his assistant and ordered him to review my case.

When I left his office, Nina was nervous. "Leonid, what did you discuss? I heard loud sounds, then soft sounds."

"Nina, they'll restore my rights soon. Our rehabilitation is coming!"

Nina beamed. Tears flooded her eyes. But our conversation was interrupted by a young officer who couldn't believe my case. Again, and again, I repeated my life's story from 1917 to 1955. He looked at me distrustfully, but he promised me to revise my case and investigate my work in Kolyma. He was my first investigator to have said goodbye. After his tone of voice, Nina and I realize we'd never regain our youth, but we could live together without the shocks and humiliations of Gulags.

After dinner, we returned to the hotel, packed, and taxied to the railroad station where we purchased tickets for the long journey to Leningrad. It was the first time we'd seen the beautiful Lake Baikal and the Ural Mountains and the vastness of Siberia.

Fifty-Five

In Leningrad

The Public Prosecutor's Office
Monday, February 20, 1956–Monday, March 12, 1956

Our railcar was boisterous with cheer and merry with conversations as the passengers admired the beautiful mountains, gushing rivers, and drank tea on the way west. A man near me talked about the Twentieth Party Congress and it a new leader, Nikita Khrushchev, who had openly denounced Stalin.

"We Russians will build a new life!" he bragged confidently.

A man objected. "Hey, friend, Lenin promised us Communism, and what did we get? Endless wars, ruinous debt, and prison camps."

As we mulled that truth, old folk songs broke out on the train crossing into Sverdlovsk, the Ural Mountains border between Asia and Europe.[1]

"Hot pies!" a young vendor shouted.

We bought four small pies. While we ate, we discussed, again, the meeting with Dubrovin and our upcoming reunion with Gennadii—Valeria was in Saratov—and the review by authorities in Leningrad. We had a lot to accomplish in a short time, and over the next four days on our journey to Moscow, we covered them repeatedly.

When the train arrived at Moscow's Yaroslavskii Railroad Station, our transfer point to Leningrad, we were surprised to find the platform bursting with jubilation. From snatches of conversations, we heard Muscovites expressing happiness at Stalin's death and the joy of seeing long-absent innocent prisoners again. With each of us carrying two bags, Nina and I left the station, crossed Komsomolskaia Square, and purchased tickets at the Leningradskii Railroad Station. We grew nervous with anticipation at seeing our son after 6,800 days, and we both took heart medications. Standing on the crowded platform, our

---

1. Sverdlovsk, a Ural Mountains city, was the name of Yekaterinburg from 1924 to 1991. Wieszynski, *The Modern Encyclopedia of Russian and Soviet History*, vol. 38 (1984), 101.

souls rejoiced when the train finally stopped by us, and we heard the announcement to board.

We went to the third railcar, took linen from an attendant for our narrow beds, and looked out at Moscow's evening lights. Before we opened the bed, Nina nestled on the bench next to the window and slept. I walked down the corridor to smoke and think.

Our Moscow-to-Leningrad fast train struggled with inertia at first but then gained traction and picked up speed. I peered out the window at the capital's flitting lights. After being confined in Kolyma for 20 years, I relished the movement, the scenery, the metronomic clacking of steel wheels on track-joints, which grew faster, rushing us home. *Home to Leningrad after two long decades in the Gulag! In seven hours, I'd see our son Gennadii. Would I recognize him—or him me? Could we communicate? My soul floated on ecstasy. And why not? A 20-year victim, and, like Dostoevskii, condemned to death by the Soviet Supreme Court twice, who wouldn't be rapturous. Life is strange. Sometimes it turns things upside down. Legs become heads; heads become legs, mental legs that walk you back through 20 years. It is hard to stand on those legs, but they are the only legs I have, and they are good to have.*

Waves of grief overcame me as I stood at the window, torn apart by anguish for all the murdered Leningradians, angst-filled for all those still imprisoned. *How can I blank out that horrible night of my arrest in 1937?! I COULDN'T! I saw Kolyma in 1938 and the "Homes of Communists" we dug, the name we gave permafrost holes we hacked and dumped bodies of our friends.*

The train stopped for two minutes in Tver, and I returned to our cabin. Soon after, I drifted off to sleep and awoke when music filled the cabin, letting passengers know that we were arriving in Leningrad, at the Moscow Railroad Station. A line quickly formed beside a small restroom, and each person asked, "Don't stay in there too long." When it was our turns, I hurriedly shaved, and Nina combed her hair.

The train stopped. We rushed outside. I spotted Gennadii, dressed in a pilot's uniform. Beside him stood a pretty, young woman and a three-year-old girl. He already had a family! As we approached, his daughter pointed at us, "Are you my grandparents?"

"Yes," Nina said joyously.

"I'm Galia," the girl replied proudly.

"Give me your hand!" I said, and Galia gave me her tiny hand. Then Gennadii's wife stepped closer. "I'm Tamara. Welcome home!"

"Thank you, Tamara," Nina said, and I added, "I hope we see you often."

Bursting with happy chatter, Tamara told us she was a dentist. Gennadii added that they live in a dormitory near Gorelovo Station, 13 miles

Fifty-Five. In Leningrad

east of Leningrad. We took a bus to the Baltic Railroad Station and a train to Gorelovo Station. On the way, Nina and I stared out the window, recalling walks, and visits with old friends.

During the train ride, I explained to Gennadii and Tamara that I must visit the authorities from the Leningrad military district to discuss my rehabilitation. When we arrived at their small dorm, Gennadii showed us another nearby room and said we could stay there as his friend was on vacation. Nina and I set our luggage in that room, and we spent the day chatting and enjoying our first lunch together in two decades.

The next morning, when Gennadii and I were at the hall outside Khrustalev's office, we meet Sergei Petrazhitskii and Yekaterina Tiagunova. Like Dubrovin, Khrustalev was friendly, and we spoke for four hours. Khrustalev did not question me as Baryshnikov and Sapozhnikov had. He spoke quietly, asking me about my life in Kolyma. I couldn't understand how he had found my former colleagues, as Petrozhitskii had become a colonel and Tiagunova had left the Red Triangle, but here they were for support. Yekaterina and Sergei explained to Khrustalev that they couldn't understand why I was ever arrested and exiled and wanted to investigate those charges. He showed us my misrepresented biography, written by Baryshnikov and Sapozhnikov, as well as my glowing references from professors at the Leningrad Automobile Institution. He said I was the sole survivor out of 86 people *arrested and exiled* from the Red Triangle Factory.

In summary, Khrustalev stated authorities arrested me for a "crime" against the Central Committee and my file had been stamped *Strictly Confidential*, something I never suspected. Many members of the Central Committee, like me, were repressed or shot to death from 1937 to 1939. Though the archive in the Public Prosecutor's Office was full of cases like mine, Khrustalev required additional time to get to the truth. He thanked us for the meeting and advised me to visit my relatives in Saratov while he reviewed my case. He concluded by saying how guilty he felt for Nina and me, but he stressed *others* did this to us.

Gennadii had waited for us in the hall. He worried that the party secretary in his military division had refused his application to the Party, but, seeing me, he set that concern aside and was delighted when I told him about Khrustalev's positive decision.

We stopped outside the building, took photos at the Neva River, and bussed to the Red Triangle Factory where the factory manager, Ivanov, hugged me and offered me my former position. He directed the payroll clerk to pay me two month's salaries for my 20 years in Kolyma and compensate me for my family's possession losses in 1937. Gennadii and I thanked Ivanov, took the money, but I refused his offer of work due to poor health.

In the hall, I mentioned to Gennadii that Nathaniel Rybak, the former technician from the factory who had testified against me, had agreed to meet us at the North Cafeteria on Nevskii Prospect. We took a tram to downtown Leningrad, and Gennadii bought us tea and pastries while I looked around for Rybak. Seeing him at a small table, I noted he'd grown heavy and his fleshy face was stubbled with whiskers. Approaching, he stood, extended a hand, and said, "Hi, Bolotov!"

"Hi, my old comrade!" I replied, refusing to shake his hand.

Rybak asked, "How's your family doing, Bolotov?"

"We're all alive, safe, and sound. My wife is with me to see our son, and we'll soon leave to visit our daughter, a student at Saratov medical institution. My son, here, graduated from the military college in Irkutsk. He's a pilot."

"You're lucky. My wife and son died of starvation in Leningrad, and I'm living with my daughter. Bolotov, do you remember the plumber, Ivan? A bomb killed him during the siege."

"Yes, I knew him well. We worked together."

Rybak then told me about the death of Viacheslav Podolskii, a former dispatcher killed in an air raid while leaving the factory's clock house.² Besides Ivan and Viacheslav Podolskii, Nikolai Sipiagin, a former factory assistant and Georgii Zhurba, a former manager, were also killed during German attacks in September 1942.³ Zhurba was defending Nevskii Patch, the key departure locale for the army on the eastern shore of the Neva River in Dubrovka.⁴

Georgii Vladimirovich Zhurba, Manager, Red Triangle Factory, April 1940 (Saint Petersburg Lyceum No. 40).

---

2. He was killed December 12, 1941. Streltsova, *Krasnyi Treugol'nik*, 132.

3. Zhurba, Georgii Vladimirovich (1904–1942), was an engineer at the Red Triangle. In July 1941, he joined the army to defend Novgorod and was commissar of the 330th infantry regiment of the 70th division of the Leningrad front.

4. From 1941 to 1943, the Nevskii Patch, an area of 1.3 miles in length and 0.5 miles in width, stretched along the Eastern shore of the Neva River in Vsevolozhsk District. The Soviets lost 250,000 killed and 140,000 wounded, while Germans only suffered from 10,000 to 40,000. Beshanov, V.V. *Leningradskaia oborona* (Moskva ACT: Minsk Harvest, 2005), 285.

Fifty-Five. In Leningrad

I listened to him, but arrest reflections filled my mind until I asked, "Why did you leave Kolyma? It seemed to me that you made good money as a colonel."

"Poor health. Plus, I was bored to death," he replied sadly. "Let's forget the past. If you want, I'll now give you a strong recommendation letter to the Party."

"I'll think about that. In the meantime, how many people did you send to the camps?"

"Bolotov, I'm shocked. Why do you think of me so badly?" He was angry.

"Because, Rybak, you are a first-class ass!" I exclaimed.

"Yes, but you returned from Kolyma. Most didn't! They either died in Kolyma or of starvation in Leningrad."

"I've heard their sad destinies. What I want to know is, why did you denounce me and so many others to the NKVD?"

"Bolotov, that's ancient history. Who cares? At that time, the NKVD officers ordered me to fill out their special forms, and *I did my job!* You all were labeled enemies of people, and I believed it. If I'd refused to, they would have arrested and exiled my family and me."

"You're a son of a bitch, Rybak. You were frightened and defamed all of us!" I snarled.

Rybak was shocked at my outburst. He stalled, gathering his thoughts. "Bolotov, do you remember our meeting in the Kolymian mine?"

"Of course. It was 1942, and I was arrested soon after our meeting and convicted to death a second time. You may not know this, but after your Kolyma visit, Suvorov, Kulikov, and Alymenko suddenly disappeared as well, never to be seen of again."

"But Bolotov, I know guards wanted to shoot you and those others," he explained quietly. He sipped some tea and munched on a piece of pastry. "Sometimes, executioners miss their targets and kill the wrong men."

"You bet they missed their target!"

We finished our tea and pastry, and Gennadii and I left the cafeteria and headed for the nearest mall for gifts. I bought a gold ring for Tamara and a *"Zorky"* camera for Gennadii.

For the next two weeks, we enjoyed meals together and visited cultural sites. Toward the end of our visit, Nina and I received a letter from Valeria, asking all five of us to visit her in Saratov. And we did.

Fifty-Six

Our New Lives Begin

Zhavoronki–Saratov–Penza
Thursday, March 15, 1956

On the train from Leningrad to Moscow, Gennadii, Tamara, Galia, Nina, and I occupied a luxury cabin. At the small table, we discussed our future meeting with the Dobronravovs. Next morning, at Leningradskii Railroad Station, Lelia Dobronravova met us. With bags in hand, we took a metro to Belorusskii Railroad Station and a local train to Zhavoronki Station, near Lelia's summer house. On the platform, her adult sons, Dmitrii and Nikolai, met us, and we walked to the house. Once there, Elena Pamfilovna treated us royally with tasty Napoleon torts. Nikolai and Gennadii laughed when I reminded them of their boyhood New Year dance around the Christmas tree in 1935. As Nikolai and Dmitrii were separated after their parents' arrests, Dmitrii grew up in Moscow and Nikolai in Nizhnii Novgorod. Nikolai graduated from the Pedagogical Institution and Studio of Moscow Art Theater.

Elena Pamfilovna told us her story about our arrests, parcels mailed to prisons, and her life in 1937. We toasted to Nikolai's, her son-in-law's memory.

After three days with the Dobronravovs, we taxied to the Paveletskii Station for the Saratov train, arriving the next morning. Valeria, my brother, Aleksandr, and sister, Zenaida, waited on the platform. They quickly recognized me. My daughter, Valeria, and I didn't recognize each other. She passed me twice, saying "Where's my Dad?" Finally, I stopped her with, "I think I'm your Dad, Leonid Bolotov," and gave her a hug. After that, we spent two, heartwarming months at Aleksandr's house.

Worried about my rehabilitation, on May 20, 1956, Nina and I returned to Leningrad for updates at the Party committee in the Smol'nyi Building and Public Prosecutor's Office.

Fifty-Six. Our New Lives Begin

Shockingly, those authorities still praised Vyshinskii, despite him ordering shot famous founders of the Soviet justice. He called them enemies of people, thereby justifying his arbitrariness and permitting judges to pass severe sentences. Vyshinskii maintained truth depends on the judges' moral and intellective abilities and the accused beaten confessions. He also defined the role of an accomplice of crime, saying if there is only a general connection with a criminal, the accomplish is guilty, enlarging the circle of accused.

On our last day in Leningrad, Nina and I strolled along the Admiralty Embankment toward the Winter Palace. The Neva River was speckled with colorful boats riding gentle waves under a cerulean-blue sky scribbled with clouds. A lemon sun bounced off a panoply of kids, laughing and galloping around the Bronze Horseman. The bite of Kolyma's cold knifing through me and tingling my skin was but a faded memory out there beyond Pluto. And yet that day, we decided to return to Kolyma to clear our names ... no matter how long it might take.

Kolyma and Seymchan had changed. Gulags were shut, watch towers demolished. People openly discussed Stalin's policy, though most regretted the loss of cheap labor and housekeepers. Most were thrilled over the Twentieth Party Congress's decisions and the return of Soviet power.

On September 30, 1956, Nina received a written notice No. 20850–56 from the Prosecutor's Office of Leningrad Military District, signed by Colonel of Justice, Khrustalev. He confirmed that on August 6, 1956, the Leningrad Military Tribunal set aside Nina's 1937 case for lack of evidence of a crime, based on Article 4, Paragraph 5 of the RSFSR Criminal Code.

In the same envelop there was a paper regarding me. *The case of Leonid Petrovich Bolotov, your husband, has been sent to the Chief Military Prosecutor's Office.*

Nina pressed the notice to her heart and cried with happiness, but we both felt terrible for Soviet absurdity and worried prosecutors might change their minds.

Months later, on December 1956, I received Notice No. 4/12/7/700 from the Far Eastern Military Tribunal, Khabarovsk signed by Colonel of Justice, Yarin. It informed me that my verdict of December 18, 1942, was set aside for lack of evidence of a crime. A few weeks later, the new year 1957 brought my final rehabilitation. The Mayor of Seymchan District gave me the notice, sent from the Supreme Court, 13 Vorovskii Street, Moscow, signed by Colonel of Justice, Kostromin.[1] It set aside my verdict of September 2, 1937, for lack of evidence of a crime.

---

1. Kostromin, Aleksandr Aleksandrovich (1903–1961). Smirnov, N.G. *Rapava, Bagirov i drugie. Antistalinskie processy 1950-kh* (Moskva: AIRO-XXI, 2014), 142.

We stayed at our home in Kolyma until March 1958, when Nina and I left to settle in Saratov. Due to her failing health, Nina received disability and retirement pensions, and, for the next 15 years, we enjoyed our old home, though summers we visited the Baltic States as doctors recommended she stay in a cool climate.

In 1973, Valeria and her husband, Viacheslav, asked us to move to Penza. We did. We lived there happily until Nina's death on December 18, 1979, from cranial sclerosis. She was buried in the Arbekov Cemetery, Grave 899, near Karpinskii Street. Her last words to me were, "Leonid, I'll be waiting for you."

Leonid Bolotov dated his manuscript on March 15, 1980. He died seven years later, on March 9, 1987, just as Mikhail Sergeevich Gorbachev's *perestroika* and *glasnost'* was dawning in the Soviet Union.

Translator-Editor's Afterword

Bolotov, Gennadii Leonidovich (May 22, 1931–October 4, 2007), graduated from Irkutsk Pilot School in 1953 and served as a military technician in Gorelovo Airport, Leningrad. Due to his father's arrest, Gennadii was refused admittance at all military schools. Later, he studied history in correspondence courses at Saratov State University, and, in the 1960s, served on the Tajik Afghan border. In 1971, Gennadii defended his Ph.D., *The Role of the Communist Party of Tadzhikistan in Military Patriotic Education of Workers*, at Tajik State University, Dushanbe. From 1973 to 1980, he taught social sciences in the Zhukov Air-Defense Academy in Tver and published three guidelines for military officers.

From 1980 to 1986, Gennadii lectured on humanities in Tver and retired as a Colonel and Associate Professor of History. In 1986, he joined his father in Penza, and it was then his father gave him this manuscript. After the publication of October 18, 1991, of a law Addressing Victims of Political Repressions, Gennadii sent his request for consideration to the Smol'nyi Building, Leningrad, as he and his sister suffered from parental political repressions.[1] Also, he wanted to return to his parents' apartment in Leningrad. Unfortunately, authorities never acted on his request.

Gennadii had three children: Galia, Aleksei, and Svetlana. Since 1995, Svetlana Bolotova, now Lana Bourret (July 10, 1969–), has lived in America with her three children, Aleksandr, Valerie, and Richard-Leonid.

Bolotova, Valeria Leonidovna (May 22, 1937–), graduated from Saratov Medical Academy, worked in Sosnovoborsk in Krasnoiarsk Province, Saratov Province, and Penza where she lived and married Alenkin, Viacheslav Mikhailovich (February 25, 1936–February 28, 2009); they have

---

1. Zakon o Reabilitatsii Zhertv Politicheskikh Repressii. Vedomosti S" ezda Soveta Narodnykh Deputatov Verkhovnogo Soveta RSFSR. Moskva: Dom Sovetov RSFSR. 1991, No. 4, statia 1428, 1690–1696.

Left to right: Nina, Svetlana, and Leonid Bolotov, 1973 (Collection of Lana Bourret).

two daughters, Elena and (June 16, 1959–) and Irina (February 25, 1963–November 10, 1998).

Dobronravov, Nikolai Petrovich (September 28, 1901–October 26, 1941), was born to a minister's family, worked as an attorney in the Arzamas District, Nizhnii Novgorod Province. In 1926, he married Lelia Doroshevskaia, moved to Leningrad to work at the Red Triangle Factory, and they settled on Vasil'evskii Island. Nikolai and Lelia had two sons, Nikolai (November 22, 1928–) and Dmitrii (January 15, 1936–May 26, 1962) before his arrest in 1937. In May 1938, he arrived in Kolyma, worked in the gold mines and died in a Magadan camp three years later.

Dobronravova, Elena (Lelia) Dmitrievna (October 2, 1904–March 1, 1994), the beautiful daughter of Dmitrii Narkisovich Doroshevskii and Elena Pamfilovna Doroshevskaia, was born in Arzamas. In 1936, she graduated after taking foreign language courses, and in 1937, she was arrested, exiled to Tomsk, and worked in the Anzhero-Sudzhensk coal mines.

Today, it is known that Lelia's brother, Doroshevskii, Dmitrii Dmitrievich (February 2, 1899–August 12, 1956), served on the battleship *General Alekseev*, which left the Black Sea in 1920 to be stationed at Rabat, Morocco. In 1936, the Doroshevskiie asked Dmitrii to discontinue his correspondence as the NKVD spied on his family members. Due to this, Lelia received her full rehabilitation in September 1956. She taught English at

Zhavoronki Station until 1960, when she retired and moved to Moscow; she died at 90.

Doroshevskaia, Elena Pamfilovna (May 29, 1873–January 2, 1967), was born into a noble family in Kamenets-Podol'sk, Ukraine. After Nikolai's arrest, she often visited him in jail and let men know that their wives had been arrested. Elena Pamfilovna saved the lives of her grandsons, Nikolai and Dmitrii, took them to Moscow, and then returned to Leningrad where she was trapped in World War II. Eventually, she was able to leave the city and live with her son Konstantin in the north. After 1948, Elena Pamfilovna lived with Lelia and died at 94.

Dobronravov, Nikolai Nikolaevich, became a famous Russian poet and married Pakhmutova, Aleksandra Nikolaevna (November 9, 1929–), a popular Russian composer. They are well-known in Russia and abroad, having received many awards.

Kolyma and Siberia Today

The Lazo mine was closed in 1954. By 2006, time and elements had destroyed the Serpantinka jail. Since 2010, At-Uriah town and Maksim Gorkii village became ghost towns. Vaskov's House was rebuilt and occupied by the Magadan Regional Duma. In 2014, the Seymchan airport building became a Russian cultural monument. In 2018, the census recorded 2,163 inhabitants in Seymchan vs. 4,087 in 1959. In November 2019, Ivan Panikarov opened a Gulag museum, *Kolyma Atlántida*, in Yagodnoye.

In 2016, geologists discovered a huge gold deposit in Irkutsk Province, Boidaibinskii District, which is estimated to last 35 years and contained vast quantities of silver and gold.

Glossary

All-Russian Central Executive Committee: the supreme legislative and administrative organ of the Russian Federation, 1917–1937

All-Russian Communist Party: official term for the Communist Party, 1903–1952 (Bolsheviks)

All-Union Young Pioneer Organization: Lenin's organization for children 10–14, 1917–1991

Arkhiv: archive

Balalaika's E string: high-pitched sound

Balanda: watery soup made of flour, bones, turnips, and rotten potatoes

Banya: sauna

Basta: *that is enough*, a commonly used Italian word in spoken Russian

Belonozhka: white-legged horse

Beregovoy Camp or **Berlag:** Shore Camp. Ironically, the root of the name, *Ber*, is identical to that of Beria, Lavrentii Pavlovich (1896–1953), Head of Soviet Security, 1941–1945

Big House: folk term for the KGB building on Liteinii (Volodarskii) Prospect 4 in Leningrad

Black Raven: NKVD's black vehicle used to transport enemies of the people to prison

Boston suit: man's suit made of high-quality wool, usually in dark colors

Burzhuika: small, round, metal stove

Cahors: red wine from the Cahors Region of France

Central Party Committee: the supreme body of the Party operated during five-year plans between the Communist Congresses, 1917–1991

Challah: egg-enriched, yeast, Jewish bread, always braided

Glossary

Chifir: strong, black, narcotic tea prized by criminals

Citizen Chief: a formal address of prisoners to supervisor guards

Cogito, ergo sum: I think therefore I am

Comrade: form of address in the USSR, 1917–1991

Corvalol: heart medication used throughout Eastern Europe, but FDA-banned in America

Cossacks: soldiers from Southeastern Russia and Ukraine, 1395 to present

Counterrevolutionary: action directed towards the overthrow of government

Delo: dossier

Dohodiaga: sick prisoner looking like a skeleton

Ezhovshchina: term derived from the last name of Ezhov, N. I., the NKVD head during the period of mass liquidations in 1937–1938. Ironically, his last name is rooted in *ezh*, which means (1) a hedgehog, (2) barbed wire entangled with stakes or iron bars, and conveys the idea that people lived behind barbed wire

Fascism: authoritarian ultranationalism often related to Mussolini and Hitler

Gena: diminutive of Gennadii

Glasnost: openness and transparency policies instituted by Mikhail Sergeevich Gorbachev in 1985

Grand piano: Gulag slang term for the fingerprint ink pad

Gusling: Leonid's nickname

Hatar: danger in Uzbek

Home of Communists: graves dug by prisoners for the dead prisoners in Kolyma

Information Bureau: Soviet News Agency, 1941–1961

Kolia: diminutive of Nikolai

Kolyma: multi-faceted term indicating a river, mountain range, region, highway, and often a metaphor, like Auschwitz, Kolyma conveys images of harsh Soviet Gulags

Komsomol: branch of the Communist Party for youth ages 14–28, 1918–1991

Kontriki: suffix, *ik*, indicates a gentle view of counterrevolutionaries

Krasnyi Treugol'nik: Red Triangle, factory and newspaper of the same name

Kulak: grain speculator and parasite of the poor

Kum: abbreviation for commissar

List: page in Russian

Makhorka: coarsely shredded tobacco

Glossary

March 8: International Women's Day, 1917 to present

May Day: International Working Day, 1918–1992

Mensheviks: anti–Bolshevik party, 1903–1925

Muzhichok: diminutive for *muzhik*, meaning small man

Opis': inventory

Osobist: member of the NKVD branch of political trustworthiness, 1918–1943

Parasha: shit barrel

Pashka: diminutive of Pavel

Perestroika: politics of democratic reforms instituted in 1985

Port 54: type of Portuguese wine

Rabotiaga: plodder

Ruble: Russian currency, paper or coin

Sabotage: capacious term for government plots in official Soviet discourse, 1931–1956

Sanka and Sasha: diminutive forms of Aleksandr

Serpatinka: jail on the Northern Pass of Chersky Ridge

Sir: in sarcastic prison discourse, the word *sir* sounds like a synonym for the words "intellectual" and "petty bourgeoisie"

Sobachnik: dog kennel in jail

Socialist Competition: one of the principles of encouraging workers to meet and overfill production targets and receive various forms of reward

Shriek: mispronounced word *srok*, or term

Stenka: diminutive of Stepan

Stlanik: Far-Eastern type of scrub pines

Stukach: informer

Tokay: Hungarian white wine

Trotskyist: political supporter of Lev Trotskii

The Trotskyist-Zinov'evite Terrorist Group: political supporters of Trotskii and Zinoviev

Ushanka: hat with ear-flaps, which can be tied up or under the chin

Valenki: high, winter boots of white, black, or gray wool

Zakhar Kuzmich: collective term for a group of men, equivalent to Tom, Dick, and Harry

Abbreviations

AP RF: *Arkhiv Presidenta Rossiskoi Federatsii,* Russian Federation Presidential Archive

Cheka: *Chrezvychainaia Komissiia,* All-Russian Extraordinary Commission, 1917–1922

CHON: *Chasti Osobogo Naznacheniia,* local police guarding industrial sites and suppressed rebellions, 1917–1925

ChTZ: shoe soles made from tires manufactured at Cheliabinsk Tractorny Zavod, 1930–1950

Dal'stroi/Dalstroy: Far North Construction Trust, 1931–1957

Duma: Lower governing house of representatives

Gulag: *Glavnoe Upravlenie Lagerei,* Main Administration of Camps, 1918–1955

GUM: *Gosudarstavennii Universalnii Magazin,* State Department Store, 1893 to present

KWD: *Kuda weter duet,* Where the Wind Blows

NKVD: *Narkomat Vnutrennykh Del or People's,* Commissariat of Internal Affairs, 1934–1946

OGPU: *Ob'edinennoie Gosudarstvennoie Politicheskoe Upravlenie,* Joint Political Directorate, 1923–1934

Politburo: *Politicheskoie Buro,* the Communist Party highest authority, 1917–1991

RSFSR: *Rossiiskaia Sovetskaia Federatvnaia Sotsialisticheskaia Respublika,* Russian Soviet Socialist Federation, 1922–1991

t.: *tom,* or a volume, referring to books

VOKhR: *voennizirovannaya okhrana,* NKVD guards, 1924–1999

Abbreviations

ZIS—5: built under license to *Zavod Imeni Stalina, ZIS*, trucks produced 1933–1941

ZEK: *zakluchenny*, a Gulag prisoner, 1920–1960

ШII, УII, ФII: Cyrillic characters used on Berlag peacoats and hats for identification instead of prisoners' names

Bibliography

Gulag Memoirs in English and Russian

Applebaum, Anne. *Gulag Voices. An Anthology.* New Haven: Yale University Press, 2011.
Bolotov, G.L. "Kamera smertnikov" [The Cell of Convicted Bombers]. *Sura* No. 4 (2000): 148–165.
Buber-Neumann, Margarete. *Under Two Dictators.* London: Pimlico, 2009.
Faludy, György. *My Happy Days in Hell.* London: Penguin Books, 2010.
Kaple, Deborah. *Gulag Boss. A Soviet Memoir.* New York: Oxford University Press, 2011, 189–193.
Kersnovskaia, Evfrosiniia. *Skol'ko stoit chelovek* [What Is the Value of a Man?]. Moskva: KoLibri, 2016.
Kodatskaia, N.I. "Ivan Fedorovich Kodatskii." *Leningradskii martyrolog 1937–1938: Kniga pamiati zhertv politicheskikh repressii* [The Leningradian Martyrologue: 1937–1938: A Book in Memory of Political Repressions Victims], ed. E.V. Vol'skii, N.I. Dering, V.N. Zaitsev, and A.I. Razumov, t. 5, *1937 god.* Sankt-Peterburg: Rossiiskaia natsional'naia biblioteka, 2002, 531–535.
Kravchenko, Victor. *I Choose Freedom. The Personal and Political Life of a Soviet Official.* New York: Charles Scribner & Sons, 1946, 485.
Larina, Anna. *This I Cannot Forget. The Memoirs of Nikolai Bukharin's Widow.* New York: W.W. Norton, 1993, 174–180, 318–322, 339, 341, 361.
Lipper, Elinor. *Eleven Years in Soviet Prison Camps.* San Francisco: Hauraki, 2015.
Margolin, Ju.B. *Puteshestvie v stranu Ze-ka* [A Journey into Ze-ka Country]. New York: Izdatel'stvo imeni Cechova, 1952, 20, 76–77.
Mokhnach, I.V. "Sinii iod" [Blue Iodine]. *Repressirovannaia nauka,* ed. M. G. Yaroshevskii. Sankt-Peterburg: Nauka, vyp. II (1994): 145–158.
Noskovich, N.A. "Vospominaniia 'pridurka'" ["Memories of 'an Idiot'"]. *Neva* No. 4 (2001): 165–183.
Petkevich, Tamara. *Memoir of a Gulag Actress.* Trans. Yasha Klots and Ross Ufberg. DeKalb: Northern Illinois University Press, 2010.
Shapiro, Yu.V.. "Kolyma i Kolymchane." *Zdravyi smysl* No. 1 (38) (2006): 45–50.

Resources in English

Applebaum, A. *Gulag: A History.* New York: Doubleday, 2003.
Artemiev, V.P. "OKR: State Security in the Soviet Armed Forces." *Military Review* 43 (1963): 21–31.
Barclay, I.Y. "Twenty Years in Beria's Hell: A Memoir." *Hawaii University International Conferences on Arts and Humanities.* Honolulu, 2012. CD-ROM, 1–7.

Bollinger, M.J. *Stalin's Slave Ships: Kolyma, the Gulag Fleet, and the Role of the West.* Westport, CT: Praeger, 2003, 80.
Chekhov, A., Reeve, B. *Sakhalin Island.* London: Alma Books, 2013.
Conquest, Robert. *The Great Terror: A Reassessment.* New York: Oxford University Press, 1990, 624.
"Correspondence of a Gulag Prisoner." A paper presented at CARTA, Kansas City, March 27, 2010.
Davies, R.V., Oleg V. Khlevniuk, E.A. Rees, Liudmila Kosheleva, and Larisa A. Rogavaya. *The Stalin-Kaganovich Correspondence 1931–36.* Russian documents trans. Steven Shabad. New Haven: Yale University Press, 2003, 168–170.
Fisher, Burton D., ed. "The Art of Slander." In *The Barber of Seville by Rossini.* Coral Gables: Opera Journeys, 2002, 68–69.
Krippes, Karl. A. *Uzbek-English Dictionary.* Kensington, MD: Dunwoody Press, 1996, 186.
Lenoe, Matthew E. *The Kirov Murder and Soviet History.* New Haven: Yale University Press, 2010, 252.
"Memoirs of a Gulag Prisoner." A paper presented at the XVIII Russian-American Seminar, St. Petersburg, May 19, 2009.
Pu Yi, Henry. *The Last Manchu: The Autobiography of Henry Pu Yi, Last Emperor of China.* New York: Skyhorse Publishing, 2010.
Rossi, Jacques. *The Gulag Handbook: An Encyclopedia Dictionary of Soviet Penitentiary Institutions and Terms Related to the Forced Labor Camp.* New York: Paragon House, 1989, 129–130, 215, 401, 435, 496, 516.
Stoecker, Sally W. *Forging Stalin's Tukhachevsky and the Politics of Military Innovations.* London: Taylor and Francis, 2018.
Solzhenitsyn, Aleksandr I. *One Day in the Life of Ivan Denisovich.* New York: Farrar, Straus and Giroux, 2005.
Stephen, Martin, and Eric Grove. *See Battles in Close-up: World War 2.* Annapolis: Naval Institute Press, 1988, 11.
Weeks, Albert L. *Russia's Life-Saver: Lend-Lease Aid to the U.S.S.R. in World War II.* Lanham, MD: Lexington Books, 2004.
Wieczynski, Joseph L., ed. *The Modern Encyclopedia of Russian and Soviet History*, vols. 1, 2, 5, 6, 7, 9, 10, 11, 12, 13, 14, 15, 16, 17, 18, 19, 20, 21, 23, 24, 26, 30, 34, 36, 37, 38, 39, 40, 41, 43, 44, 46. Gulf Breeze, FL: Academic International Press, 1976–1987.
Wieczynski, Joseph L., ed. *The Modern Encyclopedia of Russian and Soviet History.* Supplement, vols. 47, 49, 50, 52, 54. Gulf Breeze, FL: Academic International Press, 1988–1990.

Resources in German

Dehl, O. *Verratene Ideale. Zur Geschichte deutscher Emigranten in der Sowjetunion in den 30er Jahren* [Betrayed ideals. The History of German Emigrants to the Soviet Union in the 1930s]. Berlin: Trafo-Verlag Dr. Wolfgang Weist, 2000, b. 25, 208–217.

Resources in Russian

Books and Articles

Babushkin, V.F. *Dni velikikh sobytii* [The Days of the Great Events]. Saratov: Privolzhskoye knizhnoye izdatel'stvo, 1984, 168–191.
Barclay, I.Y. "Solntse vzoshlo, nachianetsia den" [The Sun Rose, the Day Begins]. *Iazykovaia situatsiia v mnogoyazychnoi polikulturnoi srede i voprosy sokhranenia iazyka v literature narodov Severnogo Kavkaza.* Karachaevsk. Karachaevo-Cherkesskii universitet imeni U.D. Alieva, p.1 (2011), 102–111.
Batsaev, I.D. "Kolymskaia griada arhipelaga Gulaga (zakluchennye)" [The Kolymian

Ridge of the GULag Archipelago (prisoners)]. *Istoricheskiie aspekty Severo-Vostoka Rossii: ekonomika, obrazovaniie, kolymskii Gulag.* Magadan: SVKNII DVO RAN, 1996, 62–63.
Batsaev, I.D., and A.G. Kozlov. *Dalstroy Trust Sevvostlag OGPU-NKVD of the USSR as Presented by Documents and in Numbers (2 parts).* Part 1 (1931–1941). Magadan: NEISRI FEB RAS, 2002, 6, 11, 15, 64, 76, 77, 159, 164, 180, 187, 273, 275, 349, 351, 360.
Batulin, P.V., and S.S. Voitikov. "Zloupotrebleniia vlastiu v organakh Voennogo kontrolia 1918–1919" [Abuse of Power in the Military Inspection Branches, 1918–1919]. *Voprosy istorii,* No. 8 (2010): 46–55.
Beshanov, V.V. *Leningradskaia oborona* [The Leningrad Siege]. Moskva ACT. Minsk Harvest, 2005, 285.
Bohanov, P.P., V.T. Agalakov, N.V. Vladimirov, and U.N. Grachev. *Zhertvy politicheskikh repressii Irkutskoi oblasti: pamiat' i preduprezhdeniie budushchemu* [Victims of Political Repressions in Irkutsk Province: A Memory and Warning to Future Generations]. Irkutsk: Irkutskaia oblastnaia tipographiia No. 1, 1999, t.2, 49.
Buianov, D.V., N.S. Lobchuk, and S.A. Noritsyna. *Istoriia administrativno-territorial'nogo delenia Stalingradskogo (Nizhnevolzhskogo) kraia, 1928–1936 гг.: spravochnik* [The History of Stalingrad (Nizhnevolzhskii) Territory Administrative Division, 1928–1936]. Volgograd: Volgogradskoye nauchnoie izdatel'stvo, 2012.
Emin, F., N. Kurganov, I. Novikov, and S. Baranov. *Van'ka Kain.* Moskva: EKSMO, 2008.
Gaidar, T.A. *Golikov Arkadii iz Arzamasa* [Golikov Arkadii from Arzamas]. Moskva: Politicheskaia literatura, 1988.
Gokhlerner, V. M., and V.K. Medvedev. *Istoriia Saratovskogo kraia 1917 -1965* [History of Saratov Province, 1917–1965]. Saratov: Saratovskii gosudarstvennii universitet, 1967, 60.
Kitaygorodskii, I. I. *Teoriia stekloobrazovaniia i metody varki stekla* [The Theory of Glass Production and Melting]. Moskva—Leningrad: Geezlegprom, 1935.
Kochnev, E.D. *Avtomibili Velikoi Otechestvennoi* [Vehicles Used During the Great Patriotic War]. Moskva: EKSMO, 2010.
Kozlov, A.G. *Iz istorii zdravookhraneniia Kolymy i Chukotki (1941–1954)* [History of Kolyma and Chukotka Health Care (1941–1954)]. Magadan: Magadanskoie knizhnoye izdatel'stvo, 1991, 92–93.
Lunacharskii, A.V. "Goete i ego vremia" [Goethe and His Time]. *Literaturnoie nasledstvo,* t.4. Moskva: Zhurnal'no-gazetnoe ob'edinenie, 1932, 5–20.
Orlov, V.P., L.P. Beliakov, Ye. M. Zablotskii. *Repressirovannye geologi* [The Repressed Geologists]. Moskva—Sankt-Peterburg: VSEGEI, 1999, 248.
Petrov, N.V. *Kto rukovodil organami gosbezopasnosti 1941–1954* [Who Directed State Security, 1941–1945]. Moskva: Zveniia, 2010, 182–183.
Platonov, S.P. *Bitva za Leningrad, 1941–1944* [The Battle for Leningrad: 1941–1944]. Moskva: Voennoie izdatel'stvo ministerstva oborony of the USSR, 1964, 194–203.
Shalimov, Yu.B.. B. *Legendy i byl' kolymskogo stekla* [The Legends of Kolyma Glass Production]. Magadan: Oblastnoe gazetnoe izdatel'stvo, 1992, 16–17, 28–40.
Shirokov, A.I. *Dal'stroi v sotsialno-ekonomicheskom razvitii Severo-Vostoka SSSR (1930–1950)* [The Role of Dal'stroi Trust in Social-Economic Development of North-East USSR (1930–1950)]. Moskva: ROSSPEN, 2014, 178.
Smirnov, N.G. *Rapava, Bagirov i drugie. Antistalinskie processy 1950-kh* [Rapava, Bagirov and others. Anti-Stalin Processes of 1950s]. Moskva: AIRO-XXI, 2014, 142.
Sokolov, U. M., ed. *Krasnoarmeiskii fol'klor* [Red Army Folklore]. Moskva: Izdatel'stvo Sovetskii pisatel,' 1938, 121–122.
Streltsova, A.L. *Krasnyi Treugol'nik* [The Red Triangle Factory]. Leningrad: Lenizdat, 1978, 96–102, 132.
Taratuta, E. A. *Istoriia dvukh knig: "Podpolnaia Rossiia" S.M. Stepniaka-Kravchinskogo i "Ovod" Ethel' Lilian Voynich* [History of Two Books: "Underground Russia" by S.M. Stepniak-Kravchinskii and "The Gadfly" by Ethel Lilian Voynich]. Moskva: Khudozhestvennaia literatura, 1987, 139–141.
Uimanov, V.N., Iu. A. Petrukhin. *Bol' liudskaia: kniga pamiati tomichei, repressirovannykh v 30–40-e i nachale 50-kh godov* [The People's Pain: A Book in Memory of Tomsk Res-

idence Repressed During 1930–1950]. Tomsk: Upravleniie AFB RF po Tomskoi oblasti, vyp. 2, 1992: 335.
Vol'skii, E.V., N.I. Dering, V.N. Zaitsev, and A.I. Razumov, eds. *Leningradskii martyrolog:1937–1938: kniga pamiati zhertv politicheskikh repressii* [The Leningradian Martyrologue: 1937–1938: A Book in Memory of Political Repressions Victims], t. 1, 3, 4, 5, 10. Sankt-Peterburg: Rossiiskaia natsional'naia biblioteka, 1995–2010.
Zakovskii, L.M. *O nekotorykh metodakh i priemakh inostrannykh razvedyvatel'nykh organov i ikh trotskistsko-bukharinskoi agentury* [Methods of the Foreign Intelligence Service and its Trotskii and Bukharin Agents]. Leningrad: Partizdat TSK VKP (b), 1937, 1–52.
Zalesskii, K.A. *Imperia Stalina* [Stalin's Empire]. Moskva: Veche, 2000, 397–398.

Dictionaries

Iablokov, A. *Istoriia glazami Krokodila. XX vek. Slova 1922–1937* [History Through the Eyes of "Krokodile": 20th century: 1922–1937 Words]. Moskva: OOO "XX Cenchury Krokodila," 2014, 66.
Serokuzov, N.N. *Slovar' voshedshikh v obikhod sokrashchennykh nazvanii* [A Dictionary of Recent Abbreviations]. Vladivostok: Typo- Lithographiia. Iosif Korot,' 1924, 9.

Encyclopedias

Keldysh, Iu.V. *Muzykal'naia entsiklopediia* [A Musical Encyclopedia]. Moskva: Izdatel'stvo "Sovetskaia entsiklopediia" 1974–1976, t.2, 861 and t.3, 226.
Kirsanova, R.M., T.G. Morozova, and V.D. Sinuikov. *Kostium v russkoi khudozhestvennoi kul'ture 18—pervoi poloviny 20 vv: opyt enciclopedii* [An Encyclopedia of Clothing in Russia's Artistic Culture from the 18th to the 20th Centuries]. Moskva: Nauchnoe izdatel'stvo "Bol'shaia Rossiiskaia entsyclopedia," 1995, 47–176.
Levtov, V.E. *Bol'shaia toponimicheskaia entsiklopediia Sankt-Peterburga: 15 000 gorodskikh imen* [An Encyclopedia of 15,000 Saint Petersburg Names]. Sankt-Peterburg: Informatsionno-izdatel'skoe agentstvo "LIK," 2013, 245.
Wieszynski, Joseph L. *The Modern Encyclopedia of Russian and Soviet History*, Vol. 1, Aachen–Anichkov. Gulf Breeze, FL: Academic International Press, 1976.
_____. *The Modern Encyclopedia of Russian and Soviet History*, Vol. 2. Anikin–Bailov Rocks. Gulf Breeze, FL: Academic International Press, 1976.
_____. *The Modern Encyclopedia of Russian and Soviet History*, Vol. 5. Bobrinskii, V.A.–Bulatovich, A.K. Gulf Breeze, FL: Academic International Press, 1977.
_____. *The Modern Encyclopedia of Russian and Soviet History*, Vol. 6. Bulavin–Chernogai Uprising of 1861. Academic International Press, 1978.
_____. *The Modern Encyclopedia of Russian and Soviet History*, Vol. 7. Chernoles Culture–Congresses of Representatives of Industry and Trade. Gulf Breeze, FL: Academic International Press, 1978.
_____. *The Modern Encyclopedia of Russian and Soviet History*, Vol. 9. Decembrists' Uprising of 1821–Russian Historiography of Dovzhenko, A.P. Gulf Breeze, FL: Academic International Press, 1978.
_____ *The Modern Encyclopedia of Russian and Soviet History*, Vol. 10. Dowbar–Musnicki, Josef –Estonia, Soviet Acquisition of. Gulf Breeze, FL: Academic International Press, 1979.
_____. *The Modern Encyclopedia of Russian and Soviet History*, Vol. 11. Estonians–Franco-Russian Treaties of 1891–1894. Gulf Breeze, FL: Academic International Press, 1979.
_____. *The Modern Encyclopedia of Russian and Soviet History*, Vol. 12. Franco-Russian Relations to 1917–Golitsyn, Dmitrii Mikhailovich. Gulf Breeze, FL: Academic International Press, 1979.
_____. *The Modern Encyclopedia of Russian and Soviet History*, Vol. 13. Golitsyn, Mikhail Mikhailovich–Helphand, Alexander Israel. Gulf Breeze, FL: Academic International Press, 1979.

_____. *The Modern Encyclopedia of Russian and Soviet History*, Vol. 14. Helsinki–Agreement of 1975–Ishimka Treasure Gulf Breeze, FL: Academic International Press, 1979.
_____. *The Modern Encyclopedia of Russian and Soviet History*, Vol. 15. Ishutin, Nikolai Andreevich–Karaimy. Gulf Breeze, FL: Academic International Press, 1980.
_____. *The Modern Encyclopedia of Russian and Soviet History*, Vol. 16. Karakala, Battle of Kievan Rus. Gulf Breeze, FL: Academic International Press, 1980.
_____. *The Modern Encyclopedia of Russian and Soviet History*, Vol. 17. Kievan Uprising of 1113–Kovalevskii, Evgraf Petrovich. Gulf Breeze, FL: Academic International Press, 1980.
_____. *The Modern Encyclopedia of Russian and Soviet History*, Vol. 18. Kovalevskii, Maksim– Maksimovich Labor Legislation in Tsarist Russia. Gulf Breeze, FL: Academic International Press, 1980.
_____. *The Modern Encyclopedia of Russian and Soviet History*, Vol. 19. Lacy, Peter–Liber, Mark. Gulf Breeze, FL: Academic International Press, 1981.
_____. *The Modern Encyclopedia of Russian and Soviet History*, Vol. 21. Makarii–Meshcherskii, Aleksei Pavlovich. Gulf Breeze, FL: Academic International Press, 1981.
_____. *The Modern Encyclopedia of Russian and Soviet History*, Vol. 23. Modernism in Russia–Museums of Regional Studies in Russia and the Soviet Union. Gulf Breeze, FL: Academic International Press, 1981.
_____. *The Modern Encyclopedia of Russian and Soviet History*, Vol. 24. Lacy, Peter–Liber, Mark. Gulf Breeze, FL: Academic International Press, 1981.
_____. *The Modern Encyclopedia of Russian and Soviet History*, Vol. 26. Oleg–Pardons in Russia and the Soviet Union. Gulf Breeze, FL: Academic International Press, 1982.
_____. *The Modern Encyclopedia of Russian and Soviet History*, Vol. 30. Profinntern–Registered Cossacks. Gulf Breeze, FL: Academic International Press, 1982.
_____. *The Modern Encyclopedia of Russian and Soviet History*, Vol. 34. Semirech'e Cossack Host–Shichko, Leonid Emmanuilovich. Gulf Breeze, FL: Academic International Press, 1983.
_____. *The Modern Encyclopedia of Russian and Soviet History*, Vol. 36. Slovo o Polku Igoreve–Soviets. Gulf Breeze, FL: Academic International Press, 1984.
_____. *The Modern Encyclopedia of Russian and Soviet History*, Vol. 37. Soviets of National Economy–Stundists. Academic International Press, 1984.
_____. *The Modern Encyclopedia of Russian and Soviet History*, Vol. 38. Sturdza, Aleksandr Skarlatovich–Ter-Egiazar'ian, Mikhail Andreevich.
_____. *The Modern Encyclopedia of Russian and Soviet History*, Vol. 39. Terek Cossack Host–Trubetskoi, Evgenii Nikolaevich. Gulf Breeze, FL: Academic International Press, 1985.
_____. *The Modern Encyclopedia of Russian and Soviet History*, Vol. 40. Trubetskoi, Nikita Yur'evich–Union of Soviet Socialist Republics, Administrative–Territorial Division of. Gulf Breeze, FL: Academic International Press, 1985.
_____. *The Modern Encyclopedia of Russian and Soviet History*, Vol. 41. Union of Soviet Socialist Republics, Chronology of–Veger, Evgenii Il'ich. Gulf Breeze, FL: Academic International Press, 1986.
_____. *The Modern Encyclopedia of Russian and Soviet History*, Vol. 43. Volkonskii, Mikhail Nikitich–Wintzingerode, Ferdinand Gullaume. Gulf Breeze, FL: Academic International Press, 1986.
_____. *The Modern Encyclopedia of Russian and Soviet History*, Vol. 44. Wipper, Robert Yur'evich–Yaroslavovo Dvorishche. Gulf Breeze, FL: Academic International Press, 1987.
_____. *The Modern Encyclopedia of Russian and Soviet History*, Vol. 46. Zemstvo Agricultural Policy–Zyriane. Supplement Abakan–Archives in the Soviet Union. Gulf Breeze, FL: Academic International Press, 1987.
_____. *The Modern Encyclopedia of Russian and Soviet History*, Vol. 49. Supplement Innokentii–"Long Burial Mounds." Gulf Breeze, FL: Academic International Press, 1988.
_____. *The Modern Encyclopedia of Russian and Soviet History*, Vol. 50. Supplement Lubianka–Novocherkassk Massacre of 1962. Gulf Breeze, FL: Academic International Press, 1989.
_____. *The Modern Encyclopedia of Russian and Soviet History*, Vol. 52. Supplement Pro-

Bibliography

gressive Party–Seregin, Vladimir Sergeevich. Gulf Breeze, FL: Academic International Press, 1990.

_____. *The Modern Encyclopedia of Russian and Soviet History*, Vol. 54. Supplement Tariffs in Pre-Revolutionary Russia–Wilno. Gulf Breeze, FL: Academic International Press, 1990.

Legal Documents

Zakon o Reabilitatsii Zhertv Politicheskikh Repressii [The Russian Law Addressing Victims of Political Repressions]. *Vedomosti S" ezda Soveta Narodnykh Deputatov Verkhovnogo Soveta RSFSR*. Moskva: Dom Sovetov RSFSR. 1991, No. 4, statia 1428, 1690–1696.

Maps

Markova, N.T. *Atlas avtomobyl'nykh dorog SSSR* [Auto Road Atlas of the USSR]. 3 ed. Moskva: Glavnoye upravleniie geodesii i kartografii pri SM SSSR, 1971, 85.

Pushkareva, M.I. *Atlas shem zheleznykh dorog SSSR* [Railroad Atlas of the USSR]. 2nd ed. Moskva: Glavnoe upravleniie geodesii i kartografii pri Sovete Ministrov SSSR. 1980.

The Yellow Pages

Ves' Leningrad: adresnaia i spravochnaia kniga [1935 Leningrad Yellow Pages]. L: Lenoblispolkom i Lensovet, 1935.

Ves' Peterburg: na 1913 god: adresnaja i spravočnaja kniga g. S. Peterburga [1913 Peterburg Yellow Pages]. SPb.: izdaniie A.S. Suvorina, 1913.

Resources in Ukrainian

Rizak, I. M., O.D. Dovganich, O.V. Khlanta. *Reabilitovani istorieiu. Zakarpatska oblast'* [Rehabilitation Through History. Zakarpatskaia Province]. Kniga 1. Uzhgorod: Vidavnictvo "Zakarpattia," 2003.

Documentaries

Kremlevskie pokhorony [The Kremlin Funeral], Juliia Satarova, Aleksei Smagluk, Sergei Kraus, Natalia Duganova, Russia, 2008–2009.

Internet Resources

The Archive of the President of the Russian Federation http://stalin.memo.ru/spiski/.
Arkhiv Rossiiskoi Akademii Nauk. Sankt-Peterburgskii filial http://db.ranar.spb.ru/ru/person/.
The Iofe Found in Sankt-Peterburg http://arch.iofe.center/.
Kadrovii sostav bezopasnosti SSSR. 1935–1939 http://nkvd.memo.ru/.
Projekt: Příběhy 20. Století http://www.pametnaroda.cz/. Project dedicated to the memorial database in Europe in cooperation with the Institute for the Study of Totalitarian Regimes and Czech Radio.

Archival Photo Albums

Photo Album Report of 1938, fund 9401, inventory 3, file 38, the Ministry of Inner Affairs, State Archive, Russian Federation, Moscow.

Dal'stroi Territories Photo Album 1942-1943, fund 9401, inventory 3, file 42, the Ministry of Inner Affairs, State Archive, Russian Federation, Moscow.

Index

Addressing Victims of Political Repressions 247
Admiralty Embankment 245
Aleksander II, Russian Emperor and Tsar 22; *see also* the Romanov dynasty
Aleksandr 131, 132
Aleksandra 212–213
Aleksandrinskii Theater 82
Aleksandrov 21, 23, 28–30, 33–35, 45, 67, 93, 97
Aleksandrovka 234
Aleksandr's house 244
Alekseev 129
Alekseev, Petr Alekseevich 45
Alenkin, Viacheslav Mikhailovich 246–247
Alenkina Elena 248
Alenkina Irina 248
All-Russian Central Executive Committee 26, 251
All-Russian Communist Party (Bolsheviks) 4; *see also* Bolshevik Party; Party
All-Union Cooperative Organization 30
All-Union Young Pioneer organization 76
Altai Mountains 230
Altynnaia Mountains 156
Alymenko (Olemenko), Lazar Evdokimovich 67, 86, 97–98, 143, 243
America 138, 247; airplanes 206; food 138, 190; trucks 167, 201
Anton 165
Antonov-Saratovskii, Vladimir Pavlovich 60
Antonov's gangs 82
Anzhero-Sudzhensk 6, 231; coal mines 224, 231, 233, 248; medical commission 233
Arbat 76
Arbekov Cemetery 246
Arctic 115, 134, 139, 143

Arctic Kolyma 5, 88, 94, 115; *see also* Kolyma
Arctic sun 208
Arkadii 211–212
Armenia 89
Arsenalnaia Naberezhnaia 53
Arsenalnaia Street Jail 221
Article Fifty-Eight 103, 113, 159, 161
Article of Conviction 86
Arzamas 248
Arzamas District 248
Arzamas Gaidar Museum 81
Arzamas Museum of History and Art 79, 80
Asbestos Factory 44
Asia 239
Atka 100, 195
Automobile Institution 18, 20, 77; *see also* Leningrad Automobile Institution
At-Uriah River 104; mines 109; *see also* Nizhnii At-Uriah
Averbakh, Sophia Mikhailovna 226
Azieva, Angelina 228

Babeikin, Iakov Iakovlevich 168–170, 184–185, 189, 193–194
Baikal, Lake 238
Balakin, Ivan Prokhorovich 67–68, 86, 90, 117
balalaika's E string 203
Balashov Air Force School 32
Baltic countries 173, 230
Baltic Railroad Station 241
Baltic Sea sailor 105, 111
Baltic States 246
Bank of Ukraine 88
Barclay, Ceylon Lorenzo 2
barracks 7
Baryshnikov, Vladimir Iakovlevich 18–20, 49–52, 55, 126, 146, 241
Bashanta 77–78, 80; onion domes 78

263

Index

Bashanta River 78
Bashkirs 36
Belonozhka 37–39
Belorussia 89, 176, 230
Belorusskii Railroad Station 244
Beregovoy Camp 193, 195, 197–198, 201; see also *Beregovoy* Laws and Ethics; Magadan's Berlag; Special Camp 5
Beregovoy Laws and Ethics 197; see also *Beregovoy* Camp; Magadan's Berlag; Special Camp 5
Berezniki Chemical Factory, Perm Province 18
Bezhetsk NKVD Prison, Tver Province 1
Big House 11
Black Raven: cars 11, 53–54, 70; trucks 73, 153–154
Black Sea 248
Black Sea Fleet 118
Board of Consumer's Society 36
Bogdanov, Mikhail Vasil'evich 67, 71, 97–99
Boidaibinskii District 249
Bold Mountains 156
Bolotov 3, 51, 63, 66, *79*, 120 198–201, 205, 207–208, 210, 218, **235**, 242–243, **248**; case 245; conversations 151, 178–180, 186; ID 77, 203; jails 18, 25, 39, 48, 59, 63, 65–66, 76, 79, 82–83, 147, 149, 152, 157, 161; letters and parcels 120–121; meetings 143, 145–146; official notice 237; relationships with prisoners 122, 127–131, 175; work 136, 140–141, 166, 170
Bolotov, Aleksandr Petrovich 3, 234–235, 244
Bolotov, Aleksei Gennadievich 247
Bolotov, Boris Petrovich *3*; family 57–58
Bolotov, Gena 81–83; see also Gennadii; Gennadii Leonidovich
Bolotov, Gennadii Leonidovich: *The Role of the Communist Party of Tadzhikistan in Military Patriotic Education of Workers* 247
Bolotov, Petr Antonovich *3, 4*, 23, 62, 224, 235
Bolotova, Anna Petrovna *3*, 58, 235
Bolotova, Elena (Aleksandr's wife) 234
Bolotova, Galia 240, 244
Bolotova, Klara Petrovna *3*, 121
Bolotova (Temiakova), Nina Alekseevna *3, 4*, 10–11, 75–*79*, 81–83, 86, 101, 156, 187, 200, 206, 208, 210, 213, 216, 218–227, 233, **235**–241, 243–246, **248**
Bolotova, Svetlana Gennadievna 247; see also Bourret, Lana

Bolotova, Tamara 240–241, 243–244
Bolotova, Valeria Leonidovna 4, **6**, 10, 122, 216, 221, 224, 233–234, 239, 243–244, 246–247
Bolotova (Cherntsova), Varvara Ivanovna *3, 4*, 62, **122**; children 232, 234–235
Bolotova, Zenaida Petrovna *3*, 234, 244
Bol'shaia Kostryzhnaia Street 60
Bol'shaia Sergievskaia Street 57
Bolshevik(s) 14, 36, 38–42; anti–Bolshevik rebellion 4; beliefs 45, 54, 56, 57, 60–61, 65, 68, 121; ideas 76; people 88
Bolshevik Club 76
Bolshevik party 4, 229; see also All-Russian Communist Party (Bolsheviks); Party
Bolshoi Theater 82
Borodnia 136–137
Bortsov Tolia 134
Boston suit 10, 12, 43
Bourret, Aleksandr 248
Bourret, Lana 3, 79, **248**; see also Bolotova, Svetlana
Bourret, Richard-Leonid 247
Bourret, Valeria 247
Brevda, Isaac Solomonovich 28, 67, 71, 90, 97, 157–159
Bronze Horseman 245
Browning 50
Buhre, Paul-Eduard 16
Bukharin, N.I. 16; *ABC of Communism* 76–77; convicted political supporters 223; son 229; views on Goethe 82; wife 226
Bulba 140–141; see also Sneetser, Mark

Cahors 83
Camp Six 145, 146
Canadian ax 166
Caucasus Mountains 34
Central Committee 90, 106, 241; see also Central Party Committee; Party Committee
Central Party Committee 19, 121; see also Central Committee; Party Committee
Cerberus 227
Chaplin, Nikolai Pavlovich 71
Cherepanov, Grigorii Petrovich 169
Cherniak, Petr Vasilievich 67
Cherntsov, Ivan *4*
Cherntsov, Mikhail Ivanovich *4*
Cherntsova, Anna
Chersky Mountain 147
Chief Military Prosecutor's Office 245
China 32, 34
Chinese kitchen items and fabrics 77, 174

Index

CHON 50
CHP 197
Christ 44
Christmas tree 244
ChTZ 102, 104, 118
Chudov, Mikhail Semenovich 30, 45, 68, 227
Citizen Chief 124, 132, 147, 155
Civil War 22, 34, 82, 121, 156, 229
Claudia 138
Collection of Angelina Azieva 228
Collection of Irina Y. Barclay 1, 5
Collection of Lana Bourret 3, 4, 6, 79, 122, 235, 248
commandant 201, 208–209; house 198, 207; order 201
Commissar 40, 56
Communism 6, 51, 62, 67, 91, 159, 239
Communist(s) 29, 39–40, 56, 149, 157, 212–213; posters 65
Communist ideas 5; hierarchy 64; penal servitude 114
Communist Youth Organization 18, 25, 51; *see also* Komsomol
Congress of the Communist Party: XXth (1956) 6, 239, 245
Cosette 152
Criminal Code of the RSFSR, Article 58, 22, 72, 108; Article 4, Paragraph 5 245
Czechoslovakia 2

Dal'stroi Territories Photo Album of 1942–1943 94, 97, 110, 137, 144, 148, 166, 168, 171, 180
Dalstroy 112, 206; Administration 94, 206; Hotel 238; major 198–200
Danilenko, Ivan 184–185; *see also* our Raskolnikov
Dante 110
Death Valley 110, 119; *see also* Valley of Death
Demon 166
Denikin, Anton Ivanovich 34
Denisov 19
Department of the Inner Affairs of Magadan Province 201
Development Industry and Geological Office 206
Devil 129
Dmitrii 111
Dobronravov, Dmitrii Nikolaevich 244, 248
Dobronravov, Nikolai Nikolaevich 249; Kolia 83; Nikolai 244, 248–249
Dobronravov, Nikolai Petrovich 67–68, 70–71, 74, 90; conversations 97–98;

death 244; family 75, *80*–83, 244, 248; toast 249
Dobronravova (Doroshevskaia), Elena Dmitrievna 79–*80*, 248; Lelia 82, 224, 231–232, 244, 248–249
Don River 78
Doroshevskaia, Elena Pamfilovna 71, *80*–83, 224, 232, 244, 248–249
Doroshevskii, Dmitrii Dmitrievich 248
Doroshevskii, Dmitrii Narkisovich *79*, 248
Doroshevskii, Konstantin Dmitrievich 249
Dostoevskii 240
Dostoevskii, Fedor Mikhailovich: *Crime and Punishment* 151
Dubrovin 238–239
Dubrovka 242
Dudergoff 81
Dul'tsev, Semen 112
Duma, Alexandre: *The Count of Monte Cristo* 104, 151
Dushanbe 247
Dybenko 27–29
Dzerzhinskii, Feliks Edmundovich (Chairman of the Cheka) 22

Eastern Front, World War II 173
Ekaterininskii Public Garden 13
Elan 122
Elektroseela Plant 19, 45
Elgen Valley 195
Eliashberg, Leon Natanovich (Leon Mordukhovich) 44
England 99
English 248
Eroshkin, Gavriil Grigorievich 67, 93, 117
Estina 230
Europe 239
Evdokimov, Aleksandr Maksimovich 67–68, 98
Ezhov, Nikolai Ivanovich 90, 96
Ezhovshchina 90; *see also* Great Purge; Reign of Terror

Fantina 152, 173
Far East 213, 217
Far Eastern Military District 238
Far Eastern Military Tribunal 245
Federal Service of State Security, Saint Petersburg and Leningrad Province 7
Ferocious 150, 152
Finnish Shingles 163
Fisherman for Sea Animal 169
Florida 2
Fokina, Yekaterina 227

266　Index

Fontanka River 19
FP 197
France 16
French rolls 173

Gaidar, Arkadii 82
General Alekseev 248
General Nikishov 174; *see also* Nikishov, Ivan Fedorovich
Gennadii 122, 216, 221, 224, 233–235, 239, 240, 241, 243–244, 247
Gennadii Leonidovich (colonel and associate professor of history) 4, 6, 247
Georgia 89–90
German government 36; army 234; attacks 242; intelligence 26; invasion and planes 165; people 86–87, 147; residents 234; shepherds 71, 73, 116, 224; siege of Leningrad 211, 232; spies 65
Germany 230
Girich, Maksim Petrovich 189
Gluzskaia, Raisa 227
Gogol, Nikolai: *Taras Bulba* 140
Golenischev 137
Golden Horn Bay 88
Golden Key Mine 176
Golden Sonka 151
Gorbachev, Mikhail Sergeevich 246
Gorelovo Airport 247
Gorelovo Station 240–241
Gorkii, Maksim 136
Gosling 37
Govorov, Leonid Aleksandrovich (Marshal) 211
Grave 899
Great Bear 153
Great October Day 72; *see also* Greatest of Soviet holidays; November 7, 1937; Soviet event
Great October holiday 120
Great Purge 5, 56, 59; *see also* Ezhovshchina; Reign of Terror
Greatest of Soviet holidays 72; *see also* Great October Day; November 7, 1937; Soviet event
Gridasova, Aleksandra Romanovna 177
Grin'ko Grigorii Fedorovich 89
Grossman, Vasilii (Vasia) 68, 74–75, 84
Gulag 27, 87, 103, 137, 168, 173, 206, 216, 223, 230, 238, 240, 245; museum 249; sentences 229; *see also* Solovetskii Islands
GUM 77
Gutnik, Anton 144
Gushchinskii, Pavel Filipovich 64–65, 68

Heaven's Gate 102
Hermitage 227
Hitler, Adolf 18
Homes of Communists 240
Hugo, Victor: *Les Misérables* 152, 173

Ignatiev 200
Ilinskaia Square 60
Ilinskaia Street 60
Information Bureau 138
Institute of Red Professorship 143
Intourist Hotel Europe 55
Irkutsk camp 2
Irkutsk pilot school 216, 242, 247
Irkutsk Province 249
Ivan 242
Ivanov 241
Ivanychev, Nikolai Vladimirovich 178, 181

Javert 152
Jews 36
John the Baptist 105
Jordan River 105

Kahnovich 227
Kaleis, Avgust Simonovich 229–230
Kaleis, Gelia 229
Kalinin, Mikhail Ivanovich 89
Kalmykian steppes 77
Kamenets-Podol'sk 249
Kamyshinskaia Street 57, 60–61
Karpetin 143–144, 146–147, 149, 238
Karpinskii Street 246
Karpov Petr 211
Kasimov 19
Kaunas 230
Kazakhstan 41, 89; exiles 229
Khabarovsk 90, 238, 245; investigator 160, 237
Khakassia 96
Khasyn, River 169
Khatynnakh 101
Khatynnakh River 150
Khmara 122
Khrushchev, Nikita 239; Secret Speech 2
Khrustalev (Colonel of Justice) 241, 245
Kian, Ivan 211
Kiev 88, 230
King 102–103; speeches 106–107, 109, 111–112
Kirov, Sergei Mironovich 59, 223; murder 64, 66
Kirovski Plant 35, 53
Kitaygorodskii, Isaak Il'ich 170
Kluchevskii 221

Kochergin, Evgenii Emelianovich 64–65, 143
Kodatskii, Ivan Fedorovich 14, 45, 68
Kolchak, Aleksandr Vasil'evich 34
Kolychev, Nikolai (Kolia) 177–178, 181
Kolyma 89, 91, 100, 103, 106, 108; jails 114, 118, 120, 126, 128–129, 164, 204–205; baby 219; climate and nature 92, 113, 129, 133–135, 245; death 248; exiles 229; gold production 136; holiday 120; home 246; locals 170; managers 219; medical doctors 158; mines 218; region 213, 216–217, 237–238, 243; roads 155; slavery and authorities 159, 169, 194, 196; terms 137, 200, 240; transportation 166, 207; tyranny 116; white nights 157; work 187; see also Arctic Kolyma
Kolyma, Ivan 201
Kolyma Atlántida 249
Kolyma Auto Road 96, 98
Kolyma Gulag's 2, 18, 28, 67
Kolyma River 97, 195, 218
Komsomol 18, 25, 51, 126, 229; uniform 103; see also Communist Young Organization
Komsomolskaia Square 239
Konstantin 234
Konstantinogradskaia Street 70
Korolev 56, 64
Korovin 112
Kosarev, Aleksandr Vasil'evich 126
Kosior, Stanislav Vikentievich 89
Kostiushko 64
Kostromin, Aleksandr Aleksandrovich 245
Kozlovskii, Ivan Semenovich 82
Krasavitsa River 167, 169
Krasavka 122
Krasnoiarsk 83, 247
Krasnyi Treugol'nik, newspaper 13, 20
Kremlin 76–77; bureaucracy 121
Kresty Prison 52–55, 103, 222
Kronstadt 34
Krupskaia, Nadezhda Konstantinovna 45
Krupskaia Sugar Factory 221
Kuhorenko 186, 188–189
Kuibyshev 211
Kulakov 146–147, 149
Kuleshov, Mikhail Fedorovich 68
Kulikov, Anatolii Mikhailovich 67, 97, 243
Kulikova, Vera 231
Kulu 92–94
Kumysnaia Glade 156
Kuzbas 136
Kuznetsov, Aleksei Aleksandrovich 225

Kuznetsov, Dmitrii 178, 180
KWD 62

Ladoga Lake 232; see Road of Life
Larchenko 219
Larin Yuri Nikolaevich 229
Larina-Bukharina, Anna Mikhailovna 226
Last Judgment Day 160
Latvia 229
Law of Three Spikes 188
Lazo, Sergei Georgievich 207; mines 209, 249
Lebedev, Sergei Vasil'evich 14
Leekhtner 88–89, 91, 97
Lekarenko, Nina Alekseevna 223; sketch: *Women in Tomsk Jail* 229
Lemeshev, Sergei Iakovlevich 82
Lend-Lease Program 138
Lenin, Vladimir Il'ich 5, 45, 239
Lenin, Vladimir Il'ich: *The State and Revolution* 77
Lenin District 222
Lenin Street 218
Leningrad 5, 11, 13, 19, 44, 59, 71, 73–75, 77, 80–81, 111, 113, 155, 159, 187, 222, 241, 243, 247–248; bureaucracy 120–121, 225, 239, 244; column 86; gynecologist 228; journey 238, 245; relatives 85; siege 232; starvation 242; train 240, 244; white nights 157; World War II 165
Leningrad Automobile Institution 241; see also Automobile Institution
Leningrad Military Tribunal 245
Leningrad State Committee 121
Leningradians 84, 93, 96, 157, 159
Leningradians' Wives Boulevard 227
Leningradskaia Pravda 230
Leningradskii Railroad Station 239, 244
Lenin's city 34; see also Simbirsk
Lenin's principles 4; interpretations 76; times 56
Leonid 216–217, 219, 221, 225, 235, 238, 244, 246
Leonid Petrovich 186–188, 193, 210, 212, 214, 217
Lepekhin, Mikhail Pavlovich 55, 59
Liteinii Bridge 50
Liteinii Prospect 11
Logunov, Ivan Petrovich 170
Lopatinskii 211
Low-Volzhskii Territory 18
Lubyanka 89
Luga 81
Lunacharskii, Anatolii Vasil'evich 82

Magadan 96, 98–99, 156, 159, 166, 177, 195, 217, 237–238; authorities 185; camp 248; exiles 230; groceries 178
Magadan *Berlag* 193; *see also Beregovoy Camp; Beregovoy Law and Ethics; Special Camp 5*
Magadan Province 167
Magadan Province Administration of Internal Affairs 237
Magadan Province Ministry of Internal Affairs 237
Magadan Regional Duma 249
Magadan-Tayga Highway 167
Magadan's Nagaev Pier 94
Maiakovskii, Vladimir Vladimirovich 76
Makarova, Anastasia 2
Maksakova, Katia 176–181
Maksim Gorkii village 136; 249
Mamedov 106, 128
Manezhnaia Square 76
Marat, battleship 99
March 8 (International Women's Day) 212
Mariinsk 230
Mariinskii Theater 82
Martyshkino 81
Marx, Karl: *Capital: Critique of Political Economy* 76
Matulevich, Ivan Osipovich 64–66, 69
May Day Holiday 213–214
Menshevik(s) 60–62
Mercader, Ramon 16
Metallic Plant 19
Mexico 16
Mezgleek 175
Miakit 195
Middle School 8
Mikhailov 71
Military Board of the Supreme Court of the USSR 161
Military Medical Academy 28
Military Tribunal of the Far East 237
Ministry of Foreign Affairs 56
Ministry of the Internal Affairs 216
Moika River 19
Mokhnachev, Vladimir Onuphrievich 211
Molotov (Scriabin), Viacheslav Mikhailovich 56, 59, 65–66, 89, 96; declaration 230
Morocco 248
Moscow 18, 71, 74, 76, 89, 154, 217, 249; authorities 149, 160, 200, 193, 201, 206, 210; case 237; journey 239; justice 245; lights 240; military district 82; occupation 147; orphans 229, 244; petition 121; train 240, 244; World War II 165
Moscow Railroad Station 240
Moscow State University 56
Moscow's Yaroslavskii Railroad Station 239
Mother Nature 228
Motherland 226
Muralov, Nikolai Ivanovich 166
Muratov 72
Murmansk 71
Muscovites 90, 96, 110, 239
Mussolini, Benito 18

Nagaev Bay 94, 96
Nakhodka Bay 217
Napoleon torts 81, 244
Narvskii Gates 82
Narvskii Prospect 83
Navy commanders 85, 111, 119
Nazi 137, 173
Neil 116
Neva River 16, 19, 49–51, 77, 82, 241–242, 245
Nevel'skoi Strait 92
Nevskii Patch 242
Nevskii Prospect 13, 242
New Year 75, 152, 244
New Year's Day 82, 154
New Year's Eve 77
Nicholas the Second, the last Russian Emperor and Tsar 121, 160; *see also* the Romanov dynasty
Nikishov, Ivan Fedorovich, the Administrative Chief of Far North Development 169–172, 174, 209; office 210; wife 177
Nikitin 222
Nikolaev, Leonid Vasil'evich 59
Nikolaevsk-on-Amur 238
Nikolaevskii District, Saratov Province 36
Nikolai 116
Nizhnii At-Uriah 100–101, 200; town 249; *see also* At-Uriah River
Nizhnii Novgorod 244
Nizhnii Novgorod Province 248
NKVD 6, 10–11; agents 85, 89–90, 107, 169; officers 15, 51, 54, 70–71, 248
non–Party women 212
Norilsk 230
Norilsk Camp 2 230
North Cafeteria 242
North Star 42
Northern Crimea 81
Northern Palmira 31
Northwestern Russia 71
Nosov, Nikolai Mikhailovich 169
Novaia Botrad' 2

November 7, 1937 *see* Great October Day; Greatest of Soviet holidays; Soviet event
Novosibirsk 224, 234

Obvodnii Canal 4, 10–11, 82
October Revolution 4, 17, 72, 120; tenth anniversary 76; 20th anniversary 224
Okhotnii market 76
Okhotsk Sea 89, 92–94, 97
Okhtenskii Plant 53
Oksana 182–183
Old Man 174–175; *see also* Small Child; Vasia
Old Peckerhead 113
Olga Zakharovna 235
Order of Lenin 26
Ordzhonikidze, Grigorii Konstantinovich 14, 223
Orekhova, Lubov 224
Orlov, Andrei Aleksandrovich 67
Orokutan 195
Osipov 163
Ostapchuk 230
Ozerskaia, Rosa Abramovna 227

Pacific Ocean 75, 84, 88, 92, 191
Pakhmutova, Aleksandra Nikolaevna 249
Palatka 100, 195
Panikarov, Ivan 249
Papp (Pap), Ivan 2
Papp, Maria 2
Parnachev (Captain) 193
Party 22, 26, 34, 46, 51, 54, 63–64, 68, 77, 120–121, 241, 243; bureaucracy 121; control 146; leaders 85; lies 90; membership card 121; news 89; Bolshevik party 4, 229; *see also* All-Russian Communist Party (Bolsheviks); Bolshevik(s)
Party Committee 76, 244; *see also* Central Committee; Central Party Committee
Party Secretary 222
Pashka 46
Paveletskii Railroad Station 76, 244
Pavlov 19
Pavlov, Vasilii Egorovich 1
Pavlova, Evdokiia Dmitrievna 1
Pedagogical Institution 45
Pedagogical Institution and Studio of Moscow Art Theater 244
Penza 246–247
People's Commissariat of Heavy Industry 68
Petr 106
Petrazhitskie 83

Petrazhitskii, Sergei 241
Petrov 184–185
Petrov, Sanka 39
Petrova, Aleksandra 232
Petrovich 157–159, 179
Photo Album Report of 1938 118
Plenary Session of January 1938 89–90
Plotnikov, Isaac Solomonovich 49–50
Plundering Socialist State Property 173
Pluto 245
Podolskii, Viacheslav 242
Pokrovsk 205
Poland 173
Polevoi, Iosif Ignatievich 170, 192
Poleznii Street 235
Poliakov, Leo *81*
Poliakov, Nikolai Ivanovich *81*–82
Poliakova-Golikova, Natalia Petrovna *81*–82
Port 54, 83
Pozyvnoi, Vasilii 112, 131–133
Pravda 64
Pruss, Vladislav Aleksandrovich 21–25, 27–28, 30, 32, 35
Pskov 96
Public Prosecutor's Office of Leningrad Military District 241, 244–245
Pushkin, Aleksandr: *Dubrovskii* 152
Puyi, Chinese Emperor (Qing dynasty) 24

Rabat 248
Raisa Mikhailovna 189
Raskolnikov 184–185; *see also* Danilenko, Ivan
Raskolnikov, Rodion 151
Razin, Stepan (Stenka) Timofeevich 37, 58
Red Army, or Army 22, 26, 73, 87, 173; commanders 101; World War II 165, 183
Red Army House 116
Red Guard(s) 36, 60–62
Red Putilovets 19
Red Square 77
Red Terror 22
Red Triangle Factory 4, 13–14, 18, 54, 64, 67–68, 77, 80, 136, 142–143, 241–242, 248
Reds 42, 156
Reign of Terror 90; *see also* Ezhovshchina; Great Purge
Revolutionary Tribunal and Committee for Registration of Bourgeoisie 36
Revolution's Red color 64
Road of Life 232; *see also* Ladoga Lake
Romanov Dynasty 121; *see also* Aleksander II; Nicholas II

Rose-Marie 80
Rostov-on-Don 77–78
Rostov Province 78
Rousseau 221
Rudnia 122
Russia 37, 78, 96,133, 159–160, 249; villages 92
Russian 17; baths 206, 209; cities 34; composer 249; cultural monument 249; folk songs 83; heads 86
Russian Federation 22, 26; *see also* Russian Soviet Federative Socialist Republic (RSFSR)
Russian National Library, Saint Petersburg 13
Russian Soviet Federative Socialist Republic 89; *see also* Russian Federation
Russians 36, 239
Rybak, Nathaniel 142–146; meeting 241–243
Rybas, Lev 176–181
Rychkov, Nikolai Mikhailovich 64
Ryvkina-Vainer, Emilia Markovna 224

Saint Petersburg 5, 16, 20, 71; *see also* Leningrad
Saint Petersburg Lyceum No. 40, 242
Sakhalin Islands 92, 151
Salsk 77–78, 80
Samara 34
Sandata 78
Sapozhnikov 19, 50–51, 241
Saratov 4, 18, 23, 25, 35–37, 57, 61–62, 65, 75, 77, 122, 155, 187, 204, 213, 231, 239; children 224; dumps 235; high school 76; home 246; journey 219, 233, 241, 243; market 83; medical institution 242; postage 199; streets 234; train 244
Saratov Executive Committee 60
Saratov German District 234
Saratov Medical Academy 247
Saratov Medical Institution 106
Saratov Pedagogical College 18, 76
Saratov Province 4, 247
Saratov Radishchev Art Museum 229
Saratov Railroad Station 216
Saratov State University 4, 18, 64, 76, 247
Schmidt, Martius 229
Schmidt, Vilma 224, 229–230
Schmidt Brothers Steam Mill 57
Scythians 37
Sea of Japan 92–93
Sedov-Nevolin 54
Serebriannikov, Vasilii Dmitrievich 67, 97, 143

Serpantinka, jail 147–150, 154–155, 160, 164, 249; yard 150
Sevastopol 118
Seventy-Two Kilometer 167
Seydewitz, Frido 170
Seymchan 200–203, 206–208, 210, 213, 217–219, 23–237–238; airport, restaurant 220, 249; memories 245; town 249
Seymchan District 245
Seymchan River 206
Shaposhnikova, Liudmila Kuzminichna 227
Shcherbakov, Aleksandr Sergeevich 211
Shelkovichnaia Street 60–61
Shevelev (Colonel) 237
Shostkinski Factory 18
Shpalernaia Prison 12, 25, 31, 43, 53–55, 57, 63, 67–69, 103
Siberia 34, 74–75, 84, 89, 92, 166, 226, 238
Sidorkevich, Kostia 103–104, 110, 112, 116, 124, 127, 129, 131
Sidorov, Fedor Alekseevich 172
Simakova, Evdokiia Semenovna 210
Simbirsk 34; *see also* Lenin's city
Sipiagin, Nikolai 242
Sir Bolotov 17–20
Siverskaia 81
Skachkova, Maria Vasil'evna 224
Skoblo, Berta Aleksandrovna 224
Skoblo, Maks Solomonovich 67, 70–71, 97–98
Slave Camp Two 102
Small Child 174–175; *see also* Old Man; Vasia
Smolenskii market 76
Smol'nyi Building 244, 247
Smol'nyi Institute 59, 81
Sneetser, Mark 120, 131, 139–140; *see also* Bulba
Sniper Stream 150
Snopikov 142
Socialist Competition 133
Socialist State Property 173
Sokolov Mountains 156
Sokolowski, Kazimir 214, 218; wife 219
Sokoulin, Vasilii Nikolaevich 170
Solovetskii Islands 74; *see* Gulag
Sortirovochnaia Railroad Station 223; *see also* Sortirovochnaia Train Station
Sortirovochnaia Train Station 73; *see also* Sortirovochnaia Railroad Station
Sosnovoborsk 247
Soviet Supreme Court 5, 60, 64, 66, 240, 245; authorities 210; brass 45; camps 87; citizenship 26, 173; court

29; custom 231; enforces 221; event 72; execution 147; glory 138; government 17, 105; Gulag literature 6–7; Hammer and Sickle 199; heroes 77, 158; hierarchy 74; justice 6, 18, 63–64, 148, 222, 245; laws 27; maps 169; officials 67, 91; penitentiary system 6; people 75, 87, 91; power 65, 91, 161, 245; prisoner 199; repressions 78; society 173; *see also* Great October Day; Greatest of Soviet holidays; November 7, 1937
Soviet Union 56, 77, 87, 138, 149, 246; *see also* Union of Soviet Socialist Republics; USSR
Soviets 230
Spasskaia Tower 77
Special Camp 5, 195; *see also* Beregovoy Camp
Srednekanskii District 101, 201
Stalin, Iosif Vissarionovich: death 237, 239; Gulags 1, 6; leadership 121–122, 147, 193, 239, 245; origin 90; repressions 6–7, 46, 59, 65–66, 89, 96; truth 126; view of Soviet sabotage 14, 53
Stalingrad 77, 229
State Department of Chemistry 4, 222
State Security 237
Stepanov 142
Strelka 195
Studebaker 201
Suvorov, Fedor Trofimovich 67, 97, 136–137, 143, 243
Suvorov Street 215, 219
Sverdlovsk 239
Syzran 34

Taiga Station 234
Tajik Afghan border 247
Tajik State University 247
Tajiks 89
Tambov Province 82
Tatars 36
TB neighbor 129
Technological Institution 46
Temiakova, Olga 83, 233–234
Temiakova, Valentina 216, 233–234
Third All-Russian Congress of *Komsomol* 229
Tiagunova, Yekaterina 241
Timbaktu 83
Tokay 83
Tolmachev Military Political Academy 49, 82
Tolmachevo 81
Tom Thumb 27
Tom Turkey 35

Tomsk 6, 71; jail 225, 227–229, 233–234; exiles 248
Tomskii Medical Institution 67
Trotskii, Lev Davidovich 11, 14, 16, 166, 223
Trotskyist 47, 230
Trotskyist-Zinov'ev's group 56
Tsarist government 5
Tsarists' policemen 227
Tsar's reign 29; *see also* Nicholas II; Romanov dynasty
Tukhachevskaia-Vladimirova, Maria Nikolaevna 226
Tukhachevskii, Mikhail Nikolaevich 26, 32–34, 82, 99; spy 32; denunciation 32; sisters 226
Turaev 221
Turkey 16
Turks 89
Tver 1–2, 240, 247
Tver Province 2
Twenties Division 50
Two Hundred Percent 138
Tyrkov 19, 30

U-shape 103
Ugodnikovskaia Street 60
Ukhnalev (Major) 201; documents 207–208, 213
Ukraine 88, 165, 218, 230, 249
Ukrainian accent 101; government 88; people 96, 104
Uncle Poop 226
Union of Soviet Socialist Republics 66; *see also* the Soviet Union; USSR
UP 197
Ural Mountains 18, 191, 238–239; Urals, 42
Ural River 41
Uralsk 41
USSR 26, 223, 232; *see also* the Soviet Union; Union of Soviet Socialist Republics
Utesov, Leonid Osipovich 82
Uzbeks 89, 103, 196

Vaishlia, Iosif Stanislavovich 68
Valentina 187
Valjean 152
Valley of Death 115, 118, 124, 157; *see also* Death Valley
Vasia 174–175; *see also* Old Man; Small Child
Vasil'ev, Naum Ivanovich 14, 18–20, 45, 68
Vasil'ev Sergei Petrovich 170

Vasil'eva 228
Vasilevskii, Aleksandr Mikhailovich (Marshal) 211
Vasil'evskii Island 248
Vaskov, Rodin Ivanovich 154
Vaskov's House 154, 157, 160, 162, 164, 249
Vedeneva, Vera Aleksandrovna 233
Ventstenostsev, Sasha 112
Viktorov, N. 61
Vladimirov, Pashka 107, 110–112, 124
Vladivostok 73, 83–85, 88, 91–94, 217; distance 118; harbor 92; transit camp 85–86, 160
Vladivostok Chemistry Institution 211
Vladivostokians 85
Voinov Street 12
VOKhR 115
Volga River 35, 37, 57, 65, 77; region 96, 155–156
Volgograd 77
Vol'ka Kain 151
Volodarskii Prospect 11
Vologda 71, 74
Voltaire 221
Volzhskii Party District, Saratov Province 36
von Goethe, Johann Wolfgang 82
Vorobieva, Natasha 187–190
Voroshilov, Kliment Efremovich 56
Vorovskii Street 245
Voynich, Ethel Lilian: *The Gadfly* 151
Vyborgskii Palace of Culture 67
Vyshinskii, Andrei Januarievich 56, 89, 106, 121, 245

War Council 225
West 5, 17

White Army 34, 53
White Cossack(s) 4, 36, 38–42, 50, 156
White Revolters 61–62, 229
Winter Palace 245
Work Plan 137
World War II 173, 206, 219, 223, 225, 230, 232, 249

Yagoda, Genrikh Grigorievich 90
Yagodnoye 145; courthouse 146; town 249
Yagodnoye Mountain Notch 144–145
Yakir, Sarra Lazarevna 226
Yampolskii 62
Yarin (Colonel of Justice) 245
Yaya Station 216, 230–231, 233
Yermakova, Maria 227
Young Pioneer's Journal 76
Youth League uniform 103

Zagumennii, Sergei Ivanovich 60
Zakarpattia Region Court 1
Zakhar Kuzmich 154
Zakovskii, Leonid Mikhailovich 14, 56
Zavod Imeni Stalina (ZIS- 5 truck) 167
Zelenin, Ivan Grigorievich 182–183
Zemskova, Aleksandra Antonovna 227
Zhavoronki Station 244, 249
Zhdanov, Andrei Aleksandrovich 225
Zheelov, Grigorii Zakharovich 67–68, 75, 113
Zheerov, Petr Ivanovich 167
Zherebak, Maria 2
Zhitomir 230
Zhukov Air-Defense Academy, Tver 247
Zhurba, Georgii Vladimirovich 242
Zorky 243

www.ingramcontent.com/pod-product-compliance
Ingram Content Group UK Ltd.
Pitfield, Milton Keynes, MK11 3LW, UK
UKHW041930140426
5217IPUK00014B/396